WILD
guide

Portugal
Hidden Places, Great Adventures
and the Good Life

Edwina Pitcher

WILD
THINGS
PUBLISHING

Ponte de São João, p40

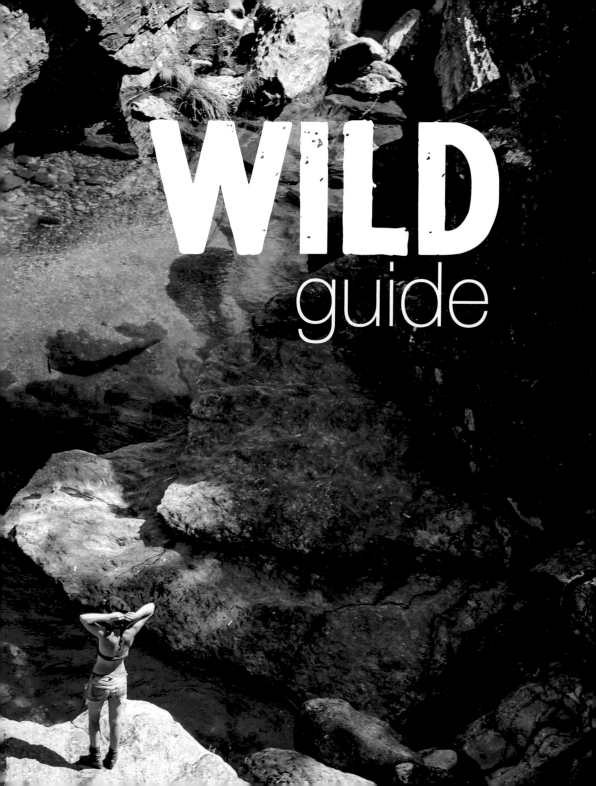

WILD
guide

Contents

Regional
Overview

Corvo

Flores

Graciosa

Faial

São Jorge

Pico

Terceira

Açores

24 p253

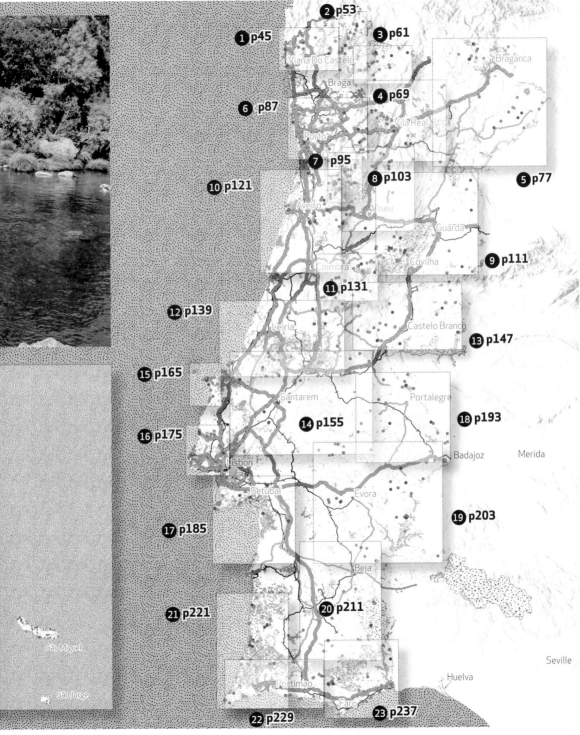

① p45
② p53
③ p61
④ p69
⑤ p77
⑥ p87
⑦ p95
⑧ p103
⑨ p111
⑩ p121
⑪ p131
⑫ p139
⑬ p147
⑭ p155
⑮ p165
⑯ p175
⑰ p185
⑱ p193
⑲ p203
⑳ p211
㉑ p221
㉒ p229
㉓ p237

Viana Do Castelo
Bragança
Braga
Vila Real
Porto
Aveiro
Viseu
Guarda
Coimbra
Covilhã
Castelo Branco
Leiria
Santarem
Portalegre
Badajoz
Merida
Lisbon
Setubal
Evora
Beja
Seville
Portimao
Huelva
Faro
São Miguel
São Jorge

Introduction

I first discovered Portugal in the autumn of 2013 by setting out on foot from Lisbon to northern Spain with an army-issue water bottle, a bivvy bag and pocket knife. Following the *caminho* to Santiago de Compostela, I crossed most of mainland Portugal. I felt its blue skies, its beating sun, its earthen terraces and tempestuous Atlantic winds off the ocean. Wild figs, grapevines and sweet chestnuts were ripening, weighing heavy on their stems and bowing over my path. I followed coastal tracks and mountain paths, carved into the land by pilgrims, fishermen and goatherds, and I found wide Roman flagstone roads, rutted by ancient cart grooves and overgrown with dense mossy woodland.

Returning again and again to this history-rich country I have discovered that hidden Portugal, away from the much-frequented coastal resorts, is a timeless and magical place. To the north and east there are wild mountains, sparkling lakes and glacial valleys; to the south and west there are dusty olive groves, secret beaches and hidden caves, and everywhere you will find rustic villages, standing stones, magical woodland and windswept hilltop castles. The people who still remain in its rural, wilder places continue to work the land in traditional ways, shepherd, bake bread and make wine, honey and olive oil. They are rich in spirit and nature's harvest. Their hospitality is perennial.

Waking up to birdsong, river mist and an early plunge into clear water is still my favourite way to start the day. As my personal *caminho* continued, often accompanied by my Portuguese friends, I have climbed to peaks and rocky summits, and seen Portugal flat as a map beneath me. From Fóia, the highest mountain of Algarve, I could see its sea-fringed edges and in Juromenha I saw the wide snaking Guadiana river defining the border with Spain. The land became my map but so did the locals' convivial desire to help with directions. I began to fully appreciate the Portuguese phrase "if you have a tongue, you can get to Rome".

Wild regions for all seasons

In springtime we rambled over the hills of northern and central Portugal (chapters 1-11) Serra da Freita, Montemuro and Alvão teem with wild flowers, exploding into joyful lilacs and yellows. Heather and gorse flower over the hills and, with the blue skies, transform the horizon into a riot of endless colour. They say heaven laughs in flowers; if so, Alentejo is in fits of hysterics as the spring fields are carpeted in deep purple with lupins growing wild under the gnarled and noble cork trees.

On summer days, the southern regions (chapters 12-23) are perfect. We wound down cliff tracks to secret beaches in Peniche, Alentejo and Sintra, deserted except for glimpses of the past, with rough rock-hewn fishermen's steps dropping into deep, still inlets, perfect for a skinny dip.

Summer is also a wonderful time to visit the northern and central regions. You can while away lazy days on sun-drenched sands or strike out from the beaten track to the rivers of Trás-os-Montes and Arganil (chapters 3, 5 & 11). The Portuguese culture of visiting *praias fluviais* – river beaches – then reaches its zenith, and Sundays are idled away on river banks, cooking lunch on the communal stone BBQs, chilling a bottle of Vinho Verde – green wine – in the sparkling river and leaping back in again after lazing in the sun.

The low evening light is at its most golden in autumn. As the summer heat eases, take a long hike along the coastal paths of Costa Vicentina or shepherds' paths through glacial valleys and over wild peaks (chapters 7-21). Autumn means harvest-time in Portugal – visit the wine-growing regions of Douro or Ribatejo to help with *vindimas*, the festival for harvesting grapes, trampling the fruit and, of course, drinking the wine.

In winter, Serra da Estrela's mountains are cloaked in snow with skiing pistes (chapter 9). This is the time to see the northern hills in bleak but beautiful greys, whites and greens, evocative of their ancient Lusitanian tribes. At the end of a day's wintry adventures, our favourite thing has been bedding down in a toasty tipi overlooking the snow-capped hills of Gerês.

Local food and ancient history

Portugal is as rich in adventures over mountains, lakes, rivers, sea and caves, as it is rich in the food and wine to fuel these adventures. In the mountains, feast on steaks, roast kid in a wood oven, mountain cheeses and smoked meats known as *fumeiro*. By the rivers, try freshwater fish. At the coast, feast on the freshest crab and grilled fish, octopus or a bubbling *caldeirada* fish stew. Kept in caves, cellars, sometimes even buried under lakes, are glorious Portuguese wines: sparkling Vinho Verde in the north, the darker wines of Douro and Dão in central regions, the lighter reds of Ribatejo, and Alentejo's mellow vintages in the south.

You will discover the best places to eat, dishes made to ancient recipes, but also rustic havens for intimate stays. Spend a week in a characterful mountain village with cobbled streets or a wild retreat on a working farm. There are treehouses built in woodlands with views of the sunrise over a river, and wilder campsites from which to stargaze.

Portugal is a place woven over with paths and stories left by Celtic tribes and Moorish settlers. It is crossed by Roman trade routes and mythic pathways of the Madonna as she appeared to our predecessors. Enduring all of this are much older footprints, stamped deeper on the stone. The footsteps of dinosaurs that ran across this coast 125 million years ago appear in southern regions (chapters 12, 16, 17 & 22), an impression left as though they were here yesterday. Time collapses in these rocks. Travel to these wild places and you can feel how thronged are these cliffs, hills, rivers and lakes with past travellers.

The end result of these journeys is this compendium of wild, secret and beautiful places across Portugal. It is packed with memories of stargazing nights, hidden coves, cool rivers, thundering waterfalls, hilltop forts and ruined castles. I hope that this book inspires many more wild adventures.

Edwina Pitcher
Lisbon, September 2016

Finding your way

Each wild place can be located using the overview map provided at the end of each chapter, along with the detailed directions, but to be sure of finding your way you'll need to use the latitude and longitude provided. This is given in decimal degrees (WGS84) and can be entered straight into any web-based mapping program, such as Google or Bing. Print out the map before you go, or save a 'screen grab' and email it to yourself. You can also enter the co-ordinates into your GPS, car satnav (enable 'decimal degrees') or your smartphone, if it has GPS. All maps apps will take decimal degrees, and the ViewRanger app will even give you turn-by-turn instructions to guide you to your point. If you have paper maps, look up the equivalent national grid reference in the conversion table at the back of the book. Approximate walk-in times are given, for one way only (we allow about 15 mins per km), and abbreviations in the directions refer to left and right (L, R) and north, east, south and west (N, E, S, W).

Wild & responsible

1. High risk of forest fires in the summertime. Don't leave any glass out in the sunshine. Even the smallest shard can spark a flame in the sun. If you see discarded bottles, please collect them.

2. A Critical Wildfire Period is announced annually, usually July–September. During this time campfires are prohibited in rural areas, allowed only in designated picnic parks or *parques de merendas* using their communal stone BBQ grills.

3. If you wash in streams or rivers, only use biodegradable soap, or none at all.

4. Park considerately.

5. Take map, compass, whistle and a water bottle when venturing into remote areas and always tell someone where you are going – do not rely on your mobile phone.

Useful phrases

hello	**olá**
good morning	**bom dia**
good afternoon	**boa tarde**
good evening	**boa noite**
please	**por favor**
thank you	**obrigado**
safe journey	**boa viagem**
where is?	**onde está?**
the beach	**a praia**
the river beach	**a praia fluvial**
the well	**o poço**
the dolmen	**a anta**
the forest	**a floresta**
the camping park	**o parque de campismo**
the picnic park	**o parque de merendas**
the footpath	**o percurso pedestre**
right	**à direita**
left	**à esquerda**
the café	**o café**
the restaurant	**o restuarante**
cup/ bottle of wine	**um copo/ uma garrafa do vinho**
a beer	**uma cerveja**
a water	**uma água**
bread	**pão**
cheese	**queijo**
smoked meat	**fumeiro**
olives	**azeitonas**
petrol station	**bomba de gasolina**

Best for
Beaches & coast

Portugal is well known for its white sand beaches. The epic coastline, stretching from Minho in the north to the tip of Sagres in the south, and on into the Algarve, is also riddled with secret coves, hidden sea caves, windswept dunes and colossal cliffs.

The coastline differs dramatically from place to place. The Costa Vicentina in the south-west offers some fabulous cliff-top hiking routes along fishermen's paths, with many detours to a secret beach, its water blue and its sand undisturbed. At Peniche, a haven for surfers, hidden beaches are interspersed between strange rocks weathered into staggering towers. There are ancient sea caves in which you can shelter and ponder the endless horizon, or others into which you can swim, or kayak, their vaulted cavities lit up by the iridescent water. At Praia da Almagreira sand dunes form red crests like a miniature Valley of the Kings.

Go wild! At Cabo Espichel there are dinosaur footprints leaving their 145 million-year-old trail up the cliff side, and on the Sintra coast you can fit your hand inside the dent of a Jurassic heel-bone. At Salir do Porto you can leap and roll down Portugal's biggest dune. Or skinny dip in the secret coves formed where the wild Arrábida hills meet the sea.

Praia da Senhora da Rocha p225

Best for Festas

The summer months are the time for *festas* in Portugal. These street parties kick off in June with Lisbon and Porto's *santos populares* and then from July to August every tiny village in the hills and valleys will have its *festa popular* with traditional *pimba* music, feasting and dancing in the streets. In Pereiro, a typical country town, the streets are strewn with petals and pungent herbs.

These festas are also a great way to sample local and seasonal gastronomy. A popular festivity is *vindimas*, essentially a wine-feast and very popular as a lot of the *adegas* – wineries and vineyards – need a hand to pick the grapes. Trample the fruit in the traditional granite *lagar*, and celebrate with plenty of wine and feasting. Taste smoked meats from over 150 Trasmontano farms at the Vinhais Fumeiro festival or celebrate all possible cherry-related cakes and wines at the cherry harvest in Resende.

See ancient traditions, sometimes superstitions, kept alive in these festivities. Dozens of colourful boats, festooned with flags, set sail over the river from Constância. At Trás-os-Montes, the *careto*, a carnival figure dressed in colourful fringes, whirls madly and chases onlookers, and in Montalegre the enigmatic witch, *bruxa*, is celebrated at their Friday the 13th party.

Best for
Skinny dipping

Stripping bare and plunging into a lake, a sparkling river or a thrillingly deep clear mountain pool is one of the most direct ways to reconnect with nature. As we bare all to the wild and immerse ourselves in it, we let it shape us, flow around us and so mould us.

Lie back to float, spread like a star, in volcanic lakes under clear skies at Lagoa Azul, or let a gentle current take you downstream as dragonflies alight on your body in Rio Couro. Strip off at a secret beach and let the waves surge around you. Feel your pulse race as you jump into a mountain pool in Gerês or swim bravely up to a thundering waterfall and let it pummel your body. Water gives us unhindered freedom of movement and many of Portugal's rivers, waterfalls and lakes – and a good number of beaches where naturism is accepted – are in secluded spots, perfect for a skinny dip which only adds to this unhindered freedom.

Ponte de São João, p40

Be safe

1 Never swim alone, and do keep a constant watch on weak swimmers.

2 Know your limits and stay close to the shoreline. Cold water will decrease your swimming range and can lead to cold cramps. People with a heart condition should avoid rapid entry into cold water.

3 Never jump into water you have not thoroughly checked for depth and obstructions.

4 Avoid strong currents, such as those found under large waterfalls, rapids or weirs: they can drag you under.

5 Always make sure you know how you will get out before you get in.

6 Wear footwear if you can.

7 Watch out for boats on any navigable river. Wear a coloured swim hat so you can be seen.

8 Avoid direct contact with blue-green algae and be wary of water quality in lowland areas during droughts and heavy rain. Cover cuts with plasters if worried, and if you develop flu-like symptoms tell your doctor you have been wild swimming.

Best for
Places to stay

Portugal's mountains and hills are riddled with little lost villages, their stone walls and cobbled streets evoking a timeless heritage, in harmony with nature. Take a rustic retreat in the hilltop villages of Comareira or Pena, and open your shutters to dawn over the Lousã hills. Or for a fairy-tale refuge, stay at the 16th century fort on the wild island of Berlengas.

Sleeping out under the stars is a magical experience and several campsites have made the experience all the more romantic. Sleep on silks and embroidered cushions in luxurious tipis on the riverbank or a secret treehouse hidden high in pine trees. Stay in a Mongolian yurt surrounded by snow-capped hills. Or put your head down in a log cabin with deer, pigs and goats in the neighbouring fields, and wake up with a morning wild swim.

Wild does not have to mean roughing it – enjoy the sensual side of nature on exquisite daybeds in magical gardens or stay in elegant farmhouses with sparkling fountains, and breakfast on local breads, honeys, jams, fruits and cakes.

Lima Escape, p53

Best for
Ancient & sacred

Before the Romans arrived in 218BC, the pages of Portugal's history were already thronged with ancient tribes. With rock carvings, standing stones and cave paintings, hill forts and tribal temples, the landscape is a rich tapestry of sacred spaces and territorial markings. To be in these places is to rekindle a sense of awe and enchantment with our Earth.

Trace a path through magical woodland to Penedo Encanto, a whale-shaped stone covered in swirling prehistoric engravings. Crawl under a megalithic dolmen and gaze up at the great stones rolled into place to honour the dead of 5,000 years ago. Under these stones you can remove yourself from the world, cradled for a moment in eternity. See the surrounding hills through Neolithic eyes at caves in Esperança and trace ochre paintings depicting hunts and dragons. Follow the Ocreza river to discover hundreds of rock carvings or climb rock-hewn steps to wild temples. Some are dedicated to millennia-old deities: Rocha da Mina, hidden in wild woodland, is given over to the healing god Endovélico; the Roman temple at Panóias, with blood channels carved in its stone altars, is dedicated to Serápis, god of the underworld.

Monsanto Templar chapel, p145

Best for
Slow food & wine

Slow food is a prerequisite of dining in Portugal: dishes are made to ancient recipes and, from farm to kitchen, cooking is a labour of love. What better way to savour the flavours than lingering with a glass of wine? Whether it's a fresh Vinho Verde from Minho or a dark deep wine from Douro, the vineyards offer a rich and varied stock.

Portugal's love for fish is unfathomable. Along the coast you can dine on stuffed squid, grilled octopus, sea bream, sea bass, cuttlefish, prawns, limpets, barnacles, sardines. But nothing beats the simple joy of a crab eaten by the sea with a glass of wine. In Peniche, try *caldeirada de peixe*, bubbling fish stew, or, near the Sado coast, razor-clam rice.

Inland, the rivers offer freshwater fish. Try grilled eels in Ribatejo or trout from the Côa. In Alentejo black pigs range free under the cork trees. Visit mountain cabins where smoked sausages – *farinheira*, *morcela* or *chouriço* – hang above open fireplaces.

Many small-scale farms keep bees, their honey tasting of rosemary, heather or sweet chestnut. Each region has its own cheeses, breads and 'conventual' cakes made with lemon, sugar and eggs. Indulge in a *cristas de galo* from Vila Real, shaped like a cockscomb, the pastry filled with a paste of almond and eggs.

Best for
Sunset hill forts & wild highs

Portugal has many mountains and hill tops, scattered with ancient hill forts and standing stones, perfect for a sunset. Climb to the highest hill at the golden hour and survey the landscape as our ancestors would have done. As the light diffuses to a deep orange haze over hills at Mosteiro de São João d'Arga, boulders catch the sun, their bright outlines casting long shadows.

At Anta das Pias, this ancient dolmen is perfectly aligned for a sunset: sit on its little hill as the air cools. Portugal has many Celtic hill forts, later Romanised, which crown its northern landscape. At Castro de Monte Mozinho you can wander ancient streets within the ruins of a Roman hill fort or sit on the time-worn steps of Castelium Marnelis, once the Roman capital of the central region.

Ruined border castles and coastal forts provide perfect places to spread your arms, lean into the wind and fill your lungs. Feel the wild Atlantic wind in your hair at Citânia de Santa Luzia. Breathe in the views from Castelo de Castro Laboreiro, a Moorish castle left to the wild, where eagles perch and lizards creep on its rocks.

Castelo de Castro Laboreiro, p50

Best for
Mountain villages

To visit the mountain villages of Portugal is to tread back to a time of harvests and honey, communal bread ovens, donkeys carrying wares and shepherd huts hidden in the hills. Many of these villages have emptied in recent years but there are a few where time seems to have stood still. Stay in a village deep in the Coimbra hills where the cows come home in the rich, evening light, brown and fawn and cream.

Other villages are even more ancient: medieval summer towns known as *brandas* are scattered over the hills of Peneda-Gerês, long-deserted, their ruins used only for animals. At Montalegre you can see ancient wolf traps, their dry stone walls echoing the slope of the hills, testifying to a forgotten way of life. In Soajo dozens of small stone *espigueiros*, corn-houses, stand sentinel on a large rock surveying the mountains.

Discover Piódão, a hilltop village built entirely from schist, or Meitriz whose slate houses ramble down to the grassy knolls of the Paiva riverbank. There are eccentric villages like Monsanto, a village crowning a rocky summit, its houses built using great boulders as walls, supporting arches, even roofs. At Ermelo little windows overlook the wide River Lima, and sweet oranges tumble over the monastery walls.

Also look out for structures created by man, such as mountain-top cairns and waymarkers that stand in some of the most obscure and remote places, as beacons for those who travel that way.

Best for
Picnics & foraging

Good, fresh local produce can be the highlight of any picnic;
it also reveals fascinating insights to an area's cultural and
natural history. With sun-drenched fields and rich earth,
Portugal provides glorious fruit and veg. Visit the Douro
region in late May for cherries and elderflowers, or Alentejo
in April for its wild asparagus. In July, little wild snails are
gathered from roadside grasses throughout the country and
are delicious cooked in butter and garlic.

Search for wild clams by the rocks of Santo Cristo in the
Açores, pick wild figs and blackberries by the wayside in
Ribatejo or forage for mushrooms in the Serra do Alvão.
Indulge in soft fruit from the pop-up roadside stalls or
local shops and farmers' markets. If picking mushrooms,
remember to leave their roots (or visit the mushroom farm in
Serra da Lua).

Portugal also has a merry culture of picnicking, with many stone
picnic tables resembling altars, sheltered by ancient trees.
These *parques de merendas* are mostly signed from the road
and, more often than not, there is a river beach or a hidden
waterfall. Chill a bottle of Vinho Verde wedged between river
stones and bring food to grill on the communal BBQs.

Soajo p52

VIANA DO CASTELO

Our perfect weekend

➜ **Float** along the River Coura at Paredes do Taboão as dragonflies alight on your body

➜ **Lean** into the ocean winds at the hilltop fort of Santa Luzia

➜ **Banquet** on the beach with *pão de Deus*, bread of God, a heavenly loaf crowned with custard and coconut

➜ **Play** at marauding pirates around Forte do Paço on the deserted beach

➜ **Breathe** in the views from O Cervo, the great stag sculpture and symbol of Vila Nova de Cerveira

➜ **Picnic** at Anta da Barrosa, a megalithic dolmen you can still scamper inside

➜ **Prise** open a delicious *ouriço do mar*, sea urchin, bought from the Viana fishwives

➜ **Cool** a bottle of Vinho Verde in the stream by Cascata do Pincho

➜ **Skinny** dip in sapphire pools at Ponte de São João and dive through sunken sunbeams

Forests, beaches, rivers or sea: to spend one day exploring Portugal's north-westernmost district offers adventures in all of them. The Santa Luzia hill, rising up above the district's capital – also called Viana do Castelo – is named after the saint of clear-sightedness. The viewpoint shows the land like a map, its sandy beaches a yellow fringe stretching out beyond Mount Padela, and the River Lima snaking in wide curves towards the sea.

Celtic settlements once scattered these hills. You can see the circular stone foundations left by these villages high on the hills, and deft grooves made by our ancestors sharpening knives on coastal rocks. On the Santa Luzia hill, remains of Iron Age streets are inhabited now solely by sheep. Wild winds grab your clothing to fill out like sails: these are known as the *nortada,* as they come straight from the North Atlantic. North of the mouth of the Lima the sea becomes far more choppy. It's in these wilder waters that *ouriço do mar* are found, spiky little sea urchins, sold by fishwives at the Viana markets for their dense red flesh, rich as caviar.

Follow the coast south to discover many secret beaches as the woods give way to dunes and coves. Inland, the hills are riddled with rivers and streams. Famously, the Romans, reaching Viana, thought they had arrived at their promised green Elysian fields of the afterlife, and the troops were afraid to cross the Lima as they supposed it was the Lethe, river of forgetfulness. Appropriately enough, this is now the region famous for Vinho Verde, 'green' or young wine with a fresh, floral nose. At Solar do Alvarinho you can taste wines made with the region's prized Alvarinho grape. Vineyards cover the hills and you will have many opportunities to try Vinho Verde. Perhaps chill a bottle for a picnic, secured between rocks, along one of the fresh running streams.

Six o'clock is when the cows come home, so don't be surprised if horned cattle block your path. Greet the shepherdess with her twinkling eyes under a black felt hood and Viana gold earrings, with a "boa tarde", and she might just wish you good luck.

RIVERS & LAKES

1 PRAIA FLUVIAL, PAREDES DO TABOÃO
Every August these mossy banks sloping down to the River Coura are host to one of Portugal's largest rock festivals. The rest of the year the small river continues to wind slowly under shady trees with the only dancing that of the dragonflies. Cool, deep but narrow river with a shingle bed.

→ From Paredes de Coura follow signs to the Praia Fluvial. Parking.

2 mins 41.9194, -8.5667

2 COVAS BROOK
Purest mountain water pools with green grasses and babbling water over stones. Perfect for a paddle or shallow swim.

→ From the junction with N302 in Covas (Coura bridge) follow N301 E for 150m; park after the farm gate and walk R down the cobbled road until the end.

2 mins, 41.8777, -8.6864

3 RIO VEZ, ARCOS DE VALDEVEZ
Try a game of water basketball in the net attached to the old bridge here or bring a canoe to try the slalom. The river snakes around the old town here: people laze on

the riverbank, swim or sit by the bar in the sun. River lifestyle the norm here. More watersports at 'Edificio Fluvivez': call +351 936 105 317.

→ Park along the N101 by the river to the N of town. Walk down the river to the beach.

2 mins, 41.8480, -8.4163

4 ESTORÃOS
Shingle river beach and shallow water swims by the old church and sleepy town above.

→ From Ponte de Lima cross the river and take the N202 W; after 2km turn R onto M524 to Moreira do Lima and continue on the M525 until Estorãos.

1 min, 41.7856, -8.6448

5 PRAIA FLUVIAL DE PONTE DA BARCA
Share your swim with the trout in this river beach along the Lima. Pebbles, clear water and a diving pier.

→ Park near the bridge in Ponte da Barca and walk upstream through the Jardim das Poetas.

5 mins, 41.8100, -8.4174

6 BARRAGEM DE COVAS
A calm peaceful dam with wild flowers and woods. And a shady and popular fishing spot.

→ From Covas (Coura bridge) take the N301 towards Caminha. After 2km turn R over the bridge and park.

2 mins, 41.8789, -8.7058

SECRET BEACHES

7 PRAIA DO MOLEDO
Wild Atlantic waves crash in and bewilderingly huge rocks nose out to sea. The wave-washed stone is perfect for a barefoot clamber, like the surface of the moon flooded with seawater. Great for pebble and shell enthusiasts.

→ From Moledo cross the railway tracks and park near the seafront. Walk down.

5 mins, 41.8500, -8.8668

8 FORTE DO PAÇO
Sandy beach with granite outcrops and the 18th century Paço Fort built by the Count of Lippe. Play marauding pirates as you chase around the old fort.

→ On the N13 passing Paço follow the brown signs towards the coast for Forte do Paço. Park on the track.

5 mins, 41.7589, -8.8771

9 FOZ DO MINHO

Here the Rio Minho meets the sea and widens into a shallow basin fronted by dunes. Fishermen come and go in small boats over this Spanish/Portuguese river border.

→ From Caminha head S on N13 for 1km, turn R at brown sign for Foz do Minho, follow for 1km. Parking.

2 mins, 41.8682, -8.8621 🏃

WATERFALLS & ROCKPOOLS

10 PONTE DE SÃO JOÃO, RIO COURA

A scrabble down a steep stony track yields a vast azure pool. Dive from huge rocks and swim into quartz caves. Filled by the mountain spring which begins high in the hills at the monastery of São João.

→ From Covas (Coura bridge) follow the N301 W towards Caminha. After 3km you pass over an old bridge; park on the roadside, and on the R is an overgrown path down.

5 mins, 41.8764, -8.7335 🏕🗻🏊

11 CASCATA DO PINCHO

Smooth granite rocks beneath the falling waterfall form a deep diving basin. At midday the water is brilliant turquoise but thrillingly cold.

→ From Espantar head N, pass the café Caçana and continue on the cobbled road. After 750m and just before the woods, take the slip road to the L, follow downhill. Reach the pool by a short walk upstream.

5 mins, 41.7977, -8.7518 🏕🏊🛶🏕

ANCIENT & SACRED

12 ANTA DA BARROSA

This megalithic dolmen was erected in 3,000BC and the large flat stones leaning together still create a shelter. Sit cross-legged on its dusty floor as the dusk draws in. A grassy area and shady trees around provide a good picnic place.

→ From Âncora head N on the N13 towards Vila Praia de Âncora, cross the river, at the roundabout take first R onto N305, 2nd L into small R. da Barrosa; dolmen is at the end of the road on the R. Cross into the grassy area.

1 min, 41.8100, -8.8506 🚲🛶🏕

13 IGREJA DO SÃO SALVADOR, BRAVÃES

Make a pilgrimage to this church with orange trees and great views across the Lima valley. Wild animals are carved in a triumphant arch over the western door and stalk through all the masonry of this 12th century church.

13

→ From Ponte da Barca take the N203 W
towards Ponte de Lima, just after Mosteiro the
church is on your R. Parking
1 min, 41.7980, -8.4531 🏛✚

HIKING & BIKING

14 ECOVIA, RIVER LIMA

Long flat paths along the banks of the River
Lima offer perfect cycling for a sunny day.
Stop along the way for a picnic or a river dip
to cool off.

→ From E of the medieval bridge at Ponte
de Lima, follow the Ecovia signs along the
river path for 16km ending at Ponta da Barca
(41.8066, -8.4248).
45 mins, 41.7688, -8.5847 🏊🏃

15 COVAS HYDROELECTRIC STATION

On the banks of the River Coura discover
the remains of gigantic hydraulic machinery.
Built by early-20th century pioneers in
hydroelectricty, it was deactivated in 1974.
Ask for the key from the Junta de Freguesia
in Covas and you may also be offered a
guide. A signposted path along the old canal
leads to a picnic park.

→ From Covas (Coura bridge) take the N301
towards Caminha; after 4km look out for

the ruins to the R. Parking. For the Junta de
Freguesia: Av. de São Salvador, 4920-042
Covas +351 251 943111
1 min, 41.8791, -8.7179 ⛰🏊🗺🚶

SUNSET & HILLTOPS

16 MOSTEIRO DE SÃO JOÃO D'ARGA

Watch the last golden rays fall over the
valley and River Minho from this 13th
century monastery. A spring has its source
here, falling eventually to the Minho.
Peaceful, with only thronging birdsong at
dusk. Continue uphill to watch the sunset,
park at any point you think high enough and
scramble up the side from there.

→ From Arga de Baixo take the M552 towads
Santo Aginha and turn at the brown sign for
the Mosteiro. Parking.
5 mins, 41.8385, -8.7324 🏕⛰🗺✚

17 CITÂNIA DE SANTA LUZIA

If you like the wind in your hair, come here
for the *Nortada* wind. Remains of circular
Iron Age dwellings crown the summit; sheep
wander along the ancient paving between
houses. From here, notice how the Lima
divides the different seas: there are much
wilder waves to the north.

12

17

→ From behind Santuário de Santa Luzia (see 18), follow the path up and around to the Citânia. Nominal entrance fee.
10 mins, 41.7053, -8.8354

18 SANTUÁRIO DE SANTA LUZIA

Rising triumphant above Viana do Castelo is the Sanctuary of Santa Luzia, St Lucy, venerated for light and clear sight. Enjoy Luzia's views over the snaking coastline as Atlantic waves beat along its edge. Inside the church, light a votive candle from the heap of waxen eyes beneath the saint's feet.
→ Park in Viana near the station and take the Elevador de Santa Luzia up to the top.
10 mins, 41.7017, -8.8349 ▣▦

19 O CERVO

Mount Crasto is crowned by the dramatic figure of a stag, 'O Cervo', symbol of Vila Nova de Cerveira, and visible from all around. The iron sculpture by the local artist José Rodrigues commands views over the widening River Minho and its dark green valley.
→ From Vila Nova de Cerveira follow brown signs to 'O Cervo' uphill for 15 mins. Parking.
1 min, 41.9472, -8.7277 ▦▲◪

WONDERFUL WILDLIFE

20 LAGOAS DE BERTIANDOS

Discover wooden bird hides by the reedy ponds and walk along the various paths through the dense and magical woodland. English oak, black willow and alder are the dominant species. There is a great camping site here.
→ From Ponte de Lima take the N202 S towards Viana do Castelo. After 4km there is a sign for the Lagoas, turn R and follow road to entry on the L. Parking.
15 mins, 41.7645, -8.6434 ▶▲◪

21 BIRDING, ARGA DE CIMA

Good birding spots up on the mountain. Look out for rock bunting, linnets and buzzards.
→ From Arga de Cima take the road S 600m towards Mãos. Park and walk up hill.
2 mins, 41.8305, -8.6842 ▶◪▲◪

ARTS & CRAFTS

22 CONVENTO DE SÃO PAIO

Founded in 1392, the convent and gardens were rescued from abandonment in the 1970s by the artist José Rodrigues. Its old walls now house his collection of sacred

art: Hindu gods peek over the shoulders of a Madonna. Wilderness animates the convent inside and out as sculptures throng the gardens and nature-inspired artworks climb the stairs. Hidden mirrors play with the views over the mountains.

➔ From Vila Nova de Cerveira take the mountain road up towards O Cervo (see 19), continue on the road past the stag and after 3km follow signs to Convento.

5 mins, 41.9301, -8.7071 🏔️⛲🔲

WILD PICNICS

23 COMMUNITY OVEN, COVAS

Bring your meat, fish and picnic to this 19th century stone oven. Start the flames inside with pine cones and dry wood. There are a fountain and picnic tables nearby in this shady village green.

➔ Take the N302 N out of Covas (Coura bridge) for 2km, on your R.

1 min, 41.8894, -8.6995 🌲

24 ERMIDA DA SENHORA DA ENCARNAÇÃO

Picnic tables under shady trees by the chapel. BBQ, old fountains and a stage for music. Glorious views across the Minho.

➔ From Vila Nova de Cerveira take the mountain road up to the O Cervo (see 19), continue until you see signs for the Capela.

2 mins, 41.9458, -8.7297 🌲🔲🌲

25 POÇA DO CERVO

'The Hart's Pool'. A still, glassy pond with trout, frogs, butterflies and eagles. Trees lean over from grassy banks to touch the water's surface which reflects the mountains.

➔ From O Cervo (see 19), walk back along the road, turn L and sharp L.

5 mins, 41.9455, -8.7235 🌲🏊🏔️✳️

LOCAL FOOD

26 RESTAURANTE O MOINHO

Look at riverside views as the River Vade comes gushing into the Lima. This old mill is now a family-run restaurant serving a delicious mix of regional Minho dishes and seasonal specialties.

➔ From the main road through Ponte da Barca, take a L before the bridge and continue round the block. Campo do Côrro 1, 4980-614 Ponte da Barca +351 258 452035, Restauranteomoinho.pt

41.8083, -8.4222 🍽️🅱️

27 RESTAURANTE CASA ESTRELA

Dark wood, stone and cool shadows only emphasize the warmth of mother and daughter at this restaurant. Fish is cooked at an open kitchen. Choose from three daily dishes: soup, bread, fish, wine for €5.50. The Viana Chocolate Factory is long gone but the chocolate mousse here is heaven.

→ R. Mateus Barbosa 60A, 4900-508 Viana do Castelo +351 258 405 294

41.6940, -8.8255 🍴▢

28 CAFÉ DA PONTE

A family café and restaurant popular with the locals. Built by the old bridge, the River Coura runs beneath and goats graze nearby. A quiet village but if Benfica win it gets pretty noisy in here. Try chicken and chips (*frango* with *batatas fritas*) and a beer.

→ Take the N301 or N302 into Covas (Coura bridge) and park near the roundabout. The café is on the bridge.

41.8784, -8.6907 🍴

29 RESTAURANTE ADEGA DO LAGAR

Come in on a Sunday and they will have only one dish. Go with it. Family-run, it has an ancient wood oven, wine press and a generous landlord. Locally sourced meat, wine, vegetables and bread. Try the *bagaço com mel*, a strong spirit mixed with honey; more than one, and you will leave *aterrada*.

→ Ponte Covas, Covas (Coura bridge) +351 251 948064

41.8777, -8.6898 🍴▢

30 MARKET AT VIANA DO CASTELO

Fishwives sell from buckets of *ouriço do mar*, 'sea-chestnuts', so called for their prickly husks; inside is a wonderful red oyster. Eaten fresh from the sea, it's the caviar of Viana.

→ Every Friday morning around the old ramparts of the castle.

41.6883, -8.8369 🍴▢▢

31 CHURRASQUEIRAS, VILA PRAIA DE ÂNCORA

Typical food here is charcoal-grilled chicken. Cheap and delicious; ask at any churrasqueira for a chicken *para levar* (take-away) and eat on the beach after a swim.

→ Along the beaches, Vila Praia de Âncora.

41.8160, -8.8636

32 FESTA DAS VINDIMAS E DESFOLHADA

Traditional festivities surrounding harvest: picking grapes, corn and wine-making. First Saturday in October, the husband and wife

team at Camping de Covas run wine-making workshops: pick grapes, use original machinery and enjoy dinner on a long table for all in the garden.

→ Lugar de Pereiras, Covas, 4920-042 VN Cerveira +351 251 941555, Parquecampismocovas.com

41.8893, -8.6959 🍴▢▢

RUSTIC HAVENS

33 ARCOS HOUSE, CARRALCOVA

This is a tiny village composed of stone houses built for farm workers, just 15km from Arcos de Valdevez. A cluster of cottages have been restored, their low-ceilinged rooms with wooden beams are a cosy escape in the hills.

→ Lugar de Oucias, Carralcova, 4970-105 Arcos de Valdevez +351 969 804619, Arcoshouse.com

41.9041, -8.3653 🍴▢▢▢▢

WILDER CAMPSITES

34 PARQUE CAMPISMO CABEDELO

Sleep under tall pine trees that rustle in the sea wind. Wooded hills, dunes and walkways to a sandy, undeveloped beach.

→ Av. dos Trabalhadores, Cabedelo, 4900-056 Darque +351 258 322042, Inatel.pt

41.6788, -8.8230 ▢▢▢▢

35 CAMPING DE COVAS

A family-run campsite with large green fields, outdoor pool and a creative edge. They run activities around traditional activities in harvest. See also 32.

→ Lugar de Pereiras, Covas, 4920-042 V.N.Cerveira +351 251 941555 p.campismo.covas@sapo.pt

41.8877, -8.6954 ▢▢🍴▢▢

36 QUINTA DE PENTIEIROS

Bungalows and camping areas hidden in woodland with lakes, watermills, winding paths and birding huts. This is part of the Lagoas de Bertiandos wildlife conservation project (see 20)

→ Parque de Campismo, 4990-530 Arcos-Ponte de Lima +351 258 240202

41.7755, -8.6491 ▢▢▢▢▢

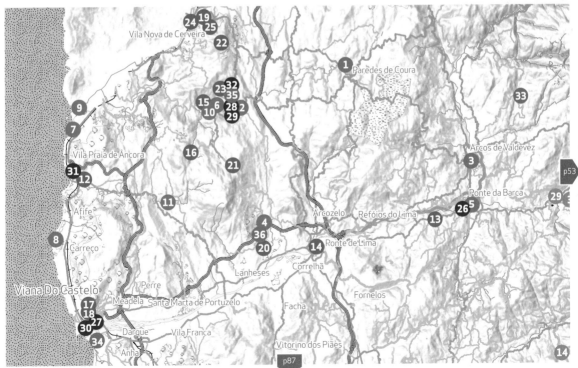

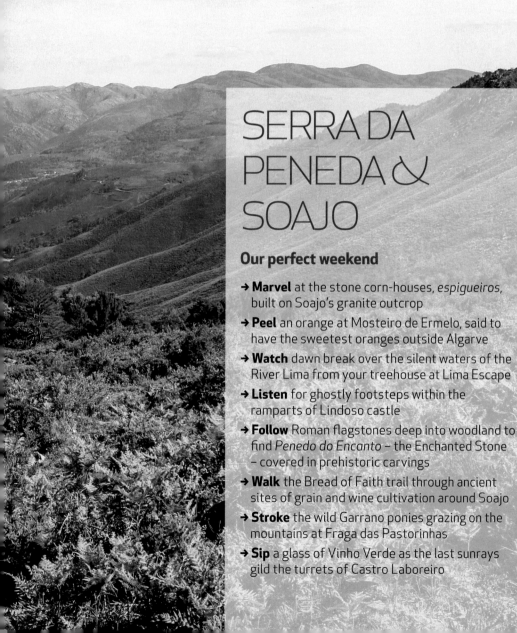

SERRA DA PENEDA & SOAJO

Our perfect weekend

→ **Marvel** at the stone corn-houses, *espigueiros*, built on Soajo's granite outcrop

→ **Peel** an orange at Mosteiro de Ermelo, said to have the sweetest oranges outside Algarve

→ **Watch** dawn break over the silent waters of the River Lima from your treehouse at Lima Escape

→ **Listen** for ghostly footsteps within the ramparts of Lindoso castle

→ **Follow** Roman flagstones deep into woodland to find *Penedo do Encanto* – the Enchanted Stone – covered in prehistoric carvings

→ **Walk** the Bread of Faith trail through ancient sites of grain and wine cultivation around Soajo

→ **Stroke** the wild Garrano ponies grazing on the mountains at Fraga das Pastorinhas

→ **Sip** a glass of Vinho Verde as the last sunrays gild the turrets of Castro Laboreiro

Eagles wheel over these mountainous regions inhabited by roe deer, Iberian wolves, wild goats and ponies. This northernmost area of Portugal is filled with hidden tors, hilltop settlements and prehistoric rock art, Roman ways and old shepherd huts. Tangled woods envelop the Roman road, Via Nova, which, in Portugal, stretches for 30km through ancestral oak trees and rare Gerês ferns, lilies, sundew and butterwort. Look out for the gold-striped salamander, water lizards and the horned viper.

The Parque Nacional da Peneda-Gerês is truly wild: it was granted National Park status as there are ecosystems here which remain undisturbed by humans. The reserve covers the plateaus of Mourela and Castro Laboreiro, but between these rise the uplands of Peneda, Soajo, Amarela and, further east, Gerês.

The unique community spirit that animates the mountain towns across the Peneda and Soajo peaks manifests its heritage with municipal ovens, shepherds' huts, canals, wolf traps, mills and *brandas* – medieval summer towns – found throughout these hills. Old ways of farming are still evident today as communities share the tasks of bread-making – local bread is known as as *pão castrejo* – for those running the mills or minding cattle on the hills. You can sign up to a bread-making workshop with Montes de Laboreiro or follow one of the many signed walking routes along the old mills. Look out for the shepherds with their dogs, of the *castro laboreiro* breed, herding the cattle.

If you walk up the Homem river, jumping over stones and dipping in the blue pools, you can see how this valley is one of many sculpted by glacial movement. U-shaped valleys, moraines and flaky rocks all bear witness to an ancient climate, far cooler than now. Or, if you fancy something more exhilarating, zip up a wetsuit and canyon down the Castro Laboreiro river and you'll slide over green stones with the tumbling water into deep, quartzy pools. Follow the river like this, along its curves and dips, and you can reach wild places without any paths, inaccessible by land and undisturbed by people.

RIVERS & WATERFALLS

1 PONTE DE DORNA

A small stone bridge of uncertain date and origin arches over the stream here. A Roman road used to connect this area. Depending on water levels it's a swim or paddle spot; grassy banks make for a relaxing picnic area.

→ From Castro Laboreiro take the M1160 S to Dorna for 4km. Turn L just before you enter the village.

2 mins, 41.9936, -8.1681 🌲👫🏊🚶

2 POÇO NEGRO, SOAJO

A tree-swing hangs over the sparkling fresh water of Poço Negro, meaning Dark Well. A cave is hidden in granite walls to one side. Large boulders are perfect for drying off in the sun with ledges for those wishing to jump in again.

→ From Soajo take the M530 out towards Paradela, past the granaries, *espigueiros*, and down the hill there is a sign which says 'Poço Negro'. Park nearby and take the steps down.

2 mins, 41.8782, -8.2582 👫🏊⛰️🧗

3 LAGOAS, ENTRE-OS-RIOS

A chain of blue pools along the River Froufe. 'Lagoa 1' has a rope-swing, 'Lagoa 2' a paddling spot, 'Lagoa 3' has diving rocks, a deep pool and towering views of the mountains either side. 'Lagoa 4' is a grassy picnic spot with heather growing between quartz rocks. Birdsong at all.

→ From Entre Ambos-os-Rios take the N203 towards Lindoso. After the bridge follow the trail signs for 'Lagoa 1' down to your R. For the rest, follow the road from Entre Ambos-os-Rios to Ermida and after 2 min take the turning to Froufe or the 'T1' sign. Follow through Froufe to find the Lagoas.

5 mins, 41.8220, -8.3011 🏊👫⛰️➕

4 LAGOAS, GERMILL

Cascades and waterfalls create deep, blue pools with quartzy, granite basins and still water. Hidden in a tangle of wild wood.

→ Park at Germill and from the chapel follow the signed walking route along the river edge until you reach the pools.

5 mins, 41.7829, -8.2650 👫⛰️➕🚶

5 MONTES DE LABOREIRO CANYONING

Zip up your wetsuit and slip over the mossy waterfalls of the Laboreiro river. See woods and rivers accessible by fin not foot. Take brave jumps into deep pools and emerge to panoramic views. A thrilling adventure for brave novices too. Canoeing, rock climbing, rappel, paint-ball, tree climbing all on offer here. Donkey walks, bread workshops and days out with a shepherdess.

→ +351 251 466 041, Montesdelaboreiro.pt

2 hrs, 42.0274, -8.1599 🏊👫⛰️📷🍴🧗

6 FISH TRAPS OF THE MINHO

Large rocky escarpments jut out into the fast flowing Minho. A feat of nature and human endeavour, the fish traps hang between the rocks.

→ There is a 6km signed linear walk along the Minho from Melgaço (42.1143, -8.2610); more info at the start point, Melgaço Tourist Office, in the square by the castle +351 251 402 440.

2.5 hrs, 42.1143, -8.2610 ⛰️🚶

ANCIENT & SACRED

7 PENEDO DO ENCANTO, LINDOSO

Prehistoric designs swirl over this ancient stone hidden deep in woodland. Barely discernible, you can trace the grooves with your fingers to 'see' them more clearly. Legend tells of Moors hiding gold in this rock; when the marks are deciphered the rock will open to reveal untold wealth. They remain to be deciphered.

→ From Lindoso take the N203/N304-1 towards Ponte da Barca. After 2km, at Parada, turn L at brown sign up to 'Penedo Encanto'. At some points your path becomes a stream. Park in Parada. Signposted from Casa do Charco, but follow the paved path when signs are missing.
30 mins, 41.8610, -8.2193 🏕️🏔️🚶

8 DOLMEN DA PORTELA DO PAU, CASTRO LABOREIRO

By the end of the 5th millennium BC the Castro Laboreiro plateau, 1,200m above sea level, was home to Neolithic communities

of shepherds. Up here, occasionally above the clouds, you can still see the funerary monuments they left behind. Known in Portuguese as '*mamoas*', they were once covered with earth to form mammary-shaped hills. Up here, the largest dolmen has zig-zagging carving inside.

→ Difficult to find, but access can be made by following the road from Rodeiro NE towards the Spanish border. After 3km park by the lake and follow the track around to R on foot for 3km.
45 mins, 42.0615, -8.1013 🏕️🏔️⚶†🚶

BORDER CASTLES

9 CASTELO DE CASTRO LABOREIRO

A wind-torn track leads to this wild castle. A 9th century Galician stronghold with pre-Roman roots turned Moorish castle; now only the eagles visit and lizards scuttle underfoot. Tread carefully along the old battlements. Spread your arms, unfurl imaginary wings and feel like an eagle wind-hovering over the blue below.

→ Before the dirt track winds up castle-wards there is a rocky promontory to your left with views of the tumbling blue Cascata do Laboreiro lost deep in woodland below. Park in

Castro Laboreiro, from the main square head down behind the pillory, cross the road, turn L, pass the museum. Dirt track to viewing rock on L, track to castle leads up R.
20 mins, 42.0231, -8.1582 🏕️🏔️⊞🅿️🚶

10 CASTELO DE MELGAÇO

Walk along the walls of this 12th century keep to take in the views of Minho. Look out for the statue of Inês Negra, a local woman and fearless defender of the castle against Castilian siege during the Portuguese Wars of Independence in 1388.

→ Follow signs to 'Castelo' in Melgaço. Parking.
1 min, 42.1146, -8.2597 🍴🍷€⊞

HIKING TRAILS

11 CURRO DA VELHA HIKING TRAIL, SERRA DA PENEDA

This 7km circular, signed trail leads through the Peneda mountains with views to the plateau of Castro Laboreiro. It leads past old shepherd huts, down flagstone paths and passes the Ribeiro de Baixo river in the Laboreiro valley.

→ Begin outside the Ranger's House (Casa do Guarda), Pousios. Parking here.
1 min, 41.9644, -8.1833 🏕️📷🅿️🚶

12 CAMINHO DO PÃO E DA FÉ, SOAJO

A 7km circular walking trail exploring survival (*pão*, bread) and faith: sites of grain and wine cultivation around Soajo, the waterfall and old mills, and crossing pilgrim paths, such as the Santiago de Compostela pilgrimage route.

→ Park in Soajo and start the walk from the town square following yellow/red signs.
2 hrs, 41.8743, -8.2628 ▲🚻⚡🚹🚶

13 TRILHO DE MEGALITISMO BRITELO

Serra Amarela has been inhabited since ancient times. This signed, circular 11km route from Britelo links the carved megalithic funerary stones that mark the beginning of human settlement 5,000BC here.

→ Park in Britelo and follow signs for Trilho de Megalitismo and yellow/red PR route signs.
3 hrs, 41.8345, -8.2902 🚻🏕️🚾🏔️🚶

14 GEIRA ROMAN WAY

Follow the Roman road, ironically called 'Via Nova', through ancient oak woodland. The paving slabs are deeply rutted by 2,000 years of cart traffic. The Roman way, linking Braga to Spanish Astorga, stretched 30km. This walk is a 9km circular, signed trail that takes you over some of the ancient

flagstones, and past mossy milestones, ruins and brooks within the woodland.

→ Start/end at church of São Sebastião, 3km S on the M535 from Terras de Bouro..
4 hrs, 41.6963, -8.2983 ▲🚻🏕️⚡🚶

15 TRILHO DA MISTURA DAS ÁGUAS

This 8km signed and circular walking route passes the Peneda, Laboreiro and Veiga rivers and makes use of a pilgrim route, smugglers' paths and the ways used by Galician workers in the Spanish Civil War. Craggy slopes lead down to untouched valleys and translucent bathing pools.

→ Begin at the church in Tibo, N from Soajo.
5 hrs, 41.9367, -8.2421 ⚡🏔️🚶

16 SANTUÁRIO DE NOSSA SENHORA DA PENEDA

According to legend the image of Our Lady was discovered in a cave nearby, giving rise to pilgrimage to this sanctuary. A thousand steps up, you can pay your homage to the hills.

→ From Soajo head N to Adrão and follow signs to Santuário da Peneda.
5 mins, 41.9737, -8.2232 🏕️🚾🏔️🚻

17 LAZER DE VEIGAS

Eagles wheel overhead at this grassy picnic spot and a narrow river curves under a small stone bridge. Picnic tables and football pitch.

→ From Lamas do Mouro follow signs to Castro Laboreiro; after 5 mins take the brown sign R to Area de Lazer.
18 mins, 42.0407, -8.1627 🚾🏕️🏕️

18 FRAGA DAS PASTORINHAS

The grandest introduction to the Serra da Peneda – the Mountain of Rock – is conjured here in its fullest. Beyond the gorge, the

great summit towers up and falls away to the River Peneda beneath. Wild ponies graze. This marks the beginning of a monumental change in landscape.

➜ From Soajo take the road N to Adrão, following signs to the church Santuário da Peneda. The miradouro lookout is en route with a small layby, 4km N of Adrão. Park and walk.

5 mins, 41.9269, -8.2373 ▣▲▲▼

MOUNTAIN TOWNS

19 MEDIEVAL SUMMER TOWN, ERMIDA

These *brandas* were used as summer homes by medieval farming folk, bringing their animals to stable in the hills. These 'lost' villages are scattered over all Peneda-Gerês and used now only for cows, filled with hay, ivy growing over the stones.

➜ Look out for the brown signs 'Branda' along roads in the park. From the viewpoint above Ermida, walk up hill and follow signs for 'Branda'.

30 mins, 41.8173, -8.2615 ▲▣▼▣

20 SOAJO

A 16th century pillory with a cheeky grinning face cut into its stone sums up the community of this small town. Famously, this town never let nobles stay "longer than the time bread takes to cool on the tip of a spear". Those who live here are those who rule. The *espigueiros* of Soajo, corn-houses, are a stunning granite army built on a fat rock overlooking the mountains.

➜ For the espigueiros follow brown signs, 500m S of Soajo on the M530.

5 mins, 41.8749, -8.2631 ▣▣▲▦

21 MOSTEIRO DO ERMELO

A 12th century Benedictine monastery on the banks of the Lima. Bells toll in a village empty but for the odd chicken. The oranges that grow here are said to be sweeter than even Alentejo oranges.

➜ S of Soajo on the M530.

2 mins, 41.8535, -8.2893 ▲▣✝▦

REGIONAL FOOD & FESTAS

22 MIRADOURO DO CASTELO

A homely restaurant with a terrace looking out over Laboreiro castle. Sip Alvarinho wine and watch the sunset light up the castle towers. Inside there's *pão castreiro frito com chouriço*, local bread, with a hard dark crust, fried with smoked meats. A good selection of local wines. All food is good 'mama food' and great traditional Portuguese dishes.

➜ Vila, 4960-061 Castro Laboreiro

+351 251 465 469

42.0274, -8.1599 ▣▣▣

23 ADEGA DO SOSSEGO, PADERNE

A bare stone, low-beamed rustic restaurant with extensive cellars. This is a good place to try the regional steaks and lamb cooked in a clay oven. Also a great place to try the local lamprey: breaded, fried, boiled, dried, roasted or with rice. A great selection of red, white and sparkling green wines.

➜ Estrada Nacional 301 Km 4, Lugar do Peso, Paderne, 4960-221 Melgaço
+351 251 404 308, Adegadosossego.com

42.1043, -8.2869 ▣▣▣

24 RESTAURANTE ESPIGUEIRO DO SOAJO

Exquisite local dishes cooked in a popular local restaurant. Try the *cabrito e anho da Serra de Soajo* (goat and lamb cooked; but pre-order ahead).

➜ Av. 25 de Abril 1425, 4970 Soajo
+351 258 576 136

41.8761, -8.2658 ▣▣

25 SOLAR DO ALVARINHO, MELGAÇO

Taste the wines from the regional Alvarinho grape in the old courtrooms of Melgaço. The town's prisons were once below, now a mural of blind Justice looks down. Your wine-tasting does not have to be blind, a guide is on hand. Try 'Reguiero' 2013, a woody example of the fresh Alvarinho grape. 'Donna Paterna' has some bite.

➜ Tv da Lage AR, 4960-556 Melgaço
+351 251 410 195

42.1141, -8.2600 ▣▣

26 FESTA DO ALVARINHO E DO FUMEIRO, MELGAÇO

A three-day-long festival celebrating the famous Vinho Verde – made mostly with the Alvarinho grape – and the region's excellent smoked meats. Also a great chance to try regional dishes of *lampreia*, lamprey, and roast goat. Mid-April.

➜ Melgaço

42.1143, -8.2579 ▣▣▣

MOUNTAIN HOUSES

27 CASA DO CHARCO, PARADA

Discover the Penedo Encanto of Lindoso (see 7) from the comfort of this traditional cottage.

➜ Caso do Charco Parada, Lindoso 4980-453, Ponte da Barca +351 919 444 905, Casadocharco.com

41.8613, -8.2193 ▣▣▲▣

28 CASA DO SERTÃO, PARADA

A cosy, traditional stone house in this tiny village. Several trails run nearby into the mountain.

→ Caso do Sertão Parada, Lindoso, 4980-453 Ponte da Barca +351 258 577 616, Casadocharco.com

41.8626, -8.2184 ⊞◿⚠🚶

WILD HAVENS & STARS

29 LIMA ESCAPE

Escape along the wilder reaches of the Lima with natural comfort. Lima Escape is set within pine woodland on the banks of the Lima as it meets the Germil and Froufe rivers. Watch the sunrise over the Serra Amarela from your treehouse with a wood-burning stove inside. 'Glamping' is also an option in a tipi with candles and blankets.

→ Lima Escape, Lugar de Igreja, 4980-312 Entre Ambos-os-Rios +351 258 588 361, info@lima-escape.pt

41.8239, -8.3174 🍴◿⚠🍽️

30 CASTELO DE LINDOSO

A border castle with a fraught history of invasion now in ruins guarded by goats. Pretty, friendly goats. This 17th century castle still has strong defensive walls, good barriers from the wind that will besiege if you wild camp here. Only for the brave to watch nightfall. Listen for steely toes on stone.

→ From Ponte da Barca take the N203 into Lindoso. Parking. 2 mins.

41.8671, -8.1991 ⊞⚠◈

31 CASA DOS CABREIROS, ROUSSAS

Amid Alvarinho vineyards with beautiful views and old stone walls, this cottage sleeps up to 12.

→ Roussas, 4960-551 Melgaço +351 962 851 205

42.1026, -8.2384 ⚠

32 LAMAS DO MOURO CAMPISMO

A beautiful, peaceful campsite set in the mountain woodland of Castro Laboreiro. A babbling brook meanders through the trees and mossy grass. Keep an eye out for a flash of orange in the treetops: red squirrels. Canyoning and adventure activities on offer.

→ Veigas de Lama, 4960-170 Lamas de Mouro +351 251 466 041, Montesdelaboreiro.pt/camping.html

42.0363, -8.1948 🍴◿⚠🍽️

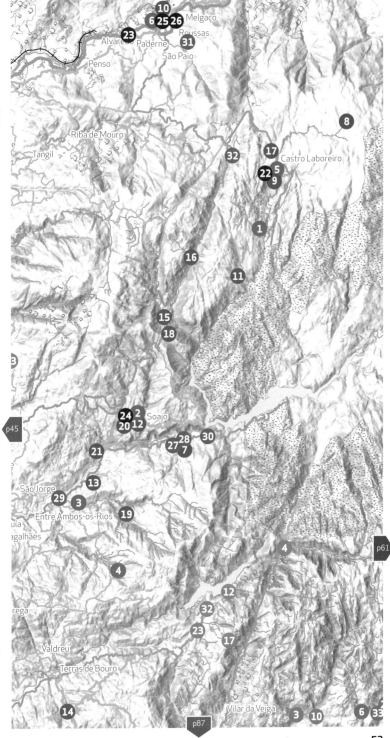

SERRA DO GERÊS & MONTALEGRE

Our perfect weekend

→ **Plunge** into the blue pool formed by the cascades at Cela Cavalos

→ **Follow** on the trail of the brown bears which roamed Gerês as late as the 17th century

→ **Soak** up the evening light filtered through the archways of the ruined monastery at Pitões das Júnias

→ **Rise** before dawn and scamper up the hills at Fafião as the sky grows pink

→ **Dance** wildly at Sexta-Feira 13, Montalegre's festival of dark tales, legends and witchcraft

→ **Dine** with the locals at Restaurante Cabaço where you can try some of the region's acclaimed *fumeiro* or smoked meats

→ **Curl** up inside a Mongolian yurt at Nomad Planet with views over snow-capped mountains

→ **Paraglide** from the Serra do Larouco, Portugal's third highest mountain

The regional name, Trás-os-Montes, means 'beyond the mountains', and here the mysticism of Montalegre, with its culture deeply rooted in the land, is greatly magnified by being 'beyond the mountains' of Gerês. Shepherdesses in thick felt hoods herd cattle from dawn until dusk. Their ancient huts, half-submerged high in the hills, appear like prehistoric tumuli. Warm, dry and womblike, these huts make the perfect wild camp.

Spy out corn-houses known as *canastros*, used to store grain for the thick crusted *pão de centeio*, rye bread. Zip up your tent at night as the *bruxa*, or witch, of Montalegre is believed to be more than just a fireside story. Be sure to follow custom and leave flowers outside, or untuck your shirt to ward off malignant spirits.

Every Friday the 13th, Montalegre comes alive with fireworks, costumed dances and *queimada*, a strong spirit infused with spices and set alight. The town celebrates its traditions with healing herbs and *fumeiro*, oak-smoked meats. You will see many Celtic parallels here, such as the Trasmontano bagpipes. The beautiful and heavy-horned *barrosã* cow is bred here. Bullfights are popular but this is still a protected and controlled breed. The roasted veal, *vitela assada*, served in any Montalegre restaurant is delicious. Chances are, they make the smoked *fumeiro* meats there too.

Beautiful waterfalls riddle the hills. Enjoy crystal waters at the cascades of Cela do Cavalos tumbling into an aquamarine pool. Or walk along the 'Wolf trail' to discover the spectacular Cascata de Pitões, falling over 30m of granite cliff.

There is a curious Montalegre legend from the time when villages left ailing dogs out for the wolves. Sick donkeys, too, would be left to the wild, and sometimes even weak old men. When the old man's time came, the son would carry the father up the hill, leaving him with bread for a day and a gaberdine cloak for the night. One day a son, having carried his father up the hill, was shocked as the father tore the gaberdine in half and handed one part back to the son. Asked if he was mad, the father replied. "For you, when your time comes." The son promptly carried him back down the hill. The wolf traps remain on these hills, a testament to this other time.

5

LAKES & RIVERS

1 PRAIA FLUVIAL, VILA DO PONTE

Grassy banks and rutted dirt roads lead down the River Rabagão. It's close to the road but no one passes this way.

→ From Montalegre take the N103 for 23km to Vila do Ponte. Park in the town and follow brown 'Moinho' signs to river, or head to 'Ponte Medieval'.

1 min, 41.7196, -7.9032 ▲⚠

2 BARRAGEM DE VENDA NOVA

The flooded River Rabagão is a perfect spot for a refreshing dip or an afternoon's fishing. The reservoir is a good source of trout for the locals.

→ Take the N103 to Venda Nova and park outside the cafés. There is a slip road between the houses to the 'Zona de Lazer' (Recreation Area).

5 mins, 41.6762, -7.9613 ⚠B

POOLS & WATERFALLS

3 POÇO AZUL, CASCATA DO ARADO

A waterfall tumbles at an altitude of 750m into this turquoise blue pool. Come here in low season for deserted swims.

→ From Portela do Homem take the N308-1 S for 15km; before River Cavado turn L onto the CM1276 for 9km following signs to Cascata do Arado.

5 mins, 41.7038, -8.1097 ▼⚠B↩⏷

4 LAGOAS, RIO HOMEM

Wild but probably the most 'known wild': boys jump with bravado from tall rocks. Follow the river up for 30 mins through this glacial valley and you will come to wilder pools.

→ Park at Portela do Homem (41.8091, -8.1316) and walk back down to the bridge.

15 mins 41.8033, -8.1288 ▼B⚠⏷

5 SETE LAGOAS

Seven deep rock pools in the River Cávado, open to the sky and surrounded by mountains.

→ From Montalegre take the M308 towards Paradela; continue on for another 7km, turn R onto unpaved road for 5km and park.

2 mins, 41.7587, -8.0270 ▲⏷⚠▼

6 CASCATA DE PINCÃES

Idyllic hidden waterfall and pool; stones under the glassy pool like hundreds of wishing-well coins. Go when the sun is high before the smooth rocks cast shadows.

→ Take the N308 into Pincães and follow the signs on Rua da Cascata for about 500m until the waterfall.

3 mins, 41.7084, -8.0553 ▲⚠⏷▼⏷

7 CELA CAVALOS

Hop over little black streams, shaded ferns and discover the bright clearing and brilliant pool. Small mills are tumble down now but would have milled flour here. Follow up the waterfall and above is another with a deeper pool for swimming.

→ Take the M308 to Cela, then take the road down past Santa Luzia Chapel (see 16) and follow the road for 4km. Park and walk 50m.

1 min, 41.7610, -7.9868 ▲⏷▼⏷▼⚠

VILLAGES & RUINS

8 CASCATA DA PITÕES

Panoramic views over the old 'wolf country' and across to the white windblown waterfall. Follow the wooden walkway for the views of the waterfall. You can take the Wolf trail from here to the *parada fojo* (wolf trap).

→ Pitões das Junias is about 22km W of Montalegre. From Montalegre take the M508 then M513, turning L at signs for Pitões das Junias. Before you enter the village turn L at

signs for Mosteiro and follow until parking area. Walk for 950m following signs.
15 mins, 41.8285, -7.9488 ⛰🚻🏊

9 SIRVOZELO

Houses are built into the side of a giant boulder in this small village with 11 inhabitants. There are probably more dogs than people here. A pretty place.

→ From Cela take the EM308 for 1km, turn R at SP and park before the village.
30 mins, 41.7706, -7.9659 ⛰🚶

10 FOJO DO FAFIÃO

This type of wolf trap exists only in the Iberian Peninsula: two tall converging dry stone walls run down the hill meeting at a pit below. Beaters would drive the wolf towards the pit. Eerily quiet, a morbid reminder of the wolf's endangered status.

→ Fafião is in the deep S of the Gerês National Park. Park at the café and walk uphill.
2 mins, 41.7036, -8.0927 ⛰🍴⊞🏃

11 FOJO DO LOBO, XERTELO

A well preserved wolf trap on the hills outside the village. Very wild but stunning views across the boulder-strewn mountains.

→ Park in Xertelo and walk 400m up the hill along the track. Fojo is on your L.
5 mins, 41.7357, -8.0150 ⛰🚻🏃

12 VILARINHO DA FURNA

When the waters are low see the ruins of the village flooded in 1972 by the Portuguese Hydro-Electricity Company, HICA. The village had Visigoth roots, but land was valued by HICA at the price of half a sardine per square metre.

→ From Campo do Geres take the N307 N, pass Parque Cerdeira and, at the first R, park and walk down the road to see the views.
30 mins, 41.7748, -8.1729 ⛰⊞🏃

13 ECOMUSEU DE BARROSO, MONTALEGRE

A museum to the collective memory of the Barroso rural traditions. Discover traditional tools, costumes and farm equipment of Portugal's bygone centuries. It is an imaginative testament to a rich heritage with workshops, new exhibits and a permanent collection. All within the old walls of Montalegre.

→ Ecomuseu de Barroso, Terreiro do Açougue 11, 5470-251 Montalegre +351 276 510 203, Ecomuseu.org
1 min, 41.8253, -7.7913 ⊞

16

HOLY & ANCIENT

14 MOSTEIRO DE SANTA MARIA DAS JÚNIAS

A 9th century monastery in the foothills of the Gerês mountains. The water canals built by Cistercian monks still run into the ruined dining hall.

→ In Pitões das Júnias follow brown sign to Mosteiro.

5 mins, 41.8311, -7.9427 🛉⊞▲✿

15 MILLS AT XERTELO

Ruins of an ancient water mill system to connect the mountain streams. There are several square stone towers and ancient wells to explore in these wild hills.

→ Xertelo is N of Cabril, on the M308. Park in the village and walk uphill.

2 mins, 41.7368, -8.0123 ▲⊞✿

16 SANTA LUZIA CHAPEL, CELA

A tiny chapel with spell-binding views across the Serra do Gerês makes a glorious picnic spot. Pilgrims to this chapel leave tiny piles of balanced stones, known as *mariolas*. Their simple presence is enchanting.

→ Cela is W of Paradela, on the M308. Park in the village and walk down to the chapel.

5 mins, 41.7666, -7.9775 ▲⊡🏕🏃

WILD WALKS

17 TRILHO DAS SILHAS DOS URSOS, GERÊS

Brown bears roamed these hills until the late 17th century. You can still see the stone structures, *silhas*, nearly 3m in height, which kept the beehives out of their reach. This 5km signed & circular walking route passes the *silhas* and swimming spots with beautiful views across the Gerês hills.

→ From Gerês, take the M533 towards Campo de Gerês. At the Lamas junction, about half way, take the forest track to the R, SP Junceda. Leave the car at the Junceda Miradore, and walk the rest of the track as far as the Casa de Junceda, then follow the walking route signs. Cm-terrasdebouro.pt/rede_trilhos_pedestres/ files/PR-11.pdf

2 hrs, 41.7456, -8.1696 ▲⊞🏃

18 TRILHO DO RABAGÃO

A 13km linear, signed walking route (PR5) which begins in Vilarinho de Negrões, on the S banks of the Rabagão reservoir, and ends at the village of Criande, taking in the ancient, rural towns of Morgade and Lamachã along the way.

14

15

→ Begin by the church at Vilarinho de Negrões and follow yellow/red signs out of town along Rua Principal.

3.5 hrs, 41.7376, -7.8013 🧍🏕️👣🍴

19 TRILHO DE D. NUNO, SALTO

The town of Salto has Roman origins and *mamoas* or megalithic tumuli are hidden in the magical woodland here. You can take the PR8 walking route, a signed 22km circular trail, through the woods. Don't forget to scatter a handful of earth if you pass a *mamoa*.

→ PR8 Trilho de D. Nuno begins in Salto at the Ecomuseu de Barroso, Rua Central 77, 5470-430 Salto +351 253 659 318

4.5 hrs, 41.6399, -7.9470 🏕️🚻

PILGRIMAGES

20 SÃO JOÃO DA FRAGA

A tiny mountain chapel with extraordinary views across the Gêres mountains. A pilgrimage is made every June from the small village of Pitões da Júnias to this chapel.

→ To reach this chapel from Pitões das Junias there is a 4.5km winding mountain track which leads from Pátio da Raposeira, the road behind Taberna Terra Celta.

1.5 hrs, 41.8307, -7.9747 ✝️🏕️🚻🅱️🔲🚶🧍

ADVENTURE ACTIVITIES

21 PARAGLIDING SERRA DO LAROUCO

The source of the River Cavado and, as the third highest mountain in Portugal at 1,535m, a popular paragliding spot. Call +351 210 848 878 for Beginners' Paragliding: Wind-cam.pt.

→ From Montalegre take the N103-9 N for 13km towards Spain. Turn R at Padornelos, and continue uphill. Park where you can, then walk.

5 mins, 41.8842, -7.7210 🏕️🔲🚻

22 CABRIL ECO RURAL

An equestrian centre where you can meet or ride the ancient breed of endangered Garrano ponies native to Galicia and northern Portugal. They can still be seen wild on these hills.

→ Rua do Passadiço 4, Lugar da Vila, 5470-013 Cabril +351 968 065 345, Ecoruralcabril@gmail.com

2 mins, 41.7138, -8.0355 👼🏕️🐾🚲

23 GERÊS EQUI'DESAFIOS

Horse trekking and adventure play park with rope swings and treetop walkways.

→ Rua de S. João 93, Campo do Gerês, 4840-030 Terras de Bouro +351 917 919 831, Equidesafios.com

1 min, 41.7503, -8.1964 🍴🚲🐾🔲🎏

REGIONAL FOOD

24 RESTAURANTE O CASTELO

Montalegre is famous for the *barrosã* breed of cattle, a wide-horned bison with a soft umber coat, which produces a tender steak, *vitela barrosã*. They serve it perfectly here, char-grilled and pink inside. Try with a glass of local red wine.

→ Terreiro Açougue 1, 5470-250 Montalegre +351 276 511 237

41.8255, -7.7914 🍴📍🅱️📶

25 RESTAURANTE CABAÇO, VILAR DE PERDIZES

A cosy restaurant behind a busy bar where the locals eat. The cook is cheerful and may pop out to chat to you. Try her *bacalhau a cabaço*. It's delicious and can be your 1,001st way to cook salted cod. A great choice of regional dishes and wines.

→ Vilar de Perdizes is on the M508 E of Montalegre. Avenida da Igreja, 5470-461 Vilar de Perdizes +351 276 536 136

41.8543, -7.6328 🍴👼📍🅱️🏕️

26 TABERNA TERRA CELTA, PITÕES DAS JÚNIAS

An ancient tavern in touch with its Celtic roots. Visit for the folk nights in this dark but lively hub of the village. Hearty food with locally sourced ingredients.

→ R. dos Caldeireiros 2, 5470-370 Pitões das Júnias +351 960 316 315

41.8417, -7.9507 📍🍴

FESTAS & FAIRS

27 FUMEIRO FESTIVAL, MONTALEGRE

A festival celebrating the heritage of fine smoked meats – *chouriça, presunto, alheria* – try the best of the best with music, dancing and other regional fare.

→ Montalegre, mid-late January.

41.8256, -7.7908 📶🍴📍📶

28 FRIDAY THE 13TH, MONTALEGRE

A festival to celebrate Montalegre's famous witch and all the wilder aspects of folklore, with a jovial twist.

→ Circus artists, fire displays, storytelling, strange costumes, dancing, street food and spell-weaving. Sextafeira13.org

41.8256, -7.7908 📶🍴📍🐾🅱️

RUSTIC HAVENS

29 CASAS DE ENTRE-PALHEIROS, SEZELHE

Three separate beautifully renovated barns with high ceilings, old beams and plenty of space for everybody. Located in the village of Sezelhe, a stone's throw from Montalegre, where the old traditions survive. A swimming pool in the garden is sheltered by a *canastro*, their traditional corn house. Beautiful views out across the hills. A real treasure of a retreat.

→ Casa Entre-Palheiros, Rua Entre-Parelheiros, Sezelhe, 5470-471 Montalegre
+351 276 518 125, Termontalegre.net
41.8131, -7.8745

WILD GLAMPING

30 NOMAD PLANET

Four traditionally painted Mongolian yurts in a field with panoramic views of the Gerês mountains. The central tipi has a kitchen and bathroom and each yurt is traditionally hand-painted with individual colours. It's stunning when it snows here and the yurts stay toasty warm with their insulation. Cycling and hiking trails nearby and 'Happiness Workshops' on offer. Exquisite attention to detail.

→ Rua do Forno 20, 5470-151 Fiães do Rio
+351 936 799 886,
Nomadplanet-portugal.com
41.7761, -7.9285

WILDER CAMPSITES

31 PARQUE DE CAMPISMO, PENEDONES

A simple campsite on the banks of the Rabagão reservoir; wake up to tranquil views across the water and take a long swim before breakfast.

→ Alto Rabagão, 5470-069 Penedones
+351 965 898 040, Aquabarroso.com
41.7572, -7.8095

32 PARQUE CAMPISMO CERDEIRA

A little village within Gerês with a welcoming family feel and a great restaurant for local dishes and wines. There is archery, a climbing wall and rappel, stone BBQs, bungalows and playing areas.

→ Rua de Cerdeira 400, Campo de Gerês, 4840-030 Terras de Bouro, Braga
+351 253 351 005, Parquecerdeira.com
41.7637, -8.1900

33 GERÊS GREEN PARK

A campsite on the wild banks of the River Cabril near several hiking trails in the national park. There are stunning mountain views and the campsite organises adventure activities such as canyoning.

→ Cabril, 5470-013 Montalegre
+351 917 007 831, Geresgreenpark.com
41.7082, -8.0417

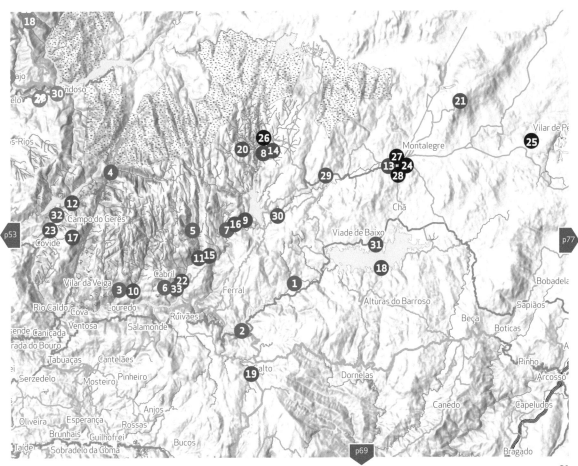

SERRA DO ALVÃO & VILA REAL

Our perfect weekend

→ **Stargaze** in Sabrosa as evening falls and night birds start up their calls. Drink dark Murça wine as the moon rises

→ **Climb** the deep Roman steps at Panóias, a temple to Serápis, and rest with your back on the sun-warmed stone

→ **Grill** a sausage on the hearth at 'A Cabana' mountain refuge, hidden in the Serra do Alvão

→ **Cower** under Fisgas de Ermelo waterfall as it cascades over 200m to the blue pool beneath

→ **Ramble** along old shepherds' tracks to Lamas de Olo and drink at the fresh fountain

→ **Picnic** along the grassy banks of the babbling River Olo at Parque de Merendas de Ermelo

→ **Breathe** in the views as the sun sets over the heather hills of Nossa Senhora da Graça

→ **Swim** in the magical waters by the hermit's chapel of São Pedro das Águias

Just north of the gentle, wine-growing Douro hills of central Portugal are the rockier, more dramatic crests and peaks of the Serra do Alvão. Water abounds in this region, bursting out as waterfalls from the mountains. At Fisgas de Ermelo the River Olo forms one of the highest waterfalls in Europe as it tumbles over rocks into green bathing pools. Explore the other waterfalls of Bilhó, Agarez and Galegos da Serra with a raft or canyoning.

The cheerful pealing of bells over the Douro hills here marks each quarter hour. On the north banks of the River Douro, the wine regions of Sabrosa and Murça fall within the same echoing web. They joke that as you leave one parish and the bells fade, you can already here the approaching peals from the next, but it's true.

This region, defined by bells, is encompassed by its rivers and fountains. Ramble through the farming villages of Lamas de Olo, Fervença or Ermelo and you'll pass countless stone fountains. These granite-built, thatched villages are surrounded by marshy wetland, *lameiros*, typical of Trás-os-Montes. Thanks to ancient irrigation systems, the land has been farmed for centuries. The livestock is still of huge value to its community, and the cows, goats and geese are all herded back home at the end of the day.

For fiery, ancient history head to Panóias, the remains of a Roman sanctuary to the Greco-Egyptian god of the underworld, Serápis. The ruins look south from Vila Real over a wild, rugged landscape. The stones' gruesome use is prescribed in Latin on their side, blood channels carved over their edge. Although there were no human victims of this resurrection cult, men and women would visit to spend the night on one of these rocks and see in the dawn as a symbol of their rebirth. Lie with your own back to the rock in the beating sun, and feel the fires, incense and euphoria of the forgotten cult of Serápis.

Vila Real has many regional peculiarities; the 'conventual' cakes, originating in convents, variations on a theme of eggs, sugar and cinnamon, are heavenly. Ask at a *pastelaria* for *cristas de galo*, *covilhetes* or *cavacórios* to fuel your adventures. The *alheira* sausage, a favourite in Portuguese mountain areas, made with blood and bread is known as *moura*. Our preferred place for *moura* is 'A Cabana', a mountain refuge deep in the Alvão woods where the meat cures on hooks by the fireplace.

5

WILD SWIMS

1 PRAIA FLUVIAL RIO RABAÇAL, VALPAÇOS

This deep, green river has wide grassy banks for a picnic or a snooze in the sun. Although crossed by the road over an arched bridge, it is still peaceful. Popular for canoeing, rafting and fishing as well as bathing.

→ From Valpaços take the R206 towards Bouça, park before the second bridge.

10 mins, 41.6305, -7.2485

2 CASCATAS DO BILHÓ

A set of waterfalls and blue pools formed by the Cabrão river. They are just off the road and continue for about 300m up where there are a few old mill houses.

→ Park in Bilhó and walk 1km S along the road to Cavernelhe.

10 mins, 41.3967, -7.8479

3 CASCATA DE GALEGOS DA SERRA

A magical waterfall that drops down from a height of about 8m into a blue green pool. Just off a fairly quiet road, it's surrounded by the typical Alvão landscape of rocky outcrops and tiered hills.

→ From Galegos da Serra take the road to Agarez for 700m until the parking area and information board.

2 mins, 41.3253, -7.7995

4 PIOCAS DAS FISGAS DE ERMELO

High jagged rocks lead down to a clear deep green pool. 'Fisgas' means 'slingshots' and the waterfall here certainly propels itself over a terrifying height. One of the tallest waterfalls in Portugal, the River Olo cascades over 200m.

→ From Ermelo head N on the N304 towards Mondim de Basto. There are a number of turnings for Fisgas. For the views and some pools turn R at the T-junction for Varzigueta (after 4km). Follow and park at signs for Piocas de Cima. Take the footpath down to the gorge. Sheer drop over cliff-face and scrabbly path.

20 mins, 41.3793, -7.8634

5 PARQUE DE MERENDAS DE ERMELO

The River Olo babbles over smooth stones and past foxgloves which line the banks in spring. The picnic area has a BBQ grill, football pitch, frogs and wild flowers. A perfect lazy Sunday picnic spot.

→ From Mondim de Basto take N304 towards Ermelo. After 20 mins see wooden plaques to 'Parque Merendas de Ermelo'. Parking.

2 mins, 41.3626, -7.8967

ANCIENT & SACRED

6 EREMITÉRIO DE SÃO PEDRO DAS ÁGUIAS

Set in the rocks by the River Távora, this hermit's chapel to St Peter of the Eagles was built in 991 to protect those fleeing from Moorish rule. Hundreds of animals carved into its stone suggest pre-Christian symbolism. Many legends abound; one is of Princess Ardinga, daughter of a Moorish king, who fell in love with a Christian knight Don Tedo and was beheaded by her father and the river ran red. But this was a long time ago, somewhere between truth and mystery. Now there is a beautiful swimming spot further along with clear, deep water and smooth stones.

→ From Granjinha follow the tiny CM1116 down to the River Távora and the hermit's chapel at the bottom.

25 mins, 41.0757, -7.5135

7 NOSSA SENHORA DA GRAÇA

From its lofty peak at 947m above sea level, the snake-backed summit bearing Santuário de Nossa Senhora da Graça can be seen throughout Mondim. A site of pilgrimage in

early September, the sanctuary has legends from Moorish conquerors, fishermen, Romans and hermits.

→ From Mondim de Basto follow the N312 N until Pedravedra, then take a slight R to follow signs uphill to Nossa Senhora. Parking.
5 mins, 41.4167, -7.9155 ▣▦✝▦

8 CHURCH BELL, TESTEIRA

A church bell that can be rung from the outside in this old schist village, typical of Alvão.

→ Relva, Corto, Cravela, Ferreiros are just some of the other mountain villages here that are worth exploring.
2 mins, 41.3507, -7.7472 ▦▣✝▦

9 SANTUÁRIO DE PANÓIAS

The remains of a 2nd century AD Roman temple to Serápis, god of the underworld. Walk around the ruins and imagine the sacrificial Roman cult performing their rites here. Climb the central altar rock and look out over the vista. A place charged with history.

→ From Vila Real take the N322 N through Mateus. Continue on the N322, pass Constantim and cross the A4, take the second L and follow signs to the Santuário. Parking.
1 min, 41.2834, -7.6819 ✝▦♺

10 BARRAGEM LAMAS DE OLO

Watch from a small peak as the sun goes down over the reservoir. As the moon rises over the open expanse, the undisturbed darkness and wildness make this is a wonderful spot for stargazing.

→ From Vila Real take the IP4. Exit N at Junction 26, and head for Borbela / Lamas Olo / Dam Alvão (M313). When you're close to the N end of Barragem Cimeira, park along the dust track and walk.
5 mins, 41.3561, -7.7941 ▦♣▣▦

11 BARREIRO

An old granite village, an *aldeia*, with a couple of *espigueiros*, granaries. A beautiful picnic spot next to a winding river in fields, on the way to Ermelo from Barreiro.

→ From Lamas de Olo turn off the M313 at signs towards Ermelo; Barreiro is en route.
5 mins, 41.3728, -7.8312 ♣▦⌖▦

12 LAMAS DE OLO

A simple rural village with granite houses and a water fountain so cool it will entirely

12

mist-up your water bottle. Livestock is an important feature of this village as are the *espigueiros*, granaries, between the houses. Take your mountain water on the signposted walking route from here (see 14).

→ If you are entering from the M313 park just outside town and walk in.

2 mins, 41.3724, -7.7956 ⊞ Ⅱ ⛰

HIKES & BIKES

13 CICLOVIA, RIVER CORGO

This cycle route follows the old railway for about 15km connecting Vila Real with Vila Pouca de Aguiar. It follows the River Corgo through the wild Marão and Alvão mountains, passing the Mateus Palace, the Roman bridge at Piscais and numerous wild spots for a dip in the Corgo river. Can also be followed on foot or by horse.

→ The cycle route begins just before the Abambres Gare Station and ends on the county boundary before Vila Pouca de Aguiar (41.4067, -7.6833).

1 hr, 41.3075, -7.7230 🚵‍♂️🚡⛰🍽🚶

14 TRILHO BARREIRO-LAMAS D'OLO

A signed, circular 13km walking trail which passes reservoirs, old stone villages, springs and rivers with their marshy *lameiros* grass, oak and pine trees.

→ From Lamas de Olo take the M313 S and turn R just before the reservoir. Park here, near the first sign, and begin the walk.

4 hrs, 41.3567, -7.7960 🚶⛰🏔🚡⊞Ⅱ

15 TRILHO AGAREZ-ARNAL

This 6.5km signed, circular trail leaves the village of Agarez and continues past grazing cattle into the mountainous area of Galegos da Serra. The path is a little more demanding, up steep hills, but the rewards are views across the valley even as far as Vila Real.

→ From Lamas de Olo take the road S into Agarez; from Agarez continue on the M1214 towards Galegos da Serra. About halfway, R, there is the first sign for the walk. Park.

1.5 hrs, 41.3225, -7.7922 🚶⛰🏔🚡⊞

16 TRILHO DO ARQUINHO

This 5km signed, linear walking route follows the Via Augusta XVII, the Roman way through woods connecting the village Possacos with Lugar da Barca on the River Rabaçal. It forms part of the Great Route 117 (GR117) which goes some 800km through Portugal and Spain. This walk is more gentle, taking you over a Roman bridge on the River Calvo, and by

11

10

orchards, vineyards and village picnic areas.

→ Start in the picnic area just E of Possacos (information board and parking). Continue on the track and cross over the R206. The walk ends where the R206 crosses the Rabaçal river at (41.6328, -7.2474).

1.25 hrs, 41.6169, -7.2692 🚶🏕️🖼️⛲

17 PARQUE FLORESTAL VILA REAL

Wild and unkempt for a city park. The River Corgo babbles by and there are plenty of picnic tables along its banks, sometimes even a tethered horse.

→ If you enter Vila Real from S along the N2, park along Avenida 1st Maio by the allotments. Walk down the narrow allotment path, along the river, and follow river until the park.

20 mins, 41.2996, -7.7403 🚶🏕️🖼️

REGIONAL WINES & FOOD

18 DOURO RIVER BOAT RIDE

Take a traditional Rabelo boat upstream as far as the mouth of the River Tua. This two-hour tour passes wine-producing farmhouses, terraced hills touching the river and vineyards – riverbanks unseen from the road. The boat will stop for you to take a swim in the Douro. An audio guide is offered, as well as a glass of Port or Moscatel.

→ Rua Marginal do Pinhão (in front of the Vintage House Hotel garden gate), 5085-037 Pinhão +351 913 129 857, Magnificodouro.pt

41.1894, -7.5441 🅿️🖼️🏊💶

19 PADARIA FLOR-CARVALHO GONÇALVES & FILHOS, COVAS DO DOURO

These tiny towns in the tiered Douro hills – Covas do Douro, Donelo, Gouvães do Douro, Calvário – all have stunning views of the Douro landscape and an untouched, hidden charm. There is a good *padaria* (bakery) at Covas do Douro where you can refuel, but it's open mornings only.

→ Rua Brasil 1, Covas do Douro 5085-205 +351 254 732 670

41.1895, -7.5943 🍴🖼️

20 ADEGA COOPERATIVA VILA REAL

Sustainable, traditional farming techniques are used to produce this award-wining Douro wine, sold here at low prices. Tawny and white port can be tried here too. Call ahead for a wine-tasting and to buy the wine.

→ Vale Frio - Folhadela, 5000-101 Vila Real +351 259 330 500, Adegavilareal.com

41.2741, -7.7191

21 QUINTA DO INFANTADO, CHANCELEIROS

This 8th-generation *adega* and vineyard has a traditional feel with bare stone and lots of ancient looking barrels. The Port made here is wonderful and the grapes are trodden in the traditional granite *lagares* rather than using modern processes. Try Roseira Douro DOC 2011, a complex, floral red wine and Quinta do Infantado Port 2011, medium dry. Call ahead for a tasting or to participate in a harvest day. Drop in any time to buy a bottle.

→ Quinta do Infantado, 5085-217 Pinhão Chanceleiros, Vila Real +351 254 738 020

41.1743, -7.5801 🍴🍷🖼️

22 RESTAURANTE 'A CABANA'

A cosy family-run cabin in the woodland of Serra do Alvão. Relax outside in seats carved in the trees. Inside homemade *alheira* sausages hang in front of the log fire. Ask for one to be grilled in the hearth and try the hearty soup and mountain bread.

→ From Vila Real take the M313 towards Lamas de Olo. Pass the lakes and A Cabana is on your L in the woods just before Lamas. 5000-142 Lamas de Olo +351 259 341 745

41.3697, -7.7980 🖼️🍴🍷

23 ADEGA SETE CONDES

A rustic restaurant, though in town, and a great place to try regional dishes, grilled *alheira* sausage, local breads and the sparkling Vinho Verde 'Nossa Senhora da Graça'.

→ Rua Velha, 4880-256 Mondim de Basto +351 255 382 342

41.4116, -7.9532 🍷🍴🐾

WILDER CAMPING & STARS

24 PARQUE DE CAMPISMO DE MONDIM DE BASTO

A beautiful woodland campsite that runs down to a river with *espigueiros* – traditional corn houses – on its banks. Horses are kept in stable nearby and it's a small stroll to the medieval bridge.

→ Lugar de Montão, 4880-187 Mondim de Basto +351 255 381 650

41.3997, -7.9519 ⛺🖼️🏕️⛺

25 PARQUE DE CAMPISMO DO RABAÇAL

A campsite on the banks of the River Rabaçal. There is a sandy river beach and woodland which gives shady pitches. Dogs, bungalows, food, bar, wifi.

→ Parque de Campismo do Rabaçal, Possacos, 5430-191 Valpaços +351 278 759 354

41.6321, -7.2475 ⛺🖼️🏊🏕️⛺

26 SABROSA

Bivvy up, wild camp and drink Murça wine under the stars then fall asleep to the distant chiming of the hilltop church bells. Wake to the low mist rising off tiered vineyards of the Douro valley.

→ Head S out of Sabrosa on the N323 until you pass the *miradouro*, a small gazebo structure. Park here and wander down a few tiers of the hillside. 5 mins.

41.2463, -7.5783 ⊞⛰⚑

27 CASA DO VISCONDE DE CHANCELEIROS

An elegant, 18th century manor house, now a guesthouse with 12 bedrooms, pool and a terrace with views over the Douro countryside. Drink a glass of Port on the terrace and watch the sun go down.

→ Casa do Visconde de Chanceleiros, 5085-2 Pinhão +351 254 730 190, Chanceleiros.com

41.1731, -7.5777 🍴⛵⚑

28 ALVÃO VILLAGE CAMPING

Overlooking the River Torno's Barragem da Falperra, this newly built camping village echoes the traditional Portuguese *aldeia*. Round stone-built *castreja* houses are elegantly furnished within. There is space for camping, caravans and campervans as well as a restaurant, bar and pool.

→ Alvão Village Camping, Lagoa da Falperra, 5450-261 Vila Pouca de Aguiar +351 259 419 038, Alvaovillagecamping.pt

41.5062, -7.6628 🍴⛵⛲⛺

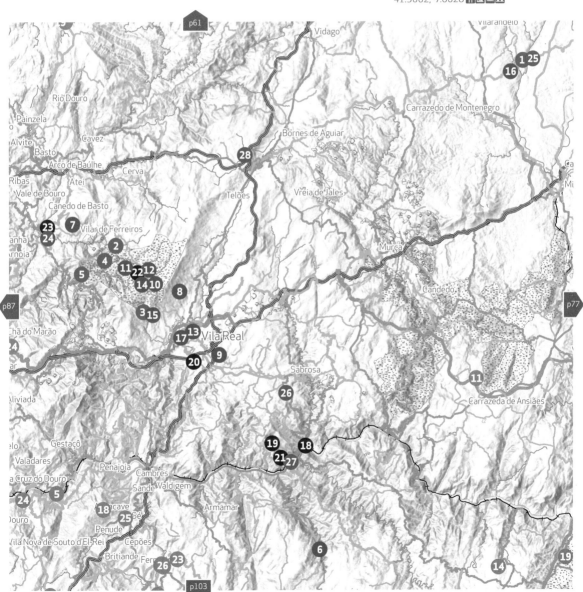

MONTESINHO & BRAGANÇA

Our perfect weekend

→ **Celebrate** the regional Miranda do Douro donkey at L Burro i L Gueiteiro festival with dancing and donkey parades

→ **Crawl** under the heavy stones of Anta da Zedes, a megalithic dolmen built some 5,000 years ago

→ **Gorge** on the smoked meats and delicious dishes made from *bísaro* pork at Feira de Fumeiro de Vinhais

→ **Watch** sunset crown the hills with gold from the dark towers of Algoso castle

→ **Marvel** at Rupestrian rock engravings some 22,000 years old in Vale do Côa

→ **Listen** out for the birdsong over the calm waters of Azibo reservoir

→ **Follow** the Roman way from Moimenta back to the wild banks of the Tuela river

→ **Look** out for wild deer as dusk falls over the Montesinho hills

→ **Picnic** on a regional fare of local cheese, smoked meats and fresh bread by Praia Fluvial de Uva

Trás-os-Montes e Alto Douro, 'Beyond the Mountains and Above the Douro', in the north-eastern tip of Portugal is as far-flung as its name suggests. This borderland, disputed for centuries, has given rise to an extraordinary culture, neither Spanish nor Portuguese but distinctly Trasmontano. So much so that their own language, Mirandese, is officially recognised and still spoken in the border towns.

The international borders disappear further under ties of friendship. One warm evening, we met a couple from the village of Rio de Onor strolling arm in arm, who had just crossed from Portugal to see her mother, who lives over in Spain. Ancient divisions disappear under familial ties and now, also, dissolved by a growing number of festivities.

The slate-built villages in the Montesinho Natural Park repose on the hills as the River Onor sparkles by on its quick paced journey. In the quiet village of Mofreita one woman insisted she show us her beehives buzzing under the chestnut trees and heavy sun. The secret to this region's abundant chestnut trees and dark honey is simple, she says: partnership. The bees pollinate the chestnuts, and the blossom feeds the honey.

Neighbouring Moimenta has ramshackle houses with lichen-covered stones and lazy donkeys nodding in the sun. A Roman way leads down the hill, along wide flagstones, and over a medieval bridge on the River Tuela. Cool off with a dip where the water is deep and fresh.

In late October the village of Sendim celebrates the Mirandese's own particular breed of donkey, the *burro da Miranda*, with street parties. But the iconic image of the region is the masked figure in a colourful fringed costume: the *careto*. At carnival, Easter or between Christmas and New Year you can see them running down the streets, whistling and whirling wildly.

Trás-os-Montes is renowned for steaks and smoked meats. Just before Lent, Vinhais has a *fumeiro* festival where hundreds of regional producers gather to sell their smoked meats: *alheira*, *chouriço*, *presunto* and *salpicão*.

At twilight these borderlands are home to wild deer. Tread quietly up the hills from Onor and you may catch a glimpse. As we crept in the near-darkness, a doe bucked out from the heather and fled over the hills. Within seconds we lost sight as she faded into the lilac-grey mountains stretching out into Spain. This is where the wild things are, heedless of borders.

RIVERS & LAKES

1 PRAIA FLUVIAL DE UVA

A wide, still river with tall trees and views up the sides of the Algoso valley. There are picnic tables here in the shade. A perfect place to unwind on the grassy banks.

→ From Vale de Algoso (between Vimioso and Mogadouro) take the road towards Uva and turn L when you cross the river.

1 min, 41.4925, -6.5259

2 PRAIA FLUVIAL DA FRAGA DA PEGADA

Dive down into the Azibo Reservoir from the long grasses of this fluvial beach. It can be busy in summer but on a quiet evening the birdsong is enchanting.

→ Turn off the N15/A4 at junction 37, following signs to Praia Fluvial/ Albufeira do Azibo and follow road 8km until beach.

2 mins, 41.5817, -6.8983

3 ECOPARK AZIBO

A hilltop getaway within the Azibo Geopark offering eco-breaks centred around the reservoir. Activities here include snorkelling, kayaking, catamaran trips and paddle boarding; all begin at the wooded banks of the Azibo Reservoir.

→ Núcleo de Salselas, 5340-400 Salselas, Macedo de Cavaleiros +351 278 448 019, Ecoparkazibo.com

1 min, 41.5592, -6.8837

4 CAIS FLUVIAL DO SENDIM

A well-guarded secret down a none-too-accessible road, dusty and steep. But the deep green Douro that sweeps out before you makes it worth all the effort.

→ From Sendim take R. do Baiunco (41.3824, -6.4193) for 5km, keeping R, down the dusty track. Before it descends too sharply, park and walk remaining distance.

20 mins, 41.3505, -6.4166

5 PRAIA FLUVIAL MIRANDA DO DOURO

Dip in the slow-moving Douro at this beach looking out to Spain.

→ From Miranda do Douro follow the N218 and signs to Praia Fluvial down the hill.

2 mins, 41.4933, -6.2689

6 PRAIA FLUVIAL FRESULFE, VINHAIS

Wide, grassy banks and granite picnic tables line the edge of this river beach on the River Tuela. A small dam widens the river before it runs on into woodland past the old mill.

Alders lean over the water and there's a diving platform further upstream.

→ From Fresulfe follow signs to the Praia Fluvial. Parking.

1 min, 41.8968, -6.9381

7 PRAIA FLUVIAL DA PONTE DE FRADES

Just before the Rabaçal river heads south out of Montesinho Natural Park, you can find this quiet beach. It's surrounded by greenery, with clear, slow water.

→ From Frades head N and then turn R at the junction. Continue for 3km along this road until you cross the river, turn L and park along dirt track.

1 min, 41.8656, -7.1195

8 PARQUE DE MERENDAS, RIO ANGUEIRA

A picnic area on the grassy banks with tables and BBQ. The occasional fisherman further upstream. Deep, cool and dark water where the river widens a little.

→ From Vimioso take the N218 E, towards Caçarelhos for about 3km, R at signs to Parque de Merendas.

5 mins, 41.5717, -6.4982

9 PRAIA FLUVIAL DA PONTE DE SOEIRA

A fluvial beach in a kink of the Tuela river. Large flat rocks jut out to form jumping platforms when the water is deep enough. Surrounded by woods and greenery.

➔ Along the N103 from Vinhais towards Bragança, pass Vila Verde as the road dips, and park before the old bridge.

2 mins, 41.8470, -6.9368 ⛰🏊

10 PONTE MEDIEVAL DA MOIMENTA

A wide paved bridge over the River Tuela. The bridge may be medieval but it is on the Roman way and its bulk and weight could withstand the cavalry. Below, the Tuela offers a deep and thrilling respite from the walk.

➔ From Igreja de São Pedro, SE of the main square in Moimenta, go L at the fountain and here begins the Via Romana. Follow the lane/stream with heavy flagstones (later changing to flat stones) winding downhill. Continue until you reach the hidden Roman bridge.

20 mins, 41.9426, -6.9696 ⛰👣🏖⛰🏊

ANCIENT & HOLY

11 ANTA DE ZEDES

A megalithic dolmen, which you can enter, with eight overlapping pillars and a roof-slab. It's known locally as Casa da Moura,

a name that testifies to folk conflation of much older history with the comparatively recent Moorish occupation. Traces of wavy carving can be seen on the inner stones.

➔ Approach Zedes village from the east on the M628 and it's 500m before the village. Park and follow signs down the dirt track.

10 mins, 41.2753, -7.2935 👣⛰🏊🌳

12 ARTE RUPESTRE DO VALE DO CÔA

This 17km stretch along the Côa river valley holds thousands of Palaeolithic rock engravings. Pictures of horses, cattle, deer, fish and human figures litter the rock. The oldest date back to almost 22,000BC, but people continued to make drawings for another 20,000 years, well into the Bronze Age. You can visit any of the 62 sites but it's best to find the information centre and choose your site. Guided tours and night tours are available, pre-book. Closed Mondays.

➔ Museu do Côa, Rua do Museu, 5150-610 Vila Nova de Foz Côa +351 279 768 260, Arte-coa.pt

1 hr, 41.0799, -7.1117 📷🚶👣⛰€

13 CASTELO DE ALGOSO

The remains of this 12th century castle stand looking out over the valleys of the Angueira and Maçãs rivers. 681m above sea level, you can see all of Trás-os-Montes and further out into Spain. A steep climb but worth it for the sunset.

➔ From Mogadouro take the N216 then N219 N and keep straight, follow signs to Vimioso, passing Azinhoso and Peso. Turn R at signs for Castelo. Park by the fountain and walk.

5 mins, 41.4614, -6.5797 📷🏰

14 CASTELO DE NUMÃO

This rocky, wild castle sits atop a hill thought to have been occupied since Lusitanian times. Its long walls follow the shape of the hill, and a watchtower and cistern remain. A dramatic, romantic place to watch the evening draw in.

➔ From Freixo de Numão, follow signs for Castelo.

1 min, 41.0686, -7.2425 🏰⛰📷

13

CAVES & RUINS

15 FORNOS DE CAL E LORGA DE DINE

This tiny village has several lime kilns half buried in the hill, easy walking from the centre and with beautiful views. Also ask here for directions to 'Lorga de Dine', a karst cave in the hillside with two chambers, used in the Bronze Age as a funerary cavity.

→ For information visit the interpretation centre in Dine. End of the road Bairro de Cima.

10 mins, 41.9111, -6.9285 🧍🚵🏔⊞

16 CASTELO DE PENAS RÓIAS

A 12th century fortress given to the Templar knights. By about 1758 it had fallen into ruin. Now overrun by the wild, it keeps its beautiful views over Azinhoso village and further out to Algoso castle.

→ From Mogadouro take the N219 N and turn off after 10km at signs for Penas Róias. Park in the village.

10 mins, 41.3922, -6.6539 🖼⊞✿

HORSES & WILDLIFE

17 CENTRO HÍPICO VINHAIS

A riding school beside the Parque Biológico entrance. You can take a lesson, a hack on horseback or a chariot ride out around the wild scenery of Montesinho.

→ See Parque Biológico de Vinhais (see 29). +351 273 771 040

1 min, 41.8585, -6.9872 🐴🐾€

18 AZIBO GEOPARK

A protected woodland area of 5,000 hectares with a reservoir in the middle. Home to hundreds of birds such as the swallow, lapwing, grebe, plover, egret, wagtail, falcon, eagle, merlin and hoopoe: bring your binoculars or keep your eyes peeled if you decide to walk one of Azibo's signed walkways.

→ From Mirandela take the A4 N towards Bragança. Take the turning to Macedo de Cavaleiros and continue through this on the N216, turning L at signs for Vale da Porca. Follow signs to the Azibo Geopark. Geoparkterrasdecavaleiros.com

2 mins, 41.5592, -6.8837 🏊🚤🏔🖼

19 MILES AWAY NATURE TOURISM

The Douro Valley is the oldest demarcated wine-growing region in the world and the Côa Valley holds the oldest known open-air, artistic expressions of mankind. Between them, that's a lot of history. Miles Away is a nature tourism company, run by locals, who will tailor an experience to your wishes, be it eagle-watching, a week's mountain trekking, a day with a shepherd or a table awaiting you – miles away on a wild riverbank – bearing the best Douro wine and food from the region.

→ Av. Dr. Artur Máximo Saraiva de Aguilar 8, 2Esq. 5150-540 Vila Nova de Foz Côa +351 938 749 528, Milesaway.pt

1 min, 41.0840, -7.1410 🐴🏔🖼🚣🍴🚴♀€

18

REGIONAL DISHES

20 RESTAURANTE FRAGA DOS TRÊS REINOS, MOIMENTA

The sort of restaurant that at lunch will simply bring you the dish they have on the stove. The grilled pork, *porco grelhado*, is very good as are the black beans with bacon. This is a great place to try local cuisine.

→ Moimenta, 5320-070 Vinhais Bragança +351 936 988 924
41.9484, -6.9750 🍴🍷

21 RESTAURANTE VASCO DA GAMA, VINHAIS

Small, quiet downstairs but upstairs there are more seats. A simple fare of local bread and dark wine in a clay pitcher while you wait. Try the *vitela assada* – oven baked meat with potatoes – and salad.

→ Rua da Calçada 24, 5320-322 Vinhais +351 931 314 251
41.8354, -7.0029 🍴🍷

22 RESTAURANTE O TURISMO, MOGADOURO

Despite its name this restaurant is popular with the locals and does amazing octopus rice, *arroz de polvo*, as well as a good number of traditional dishes and Douro house wine, at very low prices.

→ Rua de Santa Marinha, 5200-241 Mogadouro +351 279 106 558
41.3402, -6.7176 🍴🍷

MOUNTAIN FESTIVITIES

23 FEIRA DO FUMEIRO VINHAIS

With hundreds of Trasmontano producers of smoked meats, this is the best place to try the region's famous *bísaro* pig. Weekend before Lent.

→ 4730-440 Vinhais, Fumeiro.org
41.8322, -7.0085 🍴🍷🎿🏕

24 RONDA DAS ADEGAS, ATENOR

In mid-June the village of Atenor comes alive with local gastronomy, traditional arts and crafts and many local wine merchants. Try a traditional bread-making workshop or a beer-brewing workshop.

→ Rua da Igreja, Atenor.
Rondadasadegas.blogspot.pt
41.4224, -6.4804 🍴🍷🎿

25 L BURRO I L GUEITEIRO

This itinerant festival celebrates the Miranda do Douro traditions of donkeys, wandering and bagpipes. Local produce is bought and shared out on long tables and up to 20 donkeys parade into town.

→ Each year a different *aldeia* within the parishes of Miranda, Mogadouro or Vimioso hosts lunch, but the donkey parades travel to them all. Various locations. Last week of July. Aepga.pt
41.4592, -6.4448 🍴🍷🏕

RUSTIC HAVENS

26 CASA DOS PIMENTEIS

Between Vimioso and Mogadouro is a rustic, six-bedroom guest house with pool and terrace but also the traditional rooms for smoked meats, a wood oven and open fireplaces. There are beautiful walks here; within 1km you can find the River Angueira.

→ Vale de Algoso, 5230 Vimioso Domingos Pimentel +351 964 011 817, Casadospimenteis.co.pt
41.4978, -6.5395 🎿🏕🏔

27 PUIAL DE I DOURO

In the midst of the Douro International Nature Park this 19th century house, courtyard and outhouses belonged to one of the most important farms in the village of Aldeia Nova. You can glimpse the River Douro and its rugged cliff sides from here while enjoying their library stocked with Mirandese literature or their cellar stocked with Douro wine. A beautiful breakfast of cakes, Mirandese honey, jams, cheeses and hams is served every day.

→ Rua da Igreja, Aldeia Nova, 5210-170 Miranda do Douro +351 273 432 820, Turismodourorural.com
41.5405, -6.2349 🍴🎿🍷

28 CASA DE ONOR

In the heart of the Montesinho Natural Park this five-bedroom schist-built mountain house is typical of Trás-os-Montes. Just on the outskirts of the village of Rio de Onor, its wooden balcony looks out over the babbling River Onor below. You can dine on this balcony or cosy up with a book in one of the generously cushioned pews. Plenty of walks to follow up the hills nearby where you can see wild deer.

→ Aldeia de Rio de Onor, R. Central 34, 5300-821 Bragança +351 273 927 163, Casadeonor.com
41.9404, -6.6165 🍴🍺

29 PARQUE BIOLÓGICO DE VINHAIS

Set within the Montesinho Natural Park, the Parque Biológico de Vinhais makes for a very wild stay. Bunk down in one of their log cabins or take a dip with the ducks in their natural swimming pool. A centre for wildlife protection, you can learn about the native trees, fungi, soil and flowers while also getting closer to the deer, fowl, wild boar and ponies native to the surrounding area.

➜ Alto da Cidadelha, 5320 Vinhais +351 273 771 040, Parquebiologicodevinhais.com 41.8589, -6.9883 🍴🚘📶🍴⛺🏕

30 PARQUE DE CAMPISMO CEPO VERDE

A quiet campsite in the Montesinho Natural Park with beautiful mountain views and several hiking trails nearby. It is also home to the world's largest pocket knife, listed in the *Guinness Book of Records*.

➜ Lugar da Vinha do Santo, 5300-561 Gondesende Bragança +351 273 999 371, cepoverde@montesinho.com 41.8458, -6.8605 🏕📶🏕

31 PARQUE DE CAMPISMO, RIO DE ONOR

A beautiful green campsite on the banks of the River Onor and walking distance from the typical Trasmontano village of Rio de Onor. Numerous hiking trails up into the hills where you might catch a glimpse of wild deer.

➜ Aldeia de Rio de Onor, 5300-821 Bragança +351 273 927 061 41.9400, -6.6157 🍴📶⛺🏕

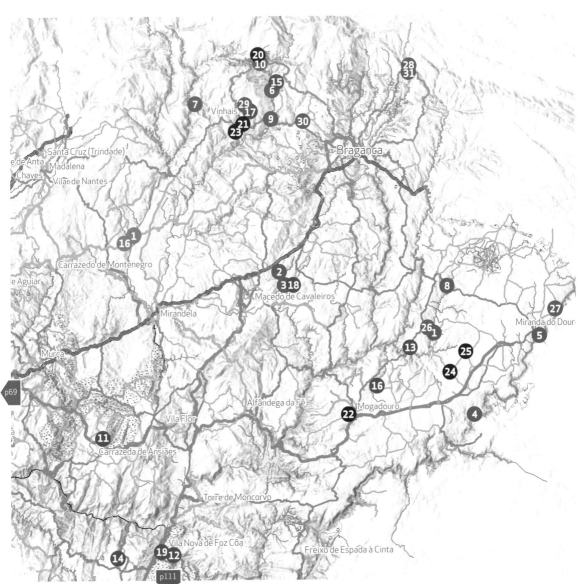

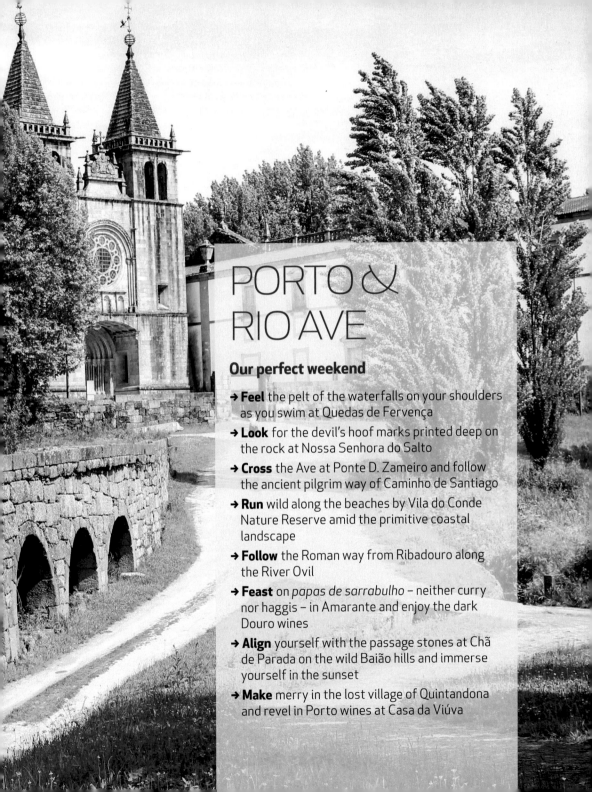

PORTO & RIO AVE

Our perfect weekend

→ **Feel** the pelt of the waterfalls on your shoulders as you swim at Quedas de Fervença

→ **Look** for the devil's hoof marks printed deep on the rock at Nossa Senhora do Salto

→ **Cross** the Ave at Ponte D. Zameiro and follow the ancient pilgrim way of Caminho de Santiago

→ **Run** wild along the beaches by Vila do Conde Nature Reserve amid the primitive coastal landscape

→ **Follow** the Roman way from Ribadouro along the River Ovil

→ **Feast** on *papas de sarrabulho* – neither curry nor haggis – in Amarante and enjoy the dark Douro wines

→ **Align** yourself with the passage stones at Chã de Parada on the wild Baião hills and immerse yourself in the sunset

→ **Make** merry in the lost village of Quintandona and revel in Porto wines at Casa da Viúva

At sunset in Porto, gold rays catch the terracotta roof tiles, the city is enflamed and mirrored in the River Douro, curling beneath. At once golden and reflected darkly in the murky depths of its river, Porto and its district's history are best understood through the glints and gleams of its rivers. Their histories are intertwined, snaking back along the watery courses from the hills of Baião, Amarante and further into the Douro region.

The river-fed vineyards would send their wines back along the river to Porto on elegant *rabelas* boats. While the union of wine and the Douro is widely celebrated, there are other forgotten narratives of the region's rivers. Old water mills, once spun by streams gushing through the hills and valleys, are scattered across the land. Their finely milled flour would produce the regional *broa*, a dense corn or rye bread with a thick crust. You used to be able to spot the millers here by the flecks of stone in their beards. You can see the mills in action in farms near Vizela or in Capela.

Pack a picnic to fuel your adventures along hiking trails up to the many pre-Roman hill forts: Terroso, Monte Padrão, Sanfins or Monte Mozinho. One trail leads to Cividade de Bagunte, an Iron Age fort surrounded by woodland; it once guarded the River Ave and is still a beautiful spot to survey the hills. You can see the remains of ancient homes, animal houses and great gateways built under Roman occupation. These forts make a magical place for a sunset.

Follow the rivers inland to Baião, where several megalithic dolmens crown the wild hills of Serra de Aboboreira, recalling ancient, wilder cultures who lived in this land. Taking the medieval road along Rota de São Bento will lead you past ruined inns up to the summit of Picotos; then return for a dip from the Aboadela river beach.

Just north of Porto, Vila do Conde is one of Portugal's oldest settlements. Phoenicians are believed to have docked here, and during the Portuguese Discoveries it excelled as a centre of shipbuilding. There's a replica galleon moored in the harbour. Walking along the coast, past the fishermen's heaped crab traps, the beaches are quiet but grooves in the rock left at São Paio by Iron Age settlers remind us that the wild is filled with voices from the past.

WILD COAST

1 VILA DO CONDE NATURE RESERVE

See the coastline as the Celts would have first seen it, uninhabited by all but the wildlife. This is 380ha of varied landscape: dunes, wetland and cliffs by the mouth of the River Ave. A great place for birdwatching, but also keep an eye out for red squirrels. You can see their presence in signs such as pine cones gnawed to the quick.

→ Park in nearby Areia and walk in. Be sure to stick to footpaths. Metro from Porto runs to 'Espaço Natureza' station 30 mins walk away.
5 mins, 41.3175, -8.7395 ⬛⬛⬛⬛⬛⬛⬛

2 SÃO PAIO

This is the only coastal Celtic settlement known in Portugal. You can see the rocks on which they sharpened their tools and possibly the remains of runic inscriptions sanctioning the passage of foreign vessels. There is a wooden walkway linking the beaches of São Paio with Praia de Labruge, both very quiet sandy coves enclosed by black rocks.

→ Park in Vila Chã by the coast and walk S along the beaches.
20 mins, 41.2822, -8.7312 ⬛⬛⬛⬛

3 NAU QUINHENTISTA

Vila do Conde was one of the most prolific centres of shipbuilding and, during the time of the Discoveries in the 15th and 16th centuries, carracks set sail to India from this harbour. Here you climb inside a replica galleon with statues of the crew – captain, scribe, chaplain, apothecary, cabin boy – about their tasks. There is even the quiet woman, a presence necessarily unknown by all but the chaplain, still hidden in her room.

→ Park near the harbour at Vila do Conde. The ship is docked opposite the boat museum. Tickets on the gangway.
2 mins, 41.3499, -8.7433 ⬛⬛⬛

4 ASSEMBLEIAS DE DEUS VILA CHÃ

Come down to these beaches to see hundreds of crab traps and fishing nets piled next to small boats. These are fishermen's beaches.

→ Turn off the N13 at signs to Vila Chã, park and walk along the seafront.
10 mins, 41.2909, -8.7333 ⬛⬛⬛

RIVERS & WATERFALLS

5 QUEDAS DE FERVENÇA

Beautiful fresh waterfalls cascade over tiers of smooth rock as the River Leça gushes through wild woodland. The water forms a pool of middling depth bordered by big smooth stones.

→ Head S from Santo Tirso along the N105 then M558-1 to Facho. The path is signed from Rua Pedras Pintas.
15 mins, 41.3023, -8.4485 ⬛⬛⬛⬛⬛⬛

6 PRAIA FLUVIAL DO TÂMEGA

Broad trees shade grassy banks by a jetty into the wide and slow River Tâmega. It is crossed by a busy bridge further down but remains peaceful at this spot. Near the pretty granite village of Barrias.

→ From Marco de Canaveses cross the Tâmega on the N211 and turn L immediately (to cross back under the road) following signs to Parque Fluvial Tâmega. After 500m follow the sand track and park.
5 mins, 41.1973, -8.1591 ⬛⬛

7 PRAIA FLUVIAL DE LARIM

A grassy park with trees and picnic tables by the River Carneiro. There are little waterfalls and bridges over the river, a popular spot with the locals.

→ Exit N15 at Larim and follow signs. Parking.
5 mins, 41.2510, -8.0344 ⬛⬛⬛

12

8 PARQUE NATURAL NOSSA SENHORA DO SALTO

The hills which flank the River Sousa form a steep, rocky gorge at this point, known as the Boca do Inferno, 'Hell's Mouth'. The river gushes through, forming deeper pools before rushing on. There is a legend that a knight was chasing a deer, in fact the devil incarnate, who leapt into this gorge. The knight and horse followed but invoked the name of Our Lady and were saved; you can still see the hoof marks left on the rock as they landed safely. A small chapel is built here, known as Our Lady of the Leap.

→ From Aguiar de Sousa take the N319-2 towards Alvre and 'Salto' is signed on your R as you cross under the A41.

2 mins, 41.1286 -8.4337 ⚑✝♿⊞

9 PRAIA FLUVIAL RUA-ABOADELA

Here the River Ovelha curves and fills before a little weir. Grassy banks provide a lovely picnic spot by this old rural village with a medieval bridge just outside Aboadela. A walking route passes through here (see 24).

→ From Amarante take the N15 to Paredes then the M574 to Rua; follow signs L to the 'Zona de Lazer'.

2 mins, 41.2775, -7.9957 ⚑✈♿⚶

HILLTOP FORTS

10 CASTRO DO MONTE PADRÃO

The occupation of this Celtic settlement began in the 9th century BC; it was inhabited until the medieval ages. Now you can take in spectacular views across the wooded hills and wander the low circular ruins.

→ The Castro is signed from Monte Córdova.

10 mins, 41.3127, -8.4490 ⊞⚶♿

11 CASTRO DE MONTE MOZINHO

This is a 1st century AD Roman hill fort with extensive groundwork, the largest of its kind in Portugal. Known locally as the 'Dead City', the entrance of the town was guarded by two giant statues of Galician warriors, now housed in the municipal museum. It commands incredible views over the Penafiel hills.

→ From Galegos take the road S towards Mosinho and after 1km turn L and follow brown signs for Castro de Monte.

5 mins, 41.1462, -8.3111 ⛰⚶⚶⊞⚶

12 CIVIDADE DE TERROSO

Known in the Middle Ages as the Earthy City, this is an enchanting spot where you can explore the remains of circular houses typical of the Celtic tribes in Iberia before Roman rule. This is one of the earliest Celtic settlements, begun in 800-900BC.

→ From Póvoa de Varzim take the N205 towards Terroso and follow signs to Cividade.

5 mins, 41.4125, -8.7205 ⛰⚶⊞⚶

13 CIVIDADE DE BAGUNTE

A Celtic hill fort hidden in eucalyptus woodland. It was later Romanised and occupied by Roman garrisons. This would have been a prominent and thriving hub, high up, guarding the entrance to the River Ave. You can walk barefoot along the remains of ancient streets, crossing worn lintels. Perfect for imaginative children to run wild.

→ From Bagunte take the N309 and then N306 north; after 1km follow brown signs to Cividade. Parking and a walk uphill.

10 mins, 41.3833, -8.6555 ⚶⊞⛰⚶⚶

14 CITÂNIA DE SANFINS

A hilltop Iron Age fort built around the 1st century BC, the circular remains of the houses are interspersed with rocky granite outcrops. Now a rambling, wild city with beautiful views.

→ Follow brown signs from Sanfins de Ferreira.

10 mins, 41.3265, -8.3856 ⊞⛰⚶⚶

15

ANCIENT & SACRED

15 MOSTEIRO DE SANTA MARIA DE POMBEIRO

This is one of the oldest monastic institutions in Portugal. Documented since 853AD, it lay along two busy medieval trade routes and was used to house pilgrims. Now a little aqueduct runs through its land; there is a gargoyled water fountain and some walking trails (see 19). The surrounding fields make a peaceful picnic spot.

➜ From Felgueiras take the N101 N for 4km and follow brown signs for Mosteiro.
5 mins, 41.3826, -8.2256 ⊞✝⊼

16 CHÃ DE PARADA

This dolmen, rising up from the Serra de Aboboreira, surveys a wild heath and is much larger inside than it appears outside. A 4.5m entry passage leads to a dark, cool recess covered by a large granite slab, placed there around 5000BC. On its walls are engravings, one known locally as 'the thing' and the other as *face oculada* (face with eyes), easier to see if you visit at night with a torch.

➜ From Baião head S towards Zona Industrial de Baião, turn R at sign 'Estações Arqueológicas' and continue up the hill. Pass

the riding centre, turn R and follow road for 6km. Alternatively, park here and walk as you will pass the Outeiro de Gregos and Meninas do Crasto dolmens (see 17 & 18), among others.
1.5 hrs, 41.2033, -8.0075 🐾⛰🎴

17 OUTEIRO DE GREGOS DOLMENS

Several tumuli, some with fallen slabs, rising up from the rocks and wind-torn heath of Serra da Aboboreira. They were built in the first half of the 4th millennium BC and command spectacular views across the Baião hills.

➜ See Chã de Parada, above.
2 mins, 41.1871, -8.0410 🐾⛰🎴🚶

18 CONJUNTO MEGALÍTICO DE MENINAS DO CRASTO

Several 4th millennium BC tumuli surround a well-preserved dolmen with a roof slab. Its name means 'Women of Crasto', *crasto* being the word for a Roman hill fort, or it could refer to the more ancient pre-Roman tribes who inhabited these wild hills.

➜ See Chã de Parada (16).
2 mins, 41.2010, -8.0211 🐾⛰🎴

18

13

HIKING & BIKING

19 CAMINHOS MEDIEVAIS WALKING TRAIL

This is a signed, circular 6km walking trail linking several medieval sites: villages, monasteries, bridges and a Roman causeway. It passes Mosteiro de Pombeiro as well as fountains, streams and the River Vizela.

→ Begins and ends at Parque de Campismo de Vila Fria (see 39).

1.5 hrs, 41.4142, -8.2349 ⬛⛰️✛⊞🚶

20 CICLOVIA DA MARGINAL ATLÂNTICA

A 4km stretch of cycle lane linking the beaches from the Forte de S. João Baptista, at the mouth of River Ave, to the Póvoa de Varzim harbour.

→ Begin at the Fort de São João.

1 hr, 41.3418, -8.7514 ⛷🚶🚴

21 ROTA DAS RAÍZES

This is a signed, 10km linear walking route from Ponte D. Zameiro (see 27), following the old Caminho de Santiago way along the River Ave, passing picturesque villages and old mills. It diverges from the Caminho and finishes at Cividade de Bagunte (see 13).

→ The walk begins at Ponte D. Zameiro (see 27) and is signed.

3 hrs, 41.3509, -8.6818 ⊞⛰️🚴✛

22 ECOPISTA DA LINHA DO TÂMEGA

Journeying to Amarante by train used to be a very romantic passage made by trundling along tracks following the River Tâmega. Now fallen into disrepair, the tracks have been given a new lease of life as a 50km cycle route between Amarante and Arco de Baúlhe.

→ Signed from Amarante train station.

3 hrs, 41.2731, -8.0833 ⛷

23 ROTA DO MARANCINHO

This signed, circular 6km walking trek leads through pine woodland interspersed with gorse flowers, following a dirt track down to a hidden paradise by the Marancinho stream. The walk continues through oak, chestnut and cork forest, with vestiges of Roman roads.

→ Begins and ends at the Igreja Românica in Gondar.

1.5 hrs, 41.2635, -8.0314 🚾⬛🚶✛

24 ROTA DE SÃO BENTO

This 12km signed and circular route passes medieval roads and ruins of ancient inns, winding up the mountain in Picotos with views across the wooded mountains of Marão and the Aboadela valley. Look out for churned earth, signs of wild boars passing this way at night.

→ Begins and ends at the Aboadela river beach (see 9 for directions).

3 hrs, 41.2774, -7.9957 🚶⛰️🍴⊞✛

25 CALÇADA ROMANA DE RIBADOURO

Follow this Roman way down paved flagstones, some 2,000 years old, leading through the beautiful Douro landscape. The way reaches north from the Douro, following

27

the River Ovil, for about 3km. It was once part of a much wider network leading to Mérida in Spain. The entrance peeks out onto the national road, signed but small so be careful not to miss it.

→ From Ribadouro take the N211 towards Porto Manso. The way is signed at 400m after the church of António de Ribadouro.
45 mins, 41.0958, -8.0825 🚶🎯🏔🔀

26 REGADIO DA POTE FERREIRA WALKING TRAIL

This signed, 3km linear route follows the Rio Ferreira past bridges, old mill houses and even an aqueduct which transports water across the steep sides of this river.

→ The walk begins at the Núcleo Museológico da Panificação (Museum of Bakery) at Ponte Ferreira, Valongo.
45 mins, 41.1883, -8.4589 🏊🎡

MILLS & MUSEUMS

27 PONTE D. ZAMEIRO

This 12th century bridge over the River Ave forms part of the Caminho de Santiago route. It is also home to a healthy number of ducks. The old men chatting on the bridge, adoptive guardians of said ducks, tend the mill house

and keep any stray ducklings inside.
→ From Bagunte take the N306 S, first L and follow, park before the old bridge.
1 min, 41.3509, -8.6817 🎡🎯🎡

28 MUSEU DA BROA

The museum is composed of six recovered and functional mills by the stream which comes rushing down over the stones into Capela village. Here you can be transported back to the time when millstones worked day and night, without stopping, producing flour that gave sustenance to our ancestors in the form of *broa*, the region's heavy cornbread.
→ From Capela, head N on N319 towards São Julião. The museum is just after the junction with M591 (leading to Figueira). Capela, Penafiel +351 933 484 761
2 mins, 41.1131, -8.3508 🎡🍴📷

29 MUSEU RURAL DO MARÃO

A museum exhibiting collections of instruments relating to the traditional tasks of rural Marão: carpentry, basket-weaving, medicine, blacksmithing, baking and exhibitions on the local *barro negro*, black clay.
→ Take the N211-1 W from Amarante. 2.5km after the junction with N210, L into the small R do Rio for 500m. Rua do Rio 503,

28

21

4600-642 Gondar +351 255 441 055, Museururaldomarao.com. Closed Mondays; 2–5.30pm Tuesday–Sunday

1 min, 41.2717, -8.1156 ⊞☷

LOCAL FOOD

30 TASQUINHA DA PONTE, AMARANTE

Step down off Amarante's cobbled streets to this dim and cosy restaurant. The *papas de sarrabulho* here is to die for. This is a traditional Minho region dish made from pigs' blood, chicken, smoked pork sausages, cumin, lemon and bread, flour or corn, served in a ceramic pot. It is strangely like a cross between curry and haggis and best accompanied with *rojões á moda do Minho*, firecracker potatoes and a glass of red Vinho Verde.

→ Rua 31 de Janeiro 193, 4600-043 Amarante +351 255 433 715

41.2686, -8.0773 ⊞▯▮

31 TASKUINHA, VILA CHÃ, PORTO

A little snack bar for the locals – with eccentric piratical embellishments – facing the beach. A nice place to enjoy the sunset and a drink.

→ Av. dos Banhos 185, 4485-850 Vila Chã, Porto

41.2900, -8.7326 ▯▮△☷

32 FESTA DE PÃO DE LÓ, MOSTEIRO DE POMBEIRO

For one weekend in late March to early April, the medieval cloisters of Mosteiro de Pombeiro (see 15) are host to this festival of sponge cakes: you can try *bolinhol de vizela*, *pão de ló de ovar* and *pão de ló de ovos moles de castelo de paiva*, among other regional specialities. There are children's workshops in bread-making and monastery-related activities .

→ Festivaldopaodelo.pt

41.3827, -8.2259 ⊞▯▮✝

33 CASA DO LAVRADOR

This is a *museu rural* and restaurant dedicated to the old ways of life in the Baião mountain villages. They keep the past alive through exhibitions, workshops, re-enactments in costume of harvest and holy festivities and, of course, through food. Here you can try local *entradas*: their *presunto e salpicão*, *cebola rachada* (stuffed onions) and the local hardy bread *broa de milho*. You have a choice of regional dishes and a truly celebratory array of puddings and wines.

→ At the W end of Gaia, on the N108, turn N onto M580, SP Corujeiras. Casa do Lavrador is the large pink building on the L. Estrada N.ª Sr.ª do Martírio 667, 4640-414, Sta Cruz do Douro, Baião +351 254 885 143 Casadolavrador.pt

41.1242, -8.0155 ⊞▯▮☷

34 CASA DO ALMOCREVE

An elegant restaurant with high granite walls, wrought iron, twisted wood furnishings and wood burning ovens. They have a great selection of wines, displayed around the room, and a selection of regional dishes. Perhaps try the *bazulaque*, a pottage with offal made in a ceramic pot. Call ahead to order the heavenly lamb, pork or veal baked in the wood oven with rice. Guest rooms available and regional cooking workshops.

→ Rua do Fontanário, Portela do Gôve, 4640-270 Baião +351 255 551 226, Casadoalmocreve.pt

41.1235, -8.0421 ▯▮☷▮⊞

35 TASQUINHA DO FUMO, ALMOFRELA

In the tiny village of Almofrela, lost in the Baião hills, is this small granite restaurant with low beams, bottles of wine and pictures of the family lining the walls. Generous portions of regional specialities served in clay pots and iron pans. In summer try the *bacalhau na brasa com batata a murro*, grilled cod with baked potatoes. In winter, they make *cozido á portuguesa e os rojões com castanhas*, stew with pork and chestnuts. The village is about 2.5km NW of Baião.

→ Almofrela, 4640-101 Baião +351 255 541 120

41.1757, -8.0571 ▯▮☷

36 CENTRO INTERPRETATIVO DA VINHA E DO VINHO, ANCEDE

Since its foundation in the 12th century, the monastery of Santo André has been intertwined with local wine production. The wine produced in its lands was sent down the Douro for export at Porto, placing Ancede on the wine map long ago. Here you can visit its small exhibition centre about the cycle of vines and wines. Try 'Lagar do Convento' Vinho Verde made from monastery-grown Avesso grapes.

→ Rua Eça de Queiroz, 4640-152 Baião +351 255 540 550

41.1019, -8.0569 ⊞☷▮€

37 WINE BAR CASA DA VIÚVA

Wine has been the physical, spiritual and fiscal sustenance for many of the inhabitants of Porto district down the ages. This history is celebrated at the village of Quintandona's 'Widow's House', an old schist stone house, once used for grain storage, now turned wine bar. Feast on local cheeses and smoked meats while you sample their cornucopia of wines.

→ Follow M592 S from Fonte Arcada, pass the M319 junction and follow brown signs to Quintadona. Rua de Quintandona, 4560-195, Lagares, Penafiel +351 255 753 603, Winebarcasadaviuva.pt

41.1338, -8.3798 🍴📷🏕️⊞

WILDER CAMPING

38 PARQUE DE CAMPISMO RURAL DE VILA FRIA

A green, friendly campsite within walking distance of the River Vizela. Grassy spots to pitch under shaded woodland, and a kids' swimming pool. A couple of signed walking routes begin here and there are beautiful wooden bungalows.

→ Rua da Raposeira, 4610-842 Felgueiras +351 255 346 403

41.3919, -8.2291 🍴⛺🗑️♨️⛰️

39 PARQUE DE CAMPISMO DO AVE

A beautifully secluded camping site on the banks of the River Ave. Dappled shade and grassy spaces, BBQ and bar, and chickens that run about free. Fresh bread delivered for breakfast.

→ About 1km S of the centre of Ferreiró. Rua da Mocha 396, 4480 – 250 Ferreiró, Vila do Conde +351 252 657 732, Campingave.net

41.3452, -8.6316 ⛺🗑️🍴⛰️♨️⛰️

RUSTIC RETREATS

40 QUINTA DE CARCAVELOS

A beautiful 17th century manor house and farm set in the Tâmega valley with magnificent views to the mountains. Wake up to a pool, a choice of nearby walks and the sweet scent of the surrounding lemon groves.

→ Rua de Carcavelos, Vila Meã, 4605-115 Amarante +351 255 734 426, Quintacarcavelos@clix.pt

41.2794, -8.1207

41 CASA DO AGUIEIRO

A little schist stone house in the village of Quintandona with two double bedrooms, kitchen and living room. It's a cosy retreat in the Penafiel hills, near a walking trail up to the Pegadinha mountain and just opposite a hidden gem of a wine bar, Casa da Viúva (see

37). An annual Broth Festival takes places here in September and 'Os Comodeantes' stage regular plays in the village.

→ Quintandona, 4560 Penafiel +351 255 752 382, geral@casaxine.org

41.1336, -8.3797 ⊞⛰️

42 CASA VALXISTO

A large, elegant guesthouse by the sleepy village of Quintandona with rooms named after fruits and flowers of the farm and decorated with rural objects, reclaimed furniture and with colours inspired by the surrounding hills. Pool and restaurant.

→ Rua Padres da Agostinha 233, 4560-195 Lagares Penafiel +351 255 752 251, Valxisto.pt

41.1354, -8.3780 🍴📷⛰️

42

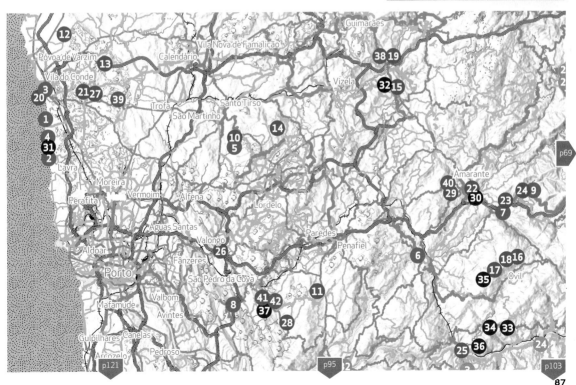

AROUCA & ALVARENGA

Our perfect weekend

→ **Picnic** on the banks of the Paiva river by the slate stone village of Meitriz

→ **Wend** your way to the wild pilgrim church Capela de São Pedro

→ **Wonder** at the strange *pedras parideiras*, 'stones that give birth'

→ **Cower** from the brink of the mountain at Portal do Inferno

→ **Bunk** down in traditional stone houses at Quinta da Vila and fling open your windows to spectacular views

→ **Discover** Drave, an abandoned mountain village, accessible only by foot

→ **Swim** up to Lovers' Isle, Ilha dos Amores, in early morning sunlight

→ **Dine** on rich *arouquesa* steak and dark red wine

→ **Brave** the rapids at the Garganta do Paiva as white water rushes out

→ **Wander** up Serra de Montemuro and pass by the old wolf traps

Around 280 million years ago a great force pushed together quartz, feldspar and biotite deep under the granite rocks in present-day Arouca. Arouca Geopark, recognised by UNESCO as a geological site of exceptional importance, is an enormous wild geology museum, its rocks valued for the clues they give as to our origins, strange predecessors and Earth's wonderful history.

These ancient events, once held deep within the rock, today surface as *pedras parideiras*, 'stones that give birth'. You can see these birthing stones at Castanheira, their glinting nodules popping out of weathered rock. Locals put them under their pillows: "they say you'll have lots of children". Whether these popping stones are understood as geological curiosities, as ancient symbols of fertility, or both, they testify to a very long history.

The history told by the geology of Arouca is strange and marvellous. More than anywhere else, the rock here holds ancient secrets about the Earth's birth, age and one of our stranger predecessors, the trilobite. These distant creatures occupied the ocean floor many million years ago and some of the largest trilobite fossils, reaching 70cm, can be seen in the slate here.

In spring, a great swathe of deep purple and yellow flowers, heather and *carqueja*, carpets the mountains of Serra de Montemuro and Serra da Freita, and weather-wizened faces crack into smiles. Wild mountain paths interlace over the hills. Follow the new Paiva walkway along the river and reach wild places hitherto inaccessible. Geological patterns left over millennia have earned its name 'the Paiva library': not only does it tell ancient stories but it resembles heavily stacked bookshelves.

Albeit carpeted in springtime flora, in May we found ourselves driving blind through heavy white cloud. We were forced to seek shelter in an abandoned mountain refuge where wind tore through the pines, cracked open shutters and howled through empty rooms. Emerging into bright sun the next day, we were re-introduced to the road we had taken: Portal do Inferno. It deserves its name, as either side of its skinny spine plunges away to devastating depths. A road for the bravest of travellers. The most intrepid souls here are the herds of mountain goats who gambol over the craggy peaks and trot away at your approach with kicks and jingling bells.

9

WATER

1 ZONA BALNEAR AREINHO

A beautiful bathing spot in the cool, clear River Paiva near a wooden walkway. Pine trees cover the steep valley sides.

→ From Vilarinho take the R326-1 E for 2km towards Miudal. At (40.9538, -8.1740) turn R and park.

2 mins, 40.9528, -8.1758 🏊🏕🚶

2 PAIVA RIVER WALKWAY

This wooden walkway, stretching 8km along the Paiva, allows previously inaccessible wild places to be seen, places such as Garganta do Paiva and Cascata das Aguieiras. It also passes fluvial beaches.

→ The walkway stretches from Espiunca (40.9929, -8.2114) to Areinho (40.9528, -8.1758).

2.5 hrs, 40.9929, -8.2114 🏕🏞🚻🛒🅿🌐

3 GARGANTA DO PAIVA

Alvarenga granite narrows the river course, and water comes rushing and tumbling out of this tightest section of the Paiva known as the river's throat. Great for canyoning and whitewater rafting in the rapids of the Aguieira waterfall upstream. Call Clube do Paiva +351 964 018 656.

→ Follow the Paiva walkway from Areinho for 3km (see 2). Clubedopaiva.com

45 mins, 40.9648, -8.1793 🏞🏃

4 PRAIA FLUVIAL DO VAU

A deep, green swimming spot in the Paiva. Nearby, the Fontão stream tumbles down into the Paiva.

→ From Canelas follow the signs for Praia Fluvial and park. Or walk from Espiunca along the Paiva walkway for 2.5km

45 mins, 40.9764, -8.1892 🏞🏊

5 PRAIA FLUVIAL DA PARADINHA

A small village with a river beach. Visit in late August for 'Sons de Água': listen to music played on the river and try the delicious regional cuisine.

→ From Alvarenga take the R326-1 towards Arouca and after 10km at a T junction take a sharp L down the narrow road to Paradinha.

2 mins, 40.9347, -8.1740 🏊🏞🍴

6 PRAIA FLUVIAL DE JANARDE

Along this stretch of the Paiva, look out for evidence of an open-air alluvial goldmine probably started in Roman times.

→ Park in Janarde and follow signs down to the river bank.

5 mins, 40.9273, -8.1481 🏊🏞

WILD WATERFALLS

7 POÇO DA SILHA

An unexpected turquoise bathing pool beneath a waterfall in the magical woodland that surrounds Manhouce.

→ Park by the bridge in Manhouce and follow the brown sign down a steep descent to the river pools.

5 mins, 40.8259, -8.2159 🏊🔦🍴🏊

8 POÇO NEGRO

Further down from Poço da Silha is this deep, green diving pool carved by cascades of the River Teixeira.

→ From the village of Sernadinha follow 'Poço Negro' signs for 1km down dirt track. Park by Carregal Dam and walk down.

5 mins, 40.8159, -8.2278 🏊🔦🏊🍴

9 CASCATA DA MIZARELA

Tumbling and roaring down 75m, this is the highest waterfall in Portugal and not exactly one you can go swimming underneath. There

is a *miradouro* viewing point, however, by the roadside and it's a sublime view across Serra da Freita.

➜ From Merujal take the M621 for 2.5km; the *miradouro* is on your R.

1 min, 40.8638, -8.2857

ANCIENT & HOLY

10 DÓLMEN DE PORTELA DE ANTA

A megalithic dolmen formed of nine lichen-covered stones and surrounded by tumuli in the Serra da Freita mountains.

➜ From Mizarela continue along the road to Gestoso. After 4km you will see a brown sign; turn L. After 500m, park and walk R uphill.

3 mins, 40.8600, -8.2595

11 IGREJA SÃO MACÁRIO

No one knows exactly when the first settlers arrived here. Legend has it that the hermit St Macárius killed a giant serpent living in a deep pit and terrorising the people. In his honour they built a chapel by his cave. He must have seen the serpent from miles away as the views are incredible. The chapel looks out to six of its 'brother' chapels on the distant hills.

➜ From Sul, along the M559, take the CM1216 N for 8km & follow brown signs for S. Macário for 1km uphill.

1 min, 40.8764, -8.0616

12 CAPELA DE SÃO PEDRO

Make a pilgrimage to this mystical chapel in the mountains. On June 29th there is a festa here for São Pedro, St Peter. You can see how popular it is as they have built an altar outside, looking over the mountains. There are several picnic tables near this 16th century church with incredible views.

➜ From Noninha drive 3km towards Casais, then L at T junction.

2 mins, 41.0086, -8.0852

COSMIC ROCKS

13 LIVRARIA DO PAIVA

Walk up the Mourinha stream to see what locals refer to as the 'Paiva Library'. Quartzite layers of rock, with Arenigian fossils, resemble giant books stacked into the mountainside.

➜ Along the Paiva walkway (see 2), W of Janarde, follow the Mourinha stream up from its confluence with the Paiva.

45 mins, 40.9202, -8.1562

14 PEDRAS PARIDEIRAS

A rare phenomenon of erosion and weathering created the granite nodules that 'pop' out, earning them the epithet 'birthing stones'. Clamber up the stony ground, like hardened lava on the mountain, and feel the deep grooves from birthed stones.

➜ From Arouca take the M511 S and pass signs for Albergaria da Serra and Mizarela, onto M621. R at brown sign for Castanheira. Parking.

3 mins, 40.8505, -8.2829

19

MAGIC MOUNTAINS

15 PORTAL DO INFERNO

This road curves gently like the mountain's spine while either side falls off to a steep drop. Breathtaking views but stick to the road on this aptly named Gateway to Hell. (Really: driving only)

→ From Arouca, take the M510 to Vila Nova do Pisco, then M567 S for 15km until it becomes Estr. do Portal do Inferno.
1 min, 40.8696, -8.1057 ⛰

16 AVELOSO

A beautiful viewpoint. In May this mountain is a thick carpet of deep purple heather and bright yellow gorse as far as the eye can see.

→ From Alvarenga take the N225 S towards Castro D'Aire; turn off L at Mosteiro and follow M550 before turning L again before Moimenta onto CM1032, to Aveloso.
5 mins, 40.9866, -8.0833 ⛰🖼🚶

17 SÃO PEDRO VELHO

Feel on top of the world at 'St Peter of the Old Rock'. 1,077m above sea level, you can see the Estrela mountains to the south, Gerês mountains to the north, Marofa mountains to the east and the Atlantic to the west.

→ Drive NW from Albergaria da Serra to M511. R, then R again at the dirt track.
2 mins, 40.8751, -8.2807 ⛰🚶📷🖼

18 PEDRAS BOROAS DO JUNQUEIRO

A rocky outcrop in the Freita mountains crowned by two enormous granite boulders. Weathering and erosion has left them fretted with polygonal cracks, resembling the district's *broa* bread.

→ From Albergaria da Serra take the road SE, first L, continue down for 500m then turn R onto cart track for 100m.
20 mins, 40.8672, -8.2612 ⛰

WILD WALKS & PICNICS

19 MINAS DE REGOUFE

Abandoned mines used for tungsten extraction in the Second World War. Now eerily silent, the ruins gaze blindly over the mountains. The signed and linear Aldeia Mágica PR walking route begins here at Regoufe and leads 4km to the abandoned village Drave, a tiny village with no roads.

→ From Arouca take the M510 joining the M567 towards Sul. After 15km follow signs to Regoufe.
5 mins, 40.8792, -8.1354 ⛰🚶▦

14

16

20 CAMINHOS DE MONTEMURO

You can only comprehend the full beauty of the Serra de Montemuro once you have its earth under your feet. Follow this circular 20km PR1 route to see the mountain's magic slowly. A day's walking will take you over mountains via Roman roads, and you will pass menhirs, wolf traps, chapels and springs.

→ Begin at the chapel of Nossa Sra. do Monte, up the road from Vila Galega (on the N225, half way between Cabril and Alvarenga) and follow the yellow/red PR1 signs from here. After 1km there is a choice of 5 paths; continue straight on for the full circuit.

6 hrs, 40.9680, -8.1241 🅰🚶⛺🚴

21 DRAVE MOUNTAIN VILLAGE

Without direct roads or electricity, the last inhabitant left this tiny mountain village with no roads in 2000. Walk here from Regoufe and discover a small river for paddling and old houses built from the traditional Lousinha stone.

→ The signed and linear Aldeia Mágica PR walking route begins at Regoufe and leads 4km to Drave. See Regoufe (19)

1 hr, 40.8615, -8.1171 ⛺🚶🅰

22 ROTA DO OURO NEGRO

This 6km, signed and linear Black Gold trail, PR8, begins at the village of Fuste and winds its way past tungsten mines and the Pena Amarela stream to the village of Rio de Frades. These abandoned mines were a rich source of tungsten, known as Portugal's 'black gold' during the Second World War.

→ The trail begins at Chapel of Sta. Catarina, Fuste, and continues through the hills to Rio de Frades (40.8762, -8.1914).

2 hrs, 40.8608, -8.3323 🅰🚶⛺🅿

23 PARQUE DE MERENDAS, PONTE DE MEITRIZ

A schist village on the banks of the Paiva, with grassy banks and picnic tables. The Rota das Tormentas passes here which, despite the name, is a beautiful signed walk.

→ Follow the route along the Paiva for 2km until the next village, Janarde, 30 mins away.

2 mins, 40.9232, -8.1292 🅰🚶⛺🅿🏕

REGIONAL DISHES

24 CASA DOS BIFES CAETANO, ALVARENGA

In the region that prides itself on its cattle, the *vitela assada* cooked here in a wood burning oven does not disappoint.

→ Albisqueiros – Alvarenga, 4540 Arouca
+351 256 955 150, Casacaetano.com
40.9689, -8.1577 🍴

25 RESTAURANTE PAIVA À VISTA

Close by the River Paiva, just a 2km walk from Areinho (see 1), this is an excellent place to try regional dishes cooked to perfection.

→ Vilarinho – Canelas, 4540-257 Arouca
+351 256 044 583
40.9528, -8.1858 🍴🅿🛏

26 ADEGA TIPICA DA PENA

A mountain retreat with stone walls, long wooden tables and hundreds of local wines and cheeses. The speciality here is *cabrito assado no forno a lenha*, roast goat from a wood oven.

→ See 11 for directions and follow signs to. Aldeia da Pena, 3660-097 S. Pedro do Sul
40.8778, -8.0787 🍴🅿⛺🅰

27 RESTAURANTE CASA NO CAMPO, ESPINHEIRO

A warm and welcoming restaurant, one of a handful of schist houses, in this tiny mountain village. Hearty mountain food and regional dishes, an excellent place to try *arouquesa* beef.

→ From Adaúfe, follow brown signs to Espinheiro. Lugar de Espinheiro, 4540-431 Moldes, Arouca +351 256 941 900
40.8927, -8.2340 🍴🅿🅰

RUSTIC HAVENS

28 QUINTA DA VILA, ALVARENGA

Throw open your bedroom windows to views of the Montemuro and Arouca Geopark mountains. An ancient vine grows by the traditional wine press house, and luxurious old stone bedrooms have deep window seats. Relax on the terrace looking out to the views or take a cool dip in the pool. The house has a rich rural history kept alive by the owner, Sr. Alfredo, and his love for the place.

→ Lugar da Vila, 4540-053 Alvarenga
+351 918 528 478, Quintadavila.pt
40.9697, -8.1684 🏨🚴🍴🅰🏊

29 QUINTA DO POMARINHO, AROUCA

A restored 19th century farmhouse with views out over Arouca Geopark.

→ Lugar de Romariz, Burgo 4540-222, Arouca
+351 256 948 198, Quintadopomarinho.com
40.9226, -8.2501 🏨🚴🍴

30 QUINTA DAS UCHAS, MANHOUCE

Old stone farmhouse with a spirit of hospitality as ancient as the Roman road on which their house is positioned. Biking, hiking, canyoning and horse riding on offer.

➜ 3660-136 Manhouce +351 932 049 093
40.8280, -8.2203 ▣◩▥

31 CASA DO PINTO

A beautiful 18th century schist stone house in a small village by Canelas. Cosy with six bedrooms and a garden - perfect for families.

➜ Canelas de Cima, 4540-252 Canelas, Arouca +351 256 949 455, Casadopinto.com
40.9676, -8.2072 ▣▥◩

WILDER CAMPING & STARS

32 ILHA DOS AMORES

Lovers' Isle is where the Paiva meets the Douro river. Stir an amorous mood and watch dusk fall over the river with distant bells tolling into the twilight hills. A beautiful place to bivvy down and watch the stars twinkle.

➜ On the N222, head E from Castelo de Paiva, cross the Paiva and turn off L towards the Douro at Escamarão. Park at the end of the road and follow dirt track out to shade of trees. 5 mins.
41.0692, -8.2595 ✦▥◩

33 PARQUE DE CAMPISMO, MERUJAL

A campsite in the heart of the Serra da Freita mountains, 1km from the River Caima.

➜ It's on the M511 NW of Albergaria da Serra. 4540-659 Merujal Arouca +351 256 947 723, Naturveredas.com
40.8734, -8.2912 ▥▣◩▵

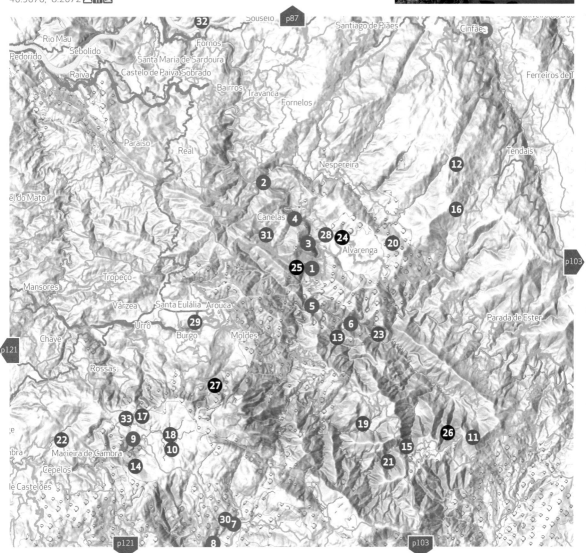

VISEU &
DOURO

Our perfect weekend

→ **Listen** to the honey bees humming through the golden hour at São João de Tarouca

→ **Spy** wild deer in the Serra das Meadas woodland

→ **Drink** dark Douro wine and feast at Restaurante Novo, Lamego

→ **Lean** into the wind at Serra do Caramulo and breathe in the endless views

→ **Taste** the warm honey of the Caramulo beekeepers

→ **Stargaze** from the megalithic dolmen, Lapa da Meruje

→ **Picnic** under the shady trees on the banks of the Douro river

→ **Jump** into the cool water at Ucanha's woodland river beach

→ **Strike** out down Roman pathways past great mossy stones and fresh springs

→ **Dive** into crystal waters at Poço Azul and dry-off on sun-warmed stone

The green, tiered hills of Viseu district slope into the south banks of the Douro river as it snakes its way, in solid curves, from east to west. The Douro has a deep connection with wine production: the river itself was used to transport the much-loved Port wine from these hills surrounding the towns of Lamego, Cinfães and Resende, to the city of Porto at the river mouth. The tributary rivers of Corgo, Tua, Varosa and Tavora define this district and encircle the heart of this Douro wine-growing region. They also branch out south, tumbling through the Castro D'Aire hills, enriching its soil and providing enchanting spots for a wild swim.

The Douro soils produce gloriously dark wines, but they also yield an abundant crop of cherries and elderberries in May. Later in the year there are harvests of dill, figs, rosemary and mushrooms. Visit the cherry festival in Resende for music, fire displays, dancing and, of course, hundreds of cherry-based cakes, sweets and wines.

Just south of Lamego is São João de Tarouca, a 12th century Cistercian monastery that has wild nature creeping into every work of art. They say the monastery had its genesis when a lightning bolt struck and marked out the foundations. This bolt is painted in now, cleaving the ceiling in two. Wander through its ruins and the herb garden: a riot of scents as lavender, thyme, mint, sage and camomile create a sanctuary for honey bees.

The broad stones of the toll bridge at Ucanha once paved the way for a busy medieval trade route, and you can see masons' signatures etched into the stones. Ucanha was the birthplace of Jose Leite de Vasconcelos (1858-1941) a theologian, ethnographer, poet and philosopher fascinated by Portugal's customs, ancient history and folklore. The toll tower has a quirky museum to his life and work; you can ask for the key at the fruit store. Further along the River Varosa is a deep green fluvial beach and a rope swing. The river runs on into magical woodland with ancient trees and moss-covered rocks.

RIVER SWIMS

1 PRAIA FLUVIAL, UCANHA

In spring, poppies and wild flowers cover the grass edging this river. Make a rope swing entry over the deep shingle-bottomed pool. Cool water escapes over the dam into luminous woodland.

→ From Ucanha follow the road down to the bridge that crosses the Varosa river. Park before the bridge.

1 min, 41.0469, -7.7488

2 PRAIA FLUVIAL, PARAÍSO

A pretty river beach with grassy banks under an arched medieval bridge.

→ Just off the N230 signed out of São João do Monte.

2 mins, 40.5969, -8.2368

3 PRAIA FLUVIAL, BESTANÇA

Waterfalls tumble over smoothed stones to form this natural pool.

→ From Cinfães follow the N222 E towards Oliveira do Douro. Don't cross the Bestança river but keep on in the direction of Pias and park.

1 min, 41.0747, -8.0718

4 PRAIA FLUVIAL, MONDIM DA BEIRA

Stone steps and ladders ramble down from the old bridge to the water's edge. There is a perfect seat carved into a tree and a children's bathing pool filled by river water. Old women chat on the bridge.

→ From Lamego take the N226 towards Tarouca, cross the River Varosa and turn R to Mondim da Beira. Follow signs to Praia Fluvial and park by bridge.

2 mins, 41.0143, -7.7503

5 PARQUE FLUVIAL, PORTO DE REI

Streams wind down through shaded woods and grassy picnic areas to join the Douro. Moored along the wide river are typical *rabelas*, cargo boats of the Douro. Take a dip in the river and gaze up at the rising Douro hills either side.

→ From Resende take the N222 E towards São Martinho. Turn L at signs for Porto de Rei and continue for 4km.

10 mins, 41.1183, -7.9128

6 PONTE DE LAGARIÇA

This simple arched Roman bridge is mirrored by the Cabrum river flowing under. It is a favourite swim spot for locals in summer, with grassy banks.

→ From Resende take the N222 W for a few minutes; at the church turn L up the M554-1 following signs to Anreade. Follow M554-1 for approx 15 mins until you see signs R to the Praia Fluvial.

1 min, 41.0637, -8.0082

7 POÇO AZUL, SANTA CRUZ DA TRAPA

Lie across sun-warmed granite boulders smoothed by this waterfall at Poço Azul. The plunging waters create a stone basin filled with a deep, azure bath.

→ From Santa Cruz da Trapa take the N227 towards Granja, and after 2 km follow brown signs for Poço Azul on your R. Park at the water tank (40.7799, -8.1617) and follow the signs downhill.

10 mins, 40.7808, -8.1650

ANCIENT & HOLY

8 DÓLMEN DA LAPA DE MERUJE

A megalithic sacred site in the Caramulo mountains. A still and bewildering place for stargazing.

→ Park in Carvalhal de Vermilhas and follow signs.

40 mins, 40.6412, -8.1392

9 SÃO JOÃO DE TAROUCA

A church with nature at its heart and creeping up the columns. The holy place has been kept through the generations by folk who tended the land and monks who studied medicinal herbs. A rich and varied herb garden survives within the ruins.

→ From Lamego follow the N226 S and continue through Mondim da Beira on the N329. Turn off at signs to the Mosteiro. Parking.
1 min, 40.9944, -7.7463 🇪🇺🏛✝

10 UCANHA

A sleepy-dog village, but the fortified bridge with its grooves worn by centuries of cart travel testifies to a more dramatic past. It was once a toll bridge and the only entrance to Mosteiro de Salzedas' lands. The tower has great views and there's a museum to the polymath José Leite de Vasconcelos, born here. Ask for the key from the fruit and veg shop to the right.

→ From Lamego head S on the N226 towards Tarouca. At the turning for Tarouca continue on the N226, crossing the river and turn L following signs for Ucanha. Park at the top once you are off the main road and walk down into town.
5 mins, 41.0481, -7.7464 🏛🍴🚜🖼

11 CAPELA, SÃO PEDRO DO SUL

Reassembled from Roman ruins in the 12th century stands this small church. Built in honour of Afonso Henriques, the first king of Portugal, to commemorate his prolonged sojourn by the healing waters here. No doubt after winning independence from Galicia and fighting the Moors, he was in need of some recuperation. Look for the mossy, strangely shaped foundation stone in the back wall, 'borrowed' from the Roman ruins nearby.

→ In Jardim de Termas, on N bank of the Vouga.
5 mins, 40.7400, -8.0935 🏛✝

WILD WALKS

12 TRILHO DA PENOITA

Beginning at the Penoita picnic park, this signed, circular 13km route PR4, takes you along shepherd tracks, past traditional villages and the Dólmen da Malhada do Cambarinho, an ancient megalithic monument built close by the source of the Alfusqueiro river. It's known locally as Casa da Orca, which mysteriously translates as 'house of the killer whale'.

→ From Ventosa, go S on M622. Cross under A25 and under IP5, then another 1km to the picnic park.
4 hrs, 40.6934, -8.1221 🚶🏕✝🐾

14

13 ROTA DOS CALEIROS ('OLD GUTTERS' WALKING ROUTE)

Beginning at the foot of Caramulinho, this 8km circular walk winds up and down between hills of 850m and 1,000m above sea level. Roman paths and ancient boulders intersect your route. Signposted.

→ See Caramulinho (16) for directions.
2 hrs, 40.5482, -8.2027 🚶♿

14 TRILHO DA SERRA DO CARAMULO

This linear 16km walking trail, PR3, reaches a peak at 1,043m above sea level on Ventoso, the Windy mountain, from where you can see the distant Serra da Estrela mountain range. It also passes the Lapa da Meruje dolmen. It ends at the River Alcofra and its medieval tower.

→ Begins in Fornelo do Monte / ends at Alcofra (40.6313, -8.1941). Go N from Caparossa on N228 for 1km, then L, signed to Fornelo.
5 hrs, 40.6427, -8.1016 🚶⛰♿📷

MAGIC MOUNTAINS

15 SERRA DO CARAMULO

Famous for its springs and sweet water, this mountain range combines great boulders, waterfalls and wooded dells. Fill your lungs as the wind pummels over the peaks of Caramulo.

→ From Agueda take the N230 E for 40km.
2 mins, 40.5873, -8.1655 🚶⛰📷

16 CARAMULINHO

The highest point of the Caramulo mountain range at 1,075m. Windy, wonderful views from this summit.

→ From Caramulo take the N230-3 W for 5km, passing Cadraço. Accessible from the road, there are 284 stone steps leading to the top.
2 mins, 40.5485, -8.2018 ⛰📷🚶

FLORA & FAUNA

17 CAMBARINHO BOTANICAL RESERVE

The densest and highest quantity of oleanders in the country to be found here. In May the mountains blossom into a riot of purples.

→ Once in Cambarinho follow signs for the Reserva Botânica. Walk the last stretch.
10 mins, 40.6725, -8.2021 ♿🚶

18 PARQUE BIOLÓGICO DA SERRA DA MEADA

A family-friendly park with native animals, such as the fox, boar, pigs, ponies and even turtles, bred and protected here. Trail routes through woodland. Look out for wild deer.

14

15

→ From Lamego follow the road north though Aldeia de São João. Follow signs for the Parque Biológico.

30 mins, 41.1042, -7.8409 ▲🚠🛶🍴🏊🎿

LOCAL FOOD & FESTAS

19 FESTA DO MEL, CARAMULO

The last weekend of August brings together beekeepers for the Caramulo Mountain's Honey Festival. Crafts, music, wines and honey, all a product of the region's flora.

→ Jardim do Santa Margarida, Caramulo

40.5719, -8.1706 🍴🎪🍷🎿

20 BEEKEEPERS IN CARAMULO

A friendly village association of beekeepers or *apicultores* who exhibit and sell their honey products here. If you are lucky, the lady in the café behind will have made her honey cake *bolo de mel*.

→ Rua do Chafariz 138, 3475-031 Caramulo

+351 232 861 496

40.5717, -8.1706 🍴🎪

21 O TASQUINHA DO MATIAS, UCANHA

Regional snacks and traditional dishes served on a veranda next to Ucanha's Roman bridge.

→ Lugar da Ponte, Ucanha, 3610-033 Tarouca

+351 254 678 241

41.0484, -7.7477 🍴🎪🔲

22 RESTAURANTE PÓVOA DÃO, SILGUEIROS

A restaurant on the banks of the River Dão, with granite stone walls and wooden furnishing. A homely, rustic atmosphere with a great selection of Dão wines. High quality regional dishes with produce from the nearby organic farm. Generous desserts.

→ Póvoa Dão-Silgueiros, 3500-546 Viseu

+351 232 958 557

40.5493, -7.9435 🍴🎪🍷🔲

23 PADARIA, MOSTEIRO DE SALZEDAS

This bakery by the village square's drinking fountain has an ancient bread oven, recently restored. Try the savoury breads and cakes baked with traditional centuries-old methods.

→ At Salzedas, park near the monastery and walk into the square. 5 mins,

41.0547, -7.7246 🍴🎪

24 RESENDE CHERRY FESTIVAL

Crafts, street shows, folklore and dancing all celebrate the cherry harvest – plenty of delicious cherry treats and Douro wines to try.

→ Last weekend of May in Resende.

41.1089, -7.9633 🍴🎪🍷🔲

25 RESTAURANTE NOVO, LAMEGO

This tiny family-run restaurant shares its forecourt with Lamego's Sé, a towering Gothic cathedral, rising incongruously opposite. This is an excellent place to try regional variations on *feijoada* and *cabritinho assado*, goat stew dishes.

→ Largo da Sé, 5100-098 Lamego

+351 254 613 166, Restaurantenovo.com

41.0966, -7.8070 🍴🎿🎪

26 MURGANHEIRA WINE, UCANHA

Douro region wine is a country to explore in itself. There are the famous dark, blood-red wines from the region such as Porca de Murça. But the wine from Murganheira is light and sparkling. Taste it, and visit their cellars carved into stone below the winery.

→ Abadia Velha, 3610-175 Ucanha

+351 254 670 185, Murganheira.com

41.0459, -7.7448 🎪🔲

RUSTIC RETREATS

27 CASA CAMPO DAS BIZARRAS, FAREJA

Located in the foothills of Serra de Montemuro, it's unknown exactly when this rural cottage was built. Its stone walls, open fireplaces and low beams give it an ancient rustic feel and make it the perfect place to cosy-up after mountain walks. 10 bedrooms.

→ Rua Capela 20, Fareja, 3600-271 Castro Daire

+351 232 386 107, Campodasbizarras.com

40.9052, -7.9140 🎿🔲

28 ALDEIA DO CODEÇAL, GOSENDE

A number of renovated but traditional stone houses in an *aldeia* where goats are still herded through the streets at dusk. Relax with a book to the clattering of hooves on cobbles outside.

→ Lugar do Codeçal – Gosende, 3600-474 Castro Daire +351 917 632 723, Aldeiadocodecal.com

41.0054, -7.9122 🍴🎪▲🔲🎿

29 QUINTA CHAVE GRANDE PARQUE DE CAMPISMO

Ten acres of sunny green terraced slopes overgrown with grapes, figs, mimosa, chestnut, hazelnut and fruit trees. They have a pool and will organise hiking trips and Douro tours.

→ Rua do Barreiro 462, Casfreires, Ferreira d'Aves, 3560-043 Satão +351 232 665 552, Chavegrande.com

40.8229, -7.6947 🍴🎪🎿▲🏔

30 CASA DOS MOINHOS DO CHÃO DO MOSTEIRO, SÃO PEDRO DO SUL

An old but renovated mill house with four rooms for a secluded break in the Estrela valley. The waters of the Zêzere flow past gently, perfect for a dip.

→ R. do Chão do Mosteiro 1, 3660-459 São Pedro do Sul +351 965 808 049, Casa-dos-moinhos.com
40.7576, -8.0604 ⛺ ⏸ ♨ ⊞

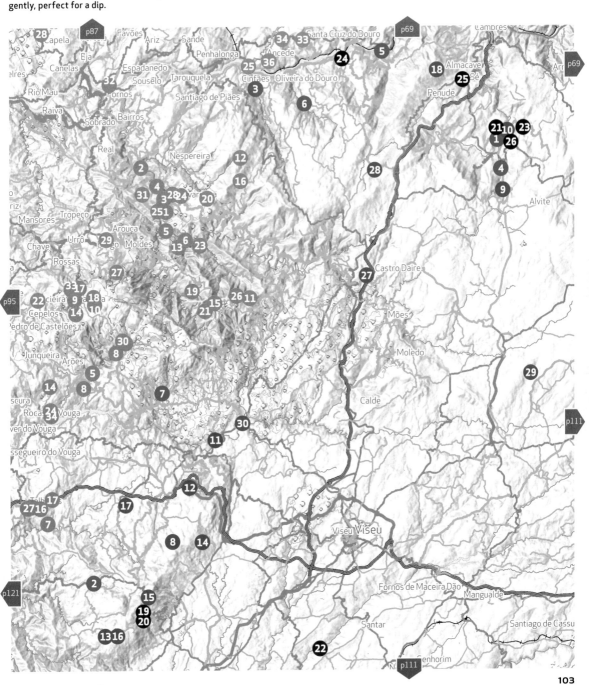

SERRA DA ESTRELA & GUARDA

Our perfect weekend

→ **Hike** along Serra da Estrela's valleys scoured by ice-bellied glaciers 20,000 years ago

→ **Swim** in the natural lakes formed beneath the Cântaros mountains

→ **Stargaze** from the summit of Torre, at 1,993m

→ **Bathe** in the mystical waters of Covão d'Ametade, thought to hold the wrecks of ancient galleons

→ **Ski** down the snowy mountains of Serra da Estrela in winter

→ **Creep** inside the Orca dolmen's megalithic burial chambers

→ **Spy** out eagles' nests and ancient rock engravings at Faia Brava

→ **Stroke** the thick, dusty hair of the *lanudos* donkeys at Castelo Rodrigo

→ **Fall** asleep to the whispering waters of the Zêzere river

The Serra da Estrela in central Portugal is the mainland's highest mountain range. *Estrela* means 'stars' and, at 1,993m above sea level, these snow-capped peaks almost touch them. The Serra is comprised of bizarrely shaped crags and boulders, glacial gorges, cromlechs, lakes, rivers and magnificent views. The mountains were first sculpted over 20,000 years ago by the gradual movement of melting ice sheets. You can walk the Zêzere, Alforda, Loriga, Covão Grande and Covão do Urso valleys, all bearing visible glacial scars down their rocky sides. In winter, snow transforms the range into a popular ski destination.

These dramatic mountains are personified by its adoptive heroes. Viriato, shepherd-warrior and chief of the last Lusitanian tribe resistant to Roman rule, and João Brandão, the Portuguese Robin Hood, were both defenders of these mountains; they came to symbolise the mountain-dwellers' defiant identity. Shepherds still roam these hills, accompanied by Serra da Estrela dogs with their distinctive golden pelt and protective nature. Emblems of protection are scattered throughout the mountains, from megaliths discovered in the Mondego river basin, to a 7m Madonna reached from steps carved into the hillside rock.

Despite being inland, Serra da Estrela has many weird and wonderful connections with the sea. It's easy to believe in these mysterious tales: certainly the silent and silver lagoons at Covão d' Ametade are a perfect setting for the Spaniard Juan Caramuel y Lobkowitz's colourful imaginings in 1639: "Of these [mountains] the most notable is called Estrela, because it was close to the stars. It is guarded by a lake and the darkness of the woods. Its water, which is sweet, flows into the Ocean, even though it is twenty leagues away... The storms which torment the seas stir up the waves on the lake very often producing the wreckage of boats, hurled from underground caves to the amazement of local inhabitants." Estrela even appears in Herman Melville's *Moby Dick* as "inland Strello Mountain", near whose summit "was said to be a lake in which the wrecks of ships floated to the surface".

Finally, Estrela cheese is said to be the best in the world. Made with sheep's milk and salt, it follows a 2,000-year-old recipe using cardoon thistle as coagulant. This is a gooey cheese inside a thick rind; eating it with local bread and red wine is a great meal.

3

WILD SWIMS

1 PRAIA FLUVIAL, SANDOMIL
Shallow water runs over pebbles at this wide, calm stretch of the River Alba by the small town of Sandomil. There is a wooden walkway to a shady café and children jump from the riverside where water momentarily deepens. Old arched stone bridge.

→ From Oliveira do Hospital take N230 S, and at the junction with N17 turn L and shortly follow signs to M506. Continue on M514 to Sandomil.

1 min, 40.3565, -7.7804 🏊🏻‍♂️🛶🍴⛱️

2 PRAIA FLUVIAL DO SABUGUEIRO
Just outside this small village where in the evening goat herders make their way down cobbled streets. A shallow swim and shingle bottom in the valley with large rocks and grassy banks.

→ From Seia take N339 into Sabugueiro. Follow the signed track down from the bridge to the fluvial beach.

5 mins, 40.4005, -7.6405 🏊🏻‍♂️🛶🍴

3 BARRAGEM VALE DO ROSSIM
Great expanse of water and, even if there are one or two other people, it's always

easy to find your own quiet corner. Scraggy olive trees run down to the stony beach. Water is deep and calmly reflects the great mountains all around.

→ From Sabugueiro take CM1125 towards Gouveia or Manteigas. After 4km turn R onto N232. After another 3km turn R down Rua Fonte do Serro.

10 mins, 40.4034, -7.5858 🏊🏻‍♂️⛱️

SACRED RIVERS

4 POÇO DO INFERNO
Known as Hell's Well, this is a plunge pool at the foot of great stone boulders in the mountainside. A waterfall pours down 10m over a narrow gorge to the dark pool. A circular, signed 2.5km walking route, PR1, leads from the waterfall through woodland and along various other streams.

→ Take the road from Caldas de Manteigas towards Cova for 7km. Park on the roadside by signs.

1 min, 40.3737, -7.5175 🚶🏻‍♂️🏊🏻‍♂️🏊🏻‍♂️

5 COVÃO D' AMETADE
Ancient glacial lagoon. Nearby the Zêzere river, which snakes 214km to the sea, has its first spring at 1,900m above sea level.

Perhaps this is where Melville imagined his skeletal sea-wrecked vessels mysteriously surfacing.

→ Just off N338, 11km S of Manteigas. Park near the hairpin bend and follow brown signs up track to the lagoon.

10 mins, 40.3285, -7.5886 🚶🏻‍♂️🏊🏻‍♂️🏔️📷

ANCIENT & SACRED

6 ANTA DA PEDRA DA ORCA, RIO TORTO
The Orca dolmen is a wonderfully complete prehistoric burial mound. It stands stolidly over views of the surrounding Mondego river basin. Some of the passageway lintels have their original cut-marks that show how their builders would have cut the stone.

→ Just off N17 (a little over 2km SW of its junction with N232), and signed from Rio Torto village.

5 mins, 40.5002, -7.6548 🌀

7 CÂNTARO MAGRO
Ice-bellied glaciers scoured the mountains into their great U-shaped valleys. Walk along the glacial routes today and marvel at the Cântaro Magro. At 1,928m above sea level it is one of the highest peaks of Serra da Estrela.

12

11

→ You can walk to a view of this peak from Covão d'Ametade (see 5) at (40.3280, -7.5873).
5 mins, 40.3283, -7.5986 🚶♿🔻

8 NASCENTE DO RIO CÔA

You can go to the source of the River Côa in Fóios, Serra das Mesas, and see this diluvial giant as a thin spring from the rocks. Amazing views out across the mountains.

→ From Fóios, cross the river and take Rua da Alcaia for 4km. At the T-junction turn R and follow signs.
5 mins, 40.2762, -6.8651 🏕♿

9 CASTELO DE VILA DO TOURO

Several medieval defensive castles line the Côa valley as this river once defined the frontier with Spain. The castles of Alfaiates, Sabugal, Sortelha, Vila do Touro and Vilar Maior are some examples, but the ruins of Vila do Touro are the wildest. This castle, given over to the Knights Templar in 1215, rises up over the village and commands strategic views of the Côa but has fallen into haunting ruins.

→ From Vila do Touro, walk up the hill for 200m.
10 mins, 40.4182, -7.1060 🏔🖼♿🔻

NATURE & WILDLIFE

10 LANUDOS DONKEYS

The outskirts of the medieval town Castelo Rodrigo, with meadows, vineyards and oak woods, are home to over 40 Mirandese donkeys. Sr Antonio looks after these endangered donkeys, which he calls *burros lanudos* because of their incredibly long woolly coats. You can visit the donkeys or call ahead to arrange a ride for small children.

→ R. da Cadeia 7, 6440-031 Castelo Rodrigo +351 964 070 183 info@casadacisterna.com
1 min, 40.8762, -6.9647 🚗♿🏕♿

11 FAIA BRAVA, CÔA VALLEY

This is a rich wilderness, devoted solely to the conservation of its wildlife. Wild Sorraia horses, deer and cattle make it their home while eagles, vultures and black storks nest on the rugged crags. There are several trails where you can discover prehistoric rock engravings, the Côa and eagles' nesting sites.

→ Organised guided tours or 2-day treks with overnight stargazing options. Atnatureza.org. The S entrance is on M607 before it crosses the Côa river from Vale de Afonsinho.
1 day, 40.9053, -7.0960 🏔♿🚶♿

SUNSET HILLTOPS

12 SENHORA DA BOA ESTRELA

Follow stone steps up to the 7m Madonna carved into the rock face of the Estrela mountains. She looks out at geological rock formations known as *queijeira* (they resemble towering slabs of cheese).

→ Along N339, 19km N of Covilhã.
3 mins, 40.3232, -7.6022 🖼🏔♿

13 TORRE DA ESTRELA

The highest peak of the mountain range and mainland Portugal, 1,993m above sea level. In the early 19th century Dom João VI

built a tower here to take it up to 2,000m. Sadly, a tarmac road leads to this summit, but the views over the glacial valleys are magnificent, especially when snow-capped.

→ Take N338 S from Manteigas and follow signs for Torre.

5 mins, 40.3218, -7.6130 🏞️🏔️❄️

14 CABEÇA DA VELHA

So called by locals, as a distinct face in the rock resembles an old woman's head. Hidden within the protected woodland of 'Mata do Desterro' this Cabeça da Velha looks out over the lands below. The woodland is rich in wildlife, cobras and frogs, as well as flora. There is also a path here to the linear, signed route PR1 which follows the River Alva for 2km.

→ From Seia take N231 S. After 3rd roundabout turn L onto EM513. Follow for 2km until you see the brown sign up hill.

10 mins, 40.3982, -7.6989 🏔️🚶❄️🐾🚗

STRIDING & GLIDING

15 LINHARES DA BEIRA PARAGLIDING

The strategic position of Linhares da Beira, with views over the entire region, has meant that it has been occupied since Lusitanian times, under Roman, then Moorish, control

until today, when it's occupied mostly by paragliders. Call Paul at Clube Vertical for a First Flight experience in tandem or for those more practiced, head to Manteigas.

→ Largo da Reboleira-Sameiro, 6260-311 Manteigas +351 967 467 746, Clubevertical.org

2 hrs, 40.4123, -7.4688 🏔️

16 GLACIAL VALLEY TRAIL

This 17km linear walk, PR6, will take you along one of the most thrilling valleys scoured by glacial movement some 20,000 years ago. Boulders rolled a millennium ago are scattered over the steep valley. The walk takes you from Manteigas, past chapels and mossy banks at Covão d' Ametade up to the great views of Senhora da Boa Estrela.

→ To begin the walk at Manteigas follow signs from Igreja São Pedro. To begin at Torre, follow signs from 40.3218, -7.6129.

4.5 hrs, 40.4003, -7.5395 🏔️❄️🏞️🚶

17 ROTA DO MACIÇO WALKING TRAIL

This 10km signed, circular walking trail, PR5, takes you past the glacial Candeeira valley and the lakes, Lagoa dos Cântaros, Lagoa da Paixão and Salgadeiras, glassily reflecting the mountains. Take care to bring a map and possibly a GPS device with you due to the

nature of this wild and demanding walk.

→ Begin at Torre (13). Manteigastrilhosverdes.com

2.5 hrs, 40.3280, -7.6066 🚶🏔️❄️📷🏞️

18 ESTÂNCIA DE SKI

Dozens of lanes to choose from, beginners lessons and various ski/accommodation packages on offer, this is Serra da Estrela's skiers' paradise.

→ Estrada Nacional 339, Apartado 332, 6200-073 Covilhã +351 275 314 727, Skiserradaestrela.com

2 mins, 40.3314, -7.6169 🏔️⛷️🍴🏞️

20

FESTAS & PICNICS

19 SIEGE OF ALMEIDA

Every year history repeats itself with this re-enactment of the French siege of Almeida castle during the Napoleonic wars. Sit atop the castle bulwarks and watch the explosions, battle and applause. Late August.

→ Almeida
40.7271, -6.9041 🖋️⊞

20 CAPELA DA NOSSA SENHORA DO ESPINHEIRO

This roadside chapel has large stone picnic tables with magnificent views across Manteigas and Gouveia.

→ From Seia take N339 E for 6km. Parking.
40.4131, -7.6726 🎋

25

BREADS & CHEESES

21 MANTEIGAS VILLAGE

To visit a town whose name actually translates as 'butters' and not to try the local dairy products would be a crime. The cheese here is famous for its wonderful gooey quality, made from goats' and sheep milk, and pours out once the hard rind is sliced.

→ Manteigas
40.4048, -7.5377 🍴

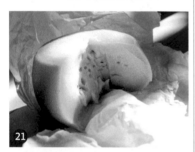

21

22 BREAD MUSEU DO PÃO, SEIA

Take a short spin through the history of bread at this museum dedicated to the loaf. You can see old regional machinery, a gallery of bread-inspired art, sacred objects and ceramics, even a reconstruction of an old Portuguese bakery. Try the different breads and grains and visit the restaurant with various dishes based on – naturally – bread.

→ Rua de Santa Ana, Quinta Fonte do Marrão, 6270-909 Seia +351 238 310 760, Museudopao.pt
40.4177, -7.6946 🍴🖋️⊞

33

REGIONAL DISHES

23 RESTAURANTE O JÚLIO, GOUVEIA

A Michelin starred restaurant with stone walls and simple decor. Try *arroz de carqueja com entrecosto*, grilled ribs with rice and gorse flowers. Or try their *cabrito com míscaros* (goat with mushrooms) and their very own *batatinhas do céu* (potatoes from heaven).

→ Rua do Loureiro 11-A, 6290-534 Gouveia +351 238 083 617, restauranteojulio@hotmail.com
40.4938, -7.5929 🍴❗

23

24 RESTAURANTE TRUTALCÔA

Mountain trout are fished straight from the River Côa outside this schist-built restaurant with a terrace and river view. There are a couple of river tanks and a lake you can visit with a bar further down.

→ Ponte de Rojões, 6320-242 Sabugal +351 271 606 227
40.3097, -6.9697 🍴🏞️

25 TABERNA DAS CALDAS, MANTEIGAS

This is a good place to sample appetizer-sized regional dishes of Manteigas. Try the *feijoca*, a bean stew with pork chouriço, pigs' ears and feet, or the *enchidos* smoked meats, and of course the local cheese.

→ Caldas de Manteigas, 6260-012 Manteigas +351 275 981 352
40.3878, -7.5452 🍴❗

26 RESTAURANTE O LAGAR, ESCALHÃO

Rustic decor, stone and wood, and in winter a strong smell of wood smoke from their fireplaces. They have a good selection of regional cheeses and smoked meats. Their cellars are well stocked with Douro wines.

→ Rua do Lagar 1, Escalhão, 6440-072 Figueira de Castelo Rodrigo +351 271 346 974
40.9448, -6.9277 🍴❗

RURAL RETREATS

27 CHÃO DO RIO, TRAVANCINHA

A group of comfortable thatched cottages in farmland surrounded by woods, wild flowers, mushrooms and the granite massifs of Serra da Estrela. This is a new-build, sustainable project – with a biological pool – that looks back to the old ways of Portuguese traditions. Fresh bread is delivered every day and local shepherds with their droves pass by regularly to graze.

→ R. da Calçada Romana, Travancinha, 6270-604 Centro Region +351 919 523 269, Chaodorio.pt
40.4188, -7.8230 ⊞🍴❗🛏️🏊

28 CASAS DO CRUZEIRO

A number of small granite houses, typical of the Estrela mountains, are now guesthouses but are kept in rural Portuguese style. There are various houses from which to choose, all in the tiny village of Sabugueiro.

→ Avenida da Igreja 5, 6270-151 Sabugueiro +351 968 578 919, Casasdocruzeiro.pt
40.4021, -7.6412 🍴❗🛏️⊞

29 CASA DA CISTERNA, FIGUEIRA DE CASTELO RODRIGO

All-stone luxury guest house with stunning views out from the centuries-old Castle Rodrigo walls. Ana and António, biologists from Lisbon, run the house with a quirky charm: the swimming pool is in fact the old castle cistern which once served as the village water tank. A different rhythm of life. See also António's donkey tours (see 10).

→ R. da Cadeia 7, 6440-031 Castelo Rodrigo +351 271 313 515, Casadacisterna.com
40.8763, -6.9647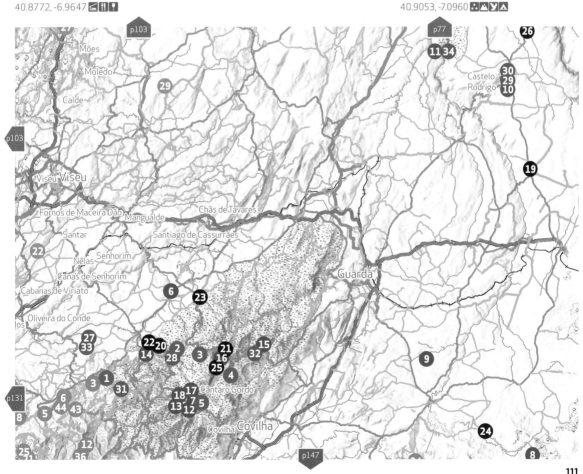

30 CASA DA AMENDOEIRA, FIGUEIRA DE CASTELO RODRIGO

This medieval guesthouse is set within the ancient walls of Castelo Roderigo with views out towards the Côa valley and the Douro Natural Park. Sleeps 12.

→ R. do Relógio 2, 6440-031 Castelo Rodrigo +351 271 313 053, Casadaamendoeira.pt
40.8772, -6.9647

31 CASA DE NASCENTE, SAZES VELHO

A number of schist-built mountain houses in this village of 11 inhabitants. Views out across Serra da Estrela. Reap the harvest of grapes, nuts and cherry trees in the garden.

→ On the M514-1 SW of Sazes da Beira. Sazes Velho 6270-351 Sazes da Beira, +351 238 951243, Casadanascente.com
40.3408, -7.7473

32 SKIPARK

Stay in one of three schist cottages by the River Zêzere as it curls around the foothills of Serra da Estrela. Take a morning dip in the crystal clear waters at the river beach or follow one of the footpaths up into the hills.

→ Largo Relva da Reboleira Sameiro, 6260-311 Sameiro, Manteigas +351 275 980 090, Skiparque.pt
40.4107, -7.4692

33 TOCA DA RAPOSA, MERUGE

Friendly, cosy campsite in the foothills of Serra da Estrela. Enjoy the treehouse. their small pool and music in the bar with local musicians.

→ Take M504-3 W of Meruge, and turn L on dirt road at blue sign. 3405-351 Meruge, Oliveira do Hospital +351 238 601 547, Toca-da-raposa.com
40.4034, -7.8268

34 STARCAMP

Stargaze with a guide to the skies in the wild hills of the Faia Brava Nature Reserve. Bivvy down and listen out for the wildlife of the mountains.

→ Off M607 W of Figueira de Castelo Rodrigo, before River Côa. Sítio da Milhoteira, Faia Brava Reserve 6440-251 Vale de Afonsinho, Guarda +351 961 336 043, Starcamp-portugal.com
40.9053, -7.0960

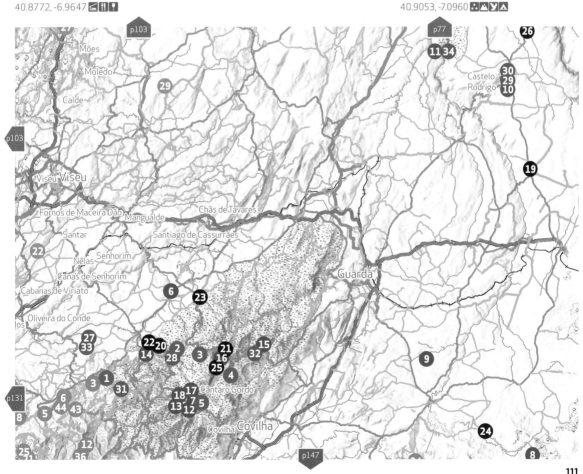

AVEIRO &
RIO VOUGA

Our perfect weekend

→ **Plunge** under the sparkling waters of Cascata da Cabreia deep within sun-dappled woodland

→ **Watch** the hills turn purple at sunset from Castelium Marnelis

→ **Crawl** under the heavy stones of Pedra Moura megalithic dolmen

→ **Picnic** under pine trees by the babbling stream in Parque de Merendas da Alombada

→ **Feast** on the hearty regional dish of *leitão*, roasted suckling pig, in Mealhada

→ **Discover** wild ruins taken over by the forest at Minas do Braçal

→ **Share** the traditional *broa* loaf, spiced with cinnamon, from Piedade

→ **Curl** up in an ancient stone house overlooking the Vouga river at Couto de Baixo

→ **Stargaze** from the wild dunes at São Jacinto

→ **Catch** sight of the dusk swallows as they dip their flight to dart over the river Alfusquiero

Aveiro is a deeply rural district bordered by the sea to one side and the mountains of Serra da Freita, Arestal and Caramulo on the other. Ascending these slopes, the district below appears as a gentle sea of hills cloaked in pine trees, receding into a blue haze. Aveiro mainly comprises small arable farmlands, with rivers snaking through its forests and vineyards. Everywhere are ancient and sacred markings left by humans on the land, from dolmens with rich engravings, to Roman roads.

The Ria de Aveiro is one of the oldest coastal lagoons in Europe and *Flor de Sal*, the region's salt, is still collected here using ancient techniques. Its saltmarshes, cane thickets, tidal mud flats and multitudes of fish make it a haven for bird life. Look out for golden plover, egrets, little bitterns, purple herons and kingfishers.

This district has also some of the purest rivers in Europe. Branching tributaries of cold water rush over gleaming ores and glinting river stones, feeding into the great River Vouga steering its course towards the sea. The Teixeira has some beautiful hidden swims under forest-filtered light. The wide blue Alfusqueiro, on the other hand, reflects the sky and, in the evening, flights of swallows come to dip and soar.

Hidden in the forest of Silva Escura – Dark Thorns – is Cascata da Cabreia. Here the River Mau plunges 25m into a quartz-blue pool. Tumbledown mills with creeping ivy resemble witches' houses. Follow the river through cork and oak woodland to Minas do Braçal where the water gushes out from the rocks so fresh it radiates iciness.

Aveiro is as thronged with ancient ruins as it is fretted with rivers. The Roman road linking Braga to Lisbon surfaces time and again across this landscape with ancient bridges, cart-worn flagstones and hilltop forts. At Cabeço do Vouga, a small hill rising above the River Marnel, you can see the excavated foundations of several Iron Age houses occupied by the Roman army. This walled town, looking out over Aveiro, is thought to be the elusive Roman capital of Talábriga. Nearby the Roman road emerges outside the village of Talhadas, meaning 'cut' or 'whittled' rock. Disguised under bright green moss, the road here is revealed as heavy flagstones thrown wildly out of line by deep forest roots. On each stone are the curved tracks left by rumbling Roman wheels.

5

HIDDEN COAST

1 DUNAS DE SÃO JACINTO

These dunes protect the Ria de Aveiro lagoon from the Atlantic. The 960ha are bordered by maritime pine woods planted in the 19th century to prevent the sand from shifting. The beach is one long clear stretch of white sand. At its southern tip is a nature reserve, home to a huge array of wintering waterfowl.

→ From Ovar take N327 S past Torreira and turn off at any sign for the beach. For nature reserve continue S. Closed 12-1pm. 3800-901 São Jacinto, Aveiro Natural.pt

2 mins, 40.6708, -8.7430

2 SÃO PEDRO DE PRAIA DE MACEDA

A sandy beach, often empty, behind pine trees and dunes. It's a scrabble down without steps to this beach.

→ From Maceda follow brown signs along the coastal road to the beach. Parking.

2 mins, 40.9207, -8.6622

RIVER SWIMS

3 PRAIA FLUVIAL DO RIO ALFUSQUEIRO

Dense woodland fringes the banks of this river. Several smooth rocks rise up from this river like whales. Perfect for sunbathing or a daring dive into the cool water. Arrive at midday to see it lit up aquamarine.

→ The beach is where M574 (A-dos-Ferreiros to Préstimo) crosses the river.

5 mins, 40.6253, -8.3615

4 PRAIA FLUVIAL DO SOUTO DO RIO

A peaceful river spot for a picnic under shady trees. The River Alfusqueiro runs fast and shallow over pebbles then deepens for longer swims. There are a few rope bridges, tunnels and swings high up in the treetops.

→ From Águeda take the N1 to Sardão, follow signs to Borralha and keep close to river for 1km.

2 mins, 40.5608, -8.4253

5 RIO TEIXEIRA

The River Teixeira is one of the cleanest rivers in Europe. At this point, just below the bridge, there is a *poço*, a well, carved by two millennia of water. Further down, the gleaming river snakes between mottled feldspar and granite worn to smooth pebbles. The river belly dips deeper again and a rope swing dangles over.

→ From Couto de Cima take M569 N to Parada and continue on the N227. Park in the lay-by just before the bridge. Follow the path down some rocks, a steep scrabble.

2 mins, 40.7957, -8.2565

6 PRAIA FLUVIAL QUINTA DO BARCO

A sandy, shaded river beach along the Vouga river. There is a café, and canoes for hire.

→ From Pessegueiro do Vouga cross the bridge and turn R; after 300m follow signs down to the Praia Fluvial. Parking.

2 mins, 40.7077, -8.3611

7 PRAIA FLUVIAL CORTEZ

This fluvial beach is formed by the widening bend of the Alfusqueiro river in the wooded valley between A-dos-Ferreiros and Préstimo. The clear, glassy river moves slowly over the shingle bottom and past its grassy banks.

→ From Destriz, take CM1608 S and W, following signs for Préstimo. About 2.5km after the Alfusqueiro bridge, double back R down a narrow road to the beach.

5 mins, 40.6500, -8.3008

8 PRAIA DO VAU, RIO TEIXEIRA

A small river beach where the Teixeira widens at its bend. Deep, green water and grassy banks.

→ Take the national road north from São João da Serra, through Conlela and follow signs for the Praia Fluvial. Parking.
5 mins, 40.7805, -8.2664 ⛱🏊🐾

9 PARQUE DE MERENDAS DA ALOMBADA

A tiny shaded picnic park deep within pine and eucalyptus woods. The river sparkles by at paddling depth, sometimes deeper.

→ From Beco follow signs to Alombada, head stright through Chãs and continue through the hills until the road dips to the bridge. Turn L.
1 min, 40.6763, -8.4117 ⛱🏔🐾

10 SERNADA DO VOUGA

The rising and waning of the Vouga is unpredictable due to new dam works but there is a nice fluvial beach just before the café here in Sernada. The river runs wide past picnic tables and a grassy camping space.

→ Cross the bridge from Machinata do Vouga and follow the dirt track down to the river before the café.
3 mins, 40.6707, -8.4535 ⛱🏊🏔🏕

11 PRAIA FLUVIAL REDONDA

A popular place for a swim but wilder, with still, clear waters further upstream. A

shaded picnic area with tables, BBQs and a pebbly entrance to the water.

→ From Águeda take the N230 E for 6km, cross the river and bear R onto N336 for 3km until Redonda. Signs on R to Praia.
5 mins, 40.5472, -8.3821 ⛱🏊🐾

SECRET WATERFALLS

12 CASCATA DA CABREIA

Walk down secret steps into woodland thick with ivy, fern and moss. Old mill-houses by the waterfall have tumbled down and now resemble witches' houses. The waterfall itself falls 25m into a blue quartz plunge pool with further streams cascading into the woodland. Sit at mossy picnic tables in this natural haven.

→ From the village of Silva Escura follow the brown sign for Cabreia. cross the stream and follow the cobbled road down. Parking.
5 mins, 40.7533, -8.3904 🚶🍴⛱🏊🐾🏔🚻

13 CASCATA QUIAIOS

A waterfall hidden behind intense lush vegetation and with thrillingly clear water cascading over limestone. A cool and refreshing dip.

→ From Quiaios Social Club (40.2144, -8.8555)

take L fork down Largo São Sebastião and continue for 1km along the dirt track.

15 mins, 40.2096, -8.8639

ANCIENT & SACRED

14 PEDRA MOURA

This Megalithic dolmen is more than 5,000 years old and is the most complete of its kind in the area. Part-buried in the earth of Serra do Arestal, you can enter the dolmen by a long corridor formed of 11 flat, granite slabs. It is on the 7km signed, circular PR8 walking route which begins in Couto de Cima.

→ From Rocas do Vouga follow brown signs for Anta.

1 min, 40.7799, -8.3098

15 'CUT STONES' OF TALHADAS

Two huge stones, one either side of the road, stand upright as though they were cleaved clean in two. There are many legends. One tells how they were cut in two by the Thunder Child walking the Caminho de Santiago. Another is that they fell apart in the earthquake at the Crucifixion. Either way, they stand iconic of a region formed by water and stone. At the other entrance to Talhadas there is a further rock, said to have once spouted miraculous water.

→ Take the national road through Talhadas and follow signs E towards Ereira. You will pass between the stones.

1 min, 40.6648, -8.3229 B

16 NECRÓPOLE MEGALÍTICA DO CHÃO REDONDO

These megalithic funerary monuments, about 5,000 years old, are hidden at the end of a vineyard path, deep within the Talhadas hills and protected by an enclosure of pine trees. The first dolmen is still partly covered by its mound, or *mamoa* but the second dolmen, while it retains its mound, is open. The long entry corridor is filled with earth and allows entrance only on hands and knees. The megaliths are without a capstone but bear their lavish decoration and zigzagging designs, clear enough for fingertips to follow.

→ From Talhadas take the road towards Ereira, and after 1km turn R at brown sign for Necrópole Megalítica. Continue down the dirt track and park near the 2nd sign. Follow path.

5 mins, 40.6639, -8.3116

17 VIA ROMANA, EREIRA

This is a surviving section of the Roman road,

built between the 2nd and 4th centuries, which connected the port of Olissipo, today Lisbon, with Braga. Wildly overgrown, at the end of a path-turned-stream, tree roots have shunted the flagstones out of place and the road resembles a surreal dream. If you visit in winter or spring, persevere to reach this road. An eerie spell surrounds these forgotten stones still deeply marked with Roman cart grooves.

→ From Talhadas follow the road past Ereira and turn R at brown sign for 'Estrada Romana'. Park at the top and walk down the L fork.

10 mins, 40.6733, -8.2973

18 MATA NACIONAL DO BUÇACO

A magical woodland planted by monks and meant to symbolise earthly paradise, it certainly comes close. Hidden trails, chapels, dense ferns and mossy oaks with twisting branches surround the 17th century palace and convent. Follow the Italian Via Sacra up the hills and into the ancient groves.

→ Follow brown signs from Luso.
2 hrs, 40.3772, -8.3637 🚻🖼️🍴🐾

FOUNTAINS & RUINS

19 PONTE VELHA DO MARNEL

Heavy flagstones and high sides fortify this old bridge. Running parallel to the national road emphasises its ancient stalwartness. Although referred to as 'Ponte Romana' by locals, the 14th century bridge was called 'the new bridge' by reference to the previous Roman bridge over the Marnel. This was once an important Roman road linking Lisbon with the northern city of Braga.

→ From Águeda, take the IC2 N. 2.5km after the Lamas do Vouga intersection, the bridge is on your R. Park in the lay-by and walk down.
1 min, 40.6327, -8.4693 🚏🚻

20 CASTELIUM MARNELIS

Also known as Cabeço do Vouga, this small hill is thought to hold the remains of the elusive city Talábriga, Roman capital of this central region. It would have been a good location as it is situated on a wooded hill looking over the meeting place of the rivers Vouga and Marnel. Although excavations have been paused, the foundations and brickwork of ancient circular houses and paths can still be seen.

→ From Lamas do Vouga follow brown signs to Estação Arqueológico. Park at the stone cross and walk up the steps.
1 min, 40.6365, -8.4641 🚻🏔️🖼️🐾

21 MINAS DO BRAÇAL

The River Mau comes from deep in the mountains near these old lead mines, bursting out with thundering freshness so cool it radiates icy air. The Braçal mines, set deep in the woods, were abandoned in 1918 after nearly a century of lead extraction, but the mining dates back to Roman times. Now you can wander the 20th century ruins, take a dip under the waterfall and look out for greater horseshoe bats.

→ From Sever do Vouga follow signs for Senhorinha and then for Minas do Braçal.

21

Follow dirt track for 2km; following red/yellow walking signs; park. Walk to the mines.
5 mins, 40.7338, -8.4005 ⛺⊞🏛

WILD WALKS

22 BIORIA

There are a number of cycling routes and walking paths in the country around Estarreja. The interpretation centre in Salreu has a birdwatching hide and cycles for hire. The Salreu Route begins here, a signed 7km circular trail passing the Aveiro Lagoon. Look out for lapwings, egrets and white storks.
➔ From Salreu follow signs to BioRia Percursos.
2 hrs, 40.7321, -8.5676 🍽⛺🚲

23 CABREIA – MINAS DO BRAÇAL TRILHO

A circular walking path with choices of 3km, 6km or 10km. The trails link the Cabreia Waterfall with the cascade at Minas do Braçal and follow the River Mau through beautiful native woodland.
➔ Start at the Cabreia waterfall (see 12).
1 hr, 40.7533, -8.3904 🏛📷

24 TRILHO DA AGUALVA

This 11km signed and circular walking route takes you through forests, hillside villages and chapels. It's all along old horse tracks and farming routes, crossing the Lordelo river (aka River Arões) at the swimming spot Poço do Pêgo Negro. A deep pool and waterfall sheltered by woodland. Look out for golden barbel fish and otters.
➔ Begin in Couto de Cima. Find an information board by the stone pillory next to the church.
3 hrs, 40.7574, -8.3072 🍽⛺🏛

BREADS & CAKES

25 LOJA DA MADALENA

This little *mercado* sells its own signature bread. The traditional *broa*, a crusty bread made with cornmeal and rye flour, is here mixed with cinnamon. Unusually, for Portugal, this variation remains savoury.
➔ R. Principal 830, Piedade
40.5574, -8.4888 🍴

26 PADARIA FLÔR DO VOUGA

This bakery specialises in regional cakes, biscuits and baked savoury treats. As all the produce is made on site, it's very reasonably priced. The cake to try is the *broa de mel e canela*. It's a honey and cinnamon bread pudding with a twist.

22

23

→ Rua Jardim 71, Sever do Vouga 3740-273
+351 234 551 212
40.7343, -8.3694 ⏷⏷

REGIONAL DISHES

27 RESTAURANTE O COUCEIRO, TALHADAS

This is the place to try local cuisine looking out over the Caramulo mountains. *Cabrito e rojões*, kid with firecracker potatoes, is delicious.

→ Talhadas do Vouga, 3740-412 Talhadas, +351 234 561 277
40.6635, -8.3276 ⏷⏷⏷

FAIRS & FESTAS & MARKETS

28 IMAGINARIUS STREET FESTIVAL

A wild street theatre and circus festival along the medieval streets. Art workshops and performances all day and late into the night. Try the town's famous *fogaça* bread, a sweet loaf resembling the medieval castle. Mid/late May.

→ Santa Maria da Feira
40.9239, -8.5423 ⏷⏷⏷⏷⏷

29 VIAGEM MEDIEVAL

For 12 days in late July-August the castle of Santa Maria da Feira retreats to life as it was in the 13th century and the reign of Afonso III. This is one of the biggest medieval fairs in Europe. Jugglers, falconry, jousts, gastronomy and encampments enliven the town.

→ Santa Maria Feira
40.9239, -8.5423 ⏷⏷⏷⏷

30 MERCADO MUNICIPAL DE ÁGUEDA

Every Saturday there is a lively market selling fresh fruit and veg, fish, smoked meats, and local cheese and breads. There are craft stalls and traditional kitchenware

→ Rua Rio Grande, 3750-137 Águeda
+351 234 624 971
40.5722, -8.4425 ⏷⏷⏷

31 FEIRA DO MIRTILO

This festival in late June celebrates the local blueberry harvest with all things blueberry-themed: cooking workshops, cakes, drinks, kids' activities, music and dancing.

→ Parque Urbano da Vila, 3740 Sever do Vouga +351 912 010 596, Feiradomirtilo.pt
40.7340, -8.3697 ⏷⏷⏷⏷

PARKS AND PICNICS

32 QUINTA DO CASTELO

Just outside the medieval town of Santa

Maria da Feira there are a few shaded picnic tables hidden behind a fountain and halfway up the mossy steps to the 9th century castle.

→ Park at the parish church (Igreja Matriz) and follow brown signs up the hill; at the fountain follow the steps up. 5 mins.
40.9221, -8.5424 ⏷⏷

33 PATEIRA DE ESPINHEL

A quiet park with picnic tables on the banks of Pateira de Fermentelos, the largest natural lake in the Iberian Peninsula. Two jetties lead out to stilt houses, perfect for a sunset over lapping waters. The circular, 10km signed trail PR1 begins here.

→ From Piedade take the main road to Espinhel and follow brown signs for Pateira. Parking. 5 mins.
40.5674, -8.5002 ⏷⏷⏷⏷

RURAL RETREATS

34 VOUGALDEIAS, COUTO DE ESTEVES

Set in an old hillside village, Vougaldeias offers several ancient renovated houses, each named after a different type of grain farmed here. The village festival in May is worth a trip. In the days before, sacks of gorse flowers are collected from the surrounding carpeted hills. At the party, streets are strewn with these *giesta* flowers.

→ Lugar do Couto de Baixo, 3740-036 Couto de Esteves, Sever do Vouga
+351 966 313 040, Vougaldeias.com
40.7523, -8.3057 ⏷⏷⏷⏷⏷

35 VALE DA SILVA VILLAS, AVEIRO

Several guesthouses and a treehouse in beautiful rural farmland with shared pool and gardens. There is the Wooden House with bare rafters and hidden nooks, the Upper House and Granny House with hammocks and open fireplaces. There is also the treehouse, a fully equipped, novel and romantic getaway in the treetops.

→ Vale da Silva, Loure, Albergaria-a-Velha
+351 916 045 055, Valedasilvavillas.com
40.6506, -8.5327 ⏷⏷⏷⏷

36 BE & SEE IN NATURE, OVAR

A one-bedroom house in the heart of the dazzling Aveiro coastal landscape. Adapted for birdwatching it has a viewpoint facing E and W in the attic. At night it becomes a bedroom with two drawer-style beds. There is a wood-burning stove and cycles. Be & See organises activities including vintage bike tours, gastronomy, night birdwatching, fishing with local fishermen and stargazing.

→ Rua de Enxemil, 3880 Ovar
+351 932 817 414, Beandseeinnature.pt
40.8457, -8.6302

WILDER CAMPSITES

37 CAMPISMO DE QUIAIOS

A beautiful camping site 500m from the beach with access to hiking and biking trails. You can relax here surrounded by the Quiaios dunes on one side and the Serra da Boa Viagem mountains on the other.

→ Rua Parque de Campismo, Praia de Quiaios,

3080-515 Figueira da Foz +351 233 910 499, Campismoquiaios.pt
40.2210, -8.8846

38 PARQUE DE CAMPISMO DE SÃO JACINTO

The municipal camping site in the heart of the Ria de Aveiro. The park faces the river and the sea beyond and is surrounded by salt marshes and pine forests.

→ Estrada Nacional 327, 3800-901 São Jacinto +351 234 331 220, Jf-saojacinto.pt
40.6801, -8.7200

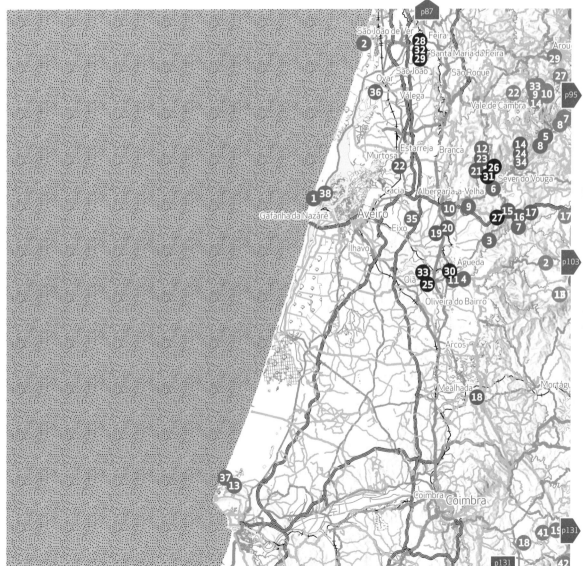

COIMBRA & ARGANIL

Our perfect weekend

→ **Wander** through the sunlit cobbled streets of Aldeia das Dez

→ **Explore** the deep green forest enclosing the hidden Fraga da Pena waterfall

→ **Shake** with laughter in the river at Ponte das Três Entradas when little fish tickle your skin

→ **Imagine** life at the old farms at Aigra Velha as you pass its ancient wolf gates

→ **Sip** from thimble-sized cups of elderflower liquor in Piódão

→ **Hike** up to the Concha da Fajão shell mown into the Fajão hilltop

→ **Catch** rainbows in the spray from Pedra da Ferida waterfall

→ **Watch** swallows dart between the rocks at Cabril do Ceira

→ **Bask** in the golden hour at Lousã castle overlooking the valley forests

→ **Run** to the hills and stay in a traditional mountain house with incredible views in Pena

Time and the hour seem to have overlooked the district of Coimbra and its mountain villages built entirely from the area's abundant slate. These villages lie scattered over the Serra do Açor mountains which, along with Serra da Estrela and Serra da Lousã, form part of Portugal's central mountain range. In summer the stones cast a haven of cool shadows and in winter the rain glosses their stony greys and yellows.

The Serra do Açor is best understood by its soaring namesake, the goshawk. Seen from above, the sweeping mountain range creates deep green folds of forest. It is a wooded region dense with pine trees. You can explore the district along hiking paths which connect the schist villages through some of the most beautiful native woodlands of Portugal.

From the hilltop village of Piódão you can walk to the valley hamlet Foz de Égua where two streams meet. Low stone bridges arch over a refreshing pool. Piódão is emblematic of a bygone way of life. Other villages – Aigra Nova, Aigra Velha, Pena and Fajão – are less well-known, but would once have been buzzing hubs of agricultural endeavour, human and animal life. A hundred years ago, when farming roles were shared, the villages had communal bread ovens and shepherding duties operated on a rotary system. If harvest was a village effort then so was the party: during Aigra Nova's chestnut festival masks would disguise the villagers, leaving them free to run wild, speaking their true thoughts in a topsy-turvy parade.

There is a heady mix of seasonal produce to try here: local honey, *bagaço* (brandy), *vinho morengueiro* (strawberry wine), chestnuts, corn bread and smoked meats. *Maranhos* – goat tripe stuffed with rice, ham and goat meat stewed in wine – are delicious. These hearty victuals make a great picnic after a bracing river swim.

Luckily, Arganil municipality is one of the most abundant places in Portugal for river swims. The Ceira and Alva rivers wind through, with countless fluvial beaches, grassy banks and shaded woodland areas. Deep in the ancient woodland of Mata da Margaraça is the Fraga da Pena waterfall. This plunges over mossy rocks into a sparkling pool. At Cabril do Ceira, the deep green river moves slowly through a stone gorge. Swim along this gorge to see swallows flit between their nests on either side of the rocks above.

LAKES & RIVERS

1 BARRAGEM SANTA LUZIA

A great expanse of still, blue water surrounded by mountains and rich in birdlife. The rare wall-creeper bird has been sighted here in the dam wall.

→ Take the N344 into Casal da Lapa (E of Cabril) and park. Follow signs to Praia Fluvial.

10 mins, 40.0901, -7.8580 🏊🚶🅿️👦🅱️

2 MOINHO DA PENA

A secluded little dell perfect for a picnic. The river, at paddling depth, babbles under rock strata like layers of collapsed cake.

→ From Serpins follow signs to Soutelo. Take the N342-3 past Soutelo and through Albergaria, turn R at signs for Comareira, through Aigra Nova/Velha until Pena. Park, following lane down to the stream. At the enormous old cork tree turn to follow stream down to mill.

5 mins, 40.1100, -8.1350 🏕️🚶⛺🏔️

3 PRAIA FLUVIAL DE SÃO GIÃO

Cool dark water under broadleaf trees. A dam holds the River Alva and it fills the deep-built sides. A grassy bank on one side and a children's slide with café on the other.

→ From Oliveira do Hospital take N230 S; at the junction with N17 turn L and follow M506, continuing on EM514 for 2km. Turn R over old stone bridge. Enter via camping, park on R.

2 mins, 40.3468, -7.8078 🍴🚶🅿️🏊👦

4 PRAIA FLUVIAL, PONTE DAS TRÊS ENTRADAS

Two rivers, the Alva and Alvôco, converge under the arches of an old stone bridge. Water so clear you can stand on the shingle bottom and watch as small fish weave between your limbs. Rowing boats for hire and a rope swing.

→ From Oliveira do Hospital take N230 S; at the junction with N17 turn R to Santa Ovaia. Turn L at Santa Ovaia onto N230 and continue to the River Alva. Park and walk down.

2 mins, 40.3070, -7.8727 🍴🚶🅿️🏊🚣

5 PRAIA FLUVIAL DE AVÔ

A Bruegel-esque swim emporium with spindly stone bridges, converging rivers, grassy banks, dogs chasing sticks, paddling pool area, rocks for leaping, sunbathing area, picnic tables and a mystical stone further upstream behind woods.

→ From Oliveira do Hospital take N230 S; at the junction with N17 turn R to Santa Ovaia. Turn L at Santa Ovaia onto N230 until a sharp-back R turn to Avô.

5 mins, 40.2943, -7.9061 🏊🚶🍴👦🏕️

6 PRAIA FLUVIAL, SÃO SEBASTIÃO DA FEIRA

Child-friendly swim with wide shallow water along the River Alva and a gentle tiered waterfall. Sandy river beach and cafe. Old wooden mill wheel further upstream.

→ From Oliveira do Hospital take N230 S; at the junction with N17 turn R towards Santa Ovaia. Turn L after 2km at sign for São Sebastião da Feira. Follow signs to Praia Fluvial.

2 mins, 40.3147, -7.8668 🏊🚶🍴

7 PRAIA FLUVIAL, CÔJA

Wide and deep water as the River Alva slows its course, trees lean over on the far side making perfect jumping platforms. The further upstream you wander, the wilder it gets. There are diving boards, a couple of slate-built bars with tables looking over the water and canoes for hire (call +351 235 729 765 or just turn up).

→ From Oliveira do Hospital take N230 S; at the junction with N17 turn R to pass Santa Ovaia. Turn L at signs for Côja. In Côja follow signs to the Praia Fluvial.

2 mins, 40.2676, -7.9954 🍴🚶👦🅱️🏊🚣

11

8

9

8 PRAIA FLUVIAL DO BARRIL DE ALVA

A shady river beach with grassy banks and a boardwalk out to a picnic island. There is a working watermill and the water is usually paddle-depth, a little deeper under the bridge.

→ From Côja (see 7) take N344 then R onto N517-1, signed for Barril de Alva, as far as the bridge. Park and walk down.

1 min, 40.2853, -7.9606 🏴‍☠️🔀🏕️🎏

9 PRAIA FLUVIAL DE MOINHOS DE ALVA

If nearby beaches are too busy, this is likely to be quieter. Tumbledown mills by the weir offers water deep enough to jump. Shingle beach and longer swims up the winding Alva.

→ From Côja (see 7) take the N344 N for 1km towards Barril de Alva. Park by the roadside and walk down R.

1 min, 40.2742, -7.9839 🎏🔀➡️

10 PRAIA FLUVIAL DA LOUÇAINHA

Deep and high-sided with wide river pools and steps down to the water. Follow further downstream to a wooded shady area.

→ From Miranda do Corvo take N17 and M556 to Vila Nova; then follow M639 and signs for Praia Fluvial da Louçainha. Parking.

2 mins, 40.0264, -8.3038 🔀🎏

11 PRAIA FLUVIAL DA PENEDA

Clear water and a rope swing upstream, shallow shingle islands and sandcastle heaven for small children further down. Dangle your feet in the water from the bar tables suspended over the river. Busy but a short walk upstream yields a wilder wooded area.

→ Park in Góis town square and walk down towards the river bridge. Walk down the W side; it's 100m on your L.

5 mins, 40.1539, -8.1121 🔀➡️🎏🏕️🎏

12 FOZ DE ÉGUA

Two small schist bridges arch over water so clear it's like swimming in crystal. A signed and circular 7km PR route leads from here to Piódão over the hills.

→ From Piódão follow signs downhill for Foz de Égua on CM1134.

2 mins, 40.2487, -7.8134 🏕️🔀➡️

13 PRAIA FLUVIAL, COLMEAL

Forests line the banks along the cool clear River Ceira. There is a shallow shingle pool under the dam and cascades, getting deeper and wilder upstream. Picnic tables and BBQ.

→ Park on the S of Colmeal bridge, walk down .

2 mins, 40.1385, -7.9987 🔀🎏🏕️

14 PRAIA FLUVIAL DA CASCALHEIRA

Great expanse of deep water due to the dam they have built here. There are diving boards, rope swings, jumping trees, fishing spots, a bar, toilet and BBQs.

→ From Arganil follow signs for Côja along EN342. After the roundabout at the end of Secarias turn L towards Mouronho and 200m ahead follow signs for Praia Fluvial Cascalheira.

5 mins, 40.2489, -8.0358 🏕️🅱️⛱️🍴♨️

15 PRAIA FLUVIAL, CABREIRA

Deep swims in a wide curve of the Ceira by the remains of an abandoned schist village. Now a couple of BBQs for communal use.

→ From Góis follow signs for Colmeal on M543. After 10 mins, pass this beach on your R. Park and walk down.

5 mins, 40.1418, -8.0662 ⛱️🏞️

16 PRAIA FLUVIAL, CAVALEIROS DE BAIXO

Deep green water in this corner of the Ceira overhung with trees. Large smooth stones line the bottom of the pool where it deepens before the tiered dam.

→ From Colmeal take the M543 N towards Texeira, turn R at signs to Casal Novo and continue until Cavaleiros de Baixo. Park in village and follow the narrow lane down.

10 mins, 40.1545, -7.9476 🏞️⛱️🏕️

17 PONTE DE FAJÃO

A shallow swim in summer and a suntrap surrounded by the wild Serra do Açor. Picnic tables on the riverbank and the shade created by olive trees make it a peaceful siesta spot.

→ From Fajão follow signs to Ponte de Fajão. Park at the bridge.

2 mins, 40.1504, -7.9114 🏞️⛱️

18 PRAIA FLUVIAL, BOGUEIRA

A deep green swim along the Ceira with a sloping gentle entrance to the water. Canoes for hire and great for pond-dipping in the stream beyond the dam.

→ From Serpins follow M552 towards Casal de Ermio. At Casal de Ermio, L at the brown sign for Praia Fluvial Bogueira. Parking.

5 mins, 40.1535, -8.2414 🅱️⛱️🍴♨️

19 CABRIL DO CEIRA

Wide, deep water of the Ceira surrounds a gorge resembling the 'clashing rocks' from the 1963 film *Jason and the Argonauts*.

Swim on your back though the gorge and look up to see swallows darting to nests either side. Beautiful deep water for jumping off the ledge under the gorge.

→ From Vila Nova da Ceira, take N342-3 SW for 4km, cross the River Ceira on R, and take the 2nd dirt track on R. Keep on the dusty track level all the way until you reach the river.
2 mins, 40.1768, -8.1748 ⛺🚣🍴🚽➕

20 PRAIA FLUVIAL DE PESSEGUEIRO

A beautiful but busy river beach with a network of bridges, dams and river-filled pools. Great little bar in the old watermill.

→ Follow brown signs from Pessegueiro.
5 mins, 40.0523, -8.0241 🅱🚣🍴🛈🚻

SECRET WATERFALLS

21 FRAGA DA PENA

Deep within magical woodland is a beautiful clear waterfall and pool. Hidden under trees are numerous secret picnic spots and earth steps to old mill houses or tiny bridges.

→ From Benfeita take M518 S towards Pardieiros, but after 1km follow signs to Fraga da Pena. Parking.
10 mins, 40.2209, -7.9359 ⛺🌲🚣🛈

22 CASCADA DA PEDRA FERIDA

Discover this waterfall by scrambling along the river path, through tangled roots and shady trees, passing an old bridge and mill ruins. Known as the 'wounded stone', this cascade has a small plunge pool beneath after the clamber up.

→ From Espinhal follow signs down and, past the large olive tree, follow the dirt track all the way to the information board; park and walk.
10 mins, 40.0197, -8.3286 ⛺🌲🚣🛈

23 POÇO DA CESTA

A beautiful swim spot with curved rocks for sunbathing thrones. Many different pools of varying depths and one great plunge pool.

→ From Cavaleiros de Cima take the road N for 500m into Casal Novo and follow signs for Poço. Keep straight, past allotments, down the side of the guesthouses.
10 mins, 40.1630, -7.9430 ⛺🚣🍴🛈🚻

CRAFTS & TRADITIONS

24 ECO-MUSEU, AIGRA NOVA

Learn about honey, the chestnut harvest, and lives governed by seasons in this museum of local traditions. If you read Portuguese, memories are recorded verbatim on the wall.

If not, there is traditional farm machinery, a wildlife museum and a plant nursery nearby.

→ From Góis take the N2 S for 5km, turn R onto N342, follow signs L to Aigra Nova. Park and walk into town, follow signs to Eco-Museu. 5 mins, 40.1201, -8.1542 ⛰🧍‍♂️⊞

25 MONTE FRIO ALPACA FARM

An alpaca farm just outside Benfeita offering alpaca treks around the beautiful landscape, picnics, wool-weaving workshops and wool-crafted gifts.

→ N of Benfeita on M518. +351 926 179 255, Montefrioalpacas.com 2 mins, 40.2320, -7.9462 🧍‍♂️🐾🍽

HIKING & BIKING

26 CANDAL PR TRAIL

This signed and circular 11km PR route begins in Candal and leads through chestnut forests, mountain villages to Lousã castle.

→ From Lousã take the N236 S towards Cerdeira and continue uphill to Candal. 3 hrs, 40.0807, -8.2034 🧍‍♂️🐶⊞⊞

27 CONCHA DE FAJÃO

The remnants of a visiting Frenchman's zealous intentions to create a Caminho de Santiago pilgrim route through Pampilhosa da Serra. The scallop shell, an ancient pilgrim symbol, is still mown into the side of the mountain and can be seen from satellites and on Google Earth. Alas the route is still a pipedream but you can walk a 4km loop (signed PR1) from Fajão's church square.

→ Park in town and walk up from the church at (40.1494, -7.9238). 1 hr, 40.1523, -7.9259 🧍‍♂️⛰🖼

28 TRANS SERRANO

Outdoor centre offering activities such as canyoning, climbing, abseiling and orienteering, as well as bread-making workshops in old mills, and olive oil tours.

→ From Góis old town cross the river and head up towards campsite; offices on R. Contacts also in the campsite. Bairro S. Paulo 2, 3330-304 Góis +351 235 778 938, Transserrano.com 1 min, 40.1556, -8.1135 🧍‍♂️🛶⛺🍽

MOUNTAIN VILLAGES

29 ALDEIA DAS DEZ

Beautiful schist-built mountain village with narrow, cobbled streets and walnut trees. Visit in October for the chestnut festival.

→ From the N230 between Avô and Alvoco das Várzeas, turn S on M508 and follow for 2.5km. 2 mins, 40.2957, -7.8669 ⊞🍴🖼🖼

30 PIÓDÃO

Wander the tangle of tiny alleys in this mountain village made entirely of schist.

→ Stone steps lead up between ancient houses, cats sleep in doorways and the white fairytale church is wonderfully incongruous with streets so narrow you can smell the history. 1 min, 40.2304, -7.8251 ⊞🍴🖼

31 AIGRA VELHA

An ancient farming village, now deserted but for a few buildings used for livestock, faces the mountains. See the remains of two gates which used to protect inhabitants from wolves.

➜ 2km S of Aigra Nova.

2 mins, 40.1107, -8.1489 ▣▲

32 ALDEIA DA PENA

Keep your faith with Pena: when you arrive it looks like a cement mistake. You have to slip in down one of the narrow alleys to discover ancient houses at strange, layered angles. Kiwi, cherry and fig trees blossom outside.

➜ 4km S of Aigra Nova.

2 mins, 40.1102, -8.1344 ▣▲

LOCAL FOOD

33 PRENSA DA RIBEIRA, CÔJA

An old olive oil press and mill-house now transformed into a restaurant by the family. Try the local cheese, various wines and, of course, olive oils at tables set around the old press and mill stones. They do several regional dishes including *costeletas de novilho,* veal cutlets made in the regional way.

➜ Rua dos Alfabres, 3305-139 Côja
+351 235 729 614
40.2669, -7.9861 ▯▮▯

34 CASA TI MARIA, GÓIS

A cosy restaurant with a friendly host cooking typical Portuguese dishes. The *bitoque* – a steak and chips with a fried egg on top – here is mouth-watering.

➜ R. Santo António 2, 3330-310 Góis
+351 912 703 071
40.1556, -8.1109 ▯▮▯

35 RESTAURANTE O PASCOAL, FAJÃO

Enjoy dinner in this little stone restaurant in the village of Fajão. Try regional specialities here such as *chanfana de cabra*, a dish from Pampilhosa da Serra of goat stewed with wine, laurel, paprika and garlic, in a *caçoilas* (black pottery) and baked in a wood oven. They also have local cheese and make a great *tigelada* for pudding (eggs, sugar and lemon baked until brown in a clay pot.)

➜ Rua das Flores, 3320 Fajão
+351 235 751 219
40.1495, -7.9229 ▯▮▯

36 RESTAURANTE FONTINHA, PIÓDÃO

In the heart of the quaint little schist-built mountain village. Here you can try hearty regional food such as goat stew in the wood oven, roast kid and smoked meats, but the locally sourced grilled trout is heavenly.

➜ Rua Eugénio Correia, 6285-018 Piódão
+351 235 731 151
40.2298, -7.8249 ▣▯▮▯▣

37 MERCADO EM BARRIL DE ALVA

Every third Saturday of the month there's this hippie-run market just outside the village by the river beach. Buy organic creams, vintage clothes, bric-a-brac, plants and delicious baked goods, fruit and veg. There might even be some circus performers.

➜ From Côja take the N344 towards Barril de Alva for 4km; the market is just before the bridge on M517-1.

40.2865, -7.9614 ▮

38 BOUTIQUE DA TUXA, CÔJA

A lively little bakery filled with many different regional cakes and heaped piles of freshly baked breads. The traditional *pão de agua*, dusty bread rolls, are exceptional in Arganil and this is an excellent vendor.

➜ Praça Dr Alberto Vale 3, 3305-150 Côja
+351 235 721 523
40.2681, -7.9888 ▮

HILLTOP RETREATS

39 CASAS DA SERRA DO AÇOR

Three beautiful schist houses in this tiny hamlet, surrounded by the stunning Açor mountain range. The River Ceira runs near and there are several hiking and biking trails.

➜ See 23 for directions to Casal Novo. Rua da Capela, Casal Novo, 3300-221 Arganil
+351 235 751 036, Casasdaserradoacor.pt
40.1622, -7.9442 ▤▮▯▣▧▯

40 CASA DE CEREJINHA, PENA

A gorgeous two-bedroomed centuries-old mountain house in Pena village built with schist stone and with a deep recessed fireplace typical of Lousã. Open your windows to incredible mountain views and step out of the front door to narrow cobbled streets winding down to the babbling river.

➜ Pena-Góis +351 914 009 194,
Casadacerejinha.wordpress.com
40.1105, -8.1348 ▯▣▣

41 JARDIM DA TIA

A beautiful chic little cottage with a veranda and fig trees in the foothills of the Serra da Lousã mountains. Enjoy the beautiful views in the morning with a basket of fresh bread, cheese and fruit with home-made jams for breakfast on the terrace. Sleeps 2-4 people.

→ Terra da Gaga, Serpins 3200-350,
Jardimdatia.com
40.1717, -8.2024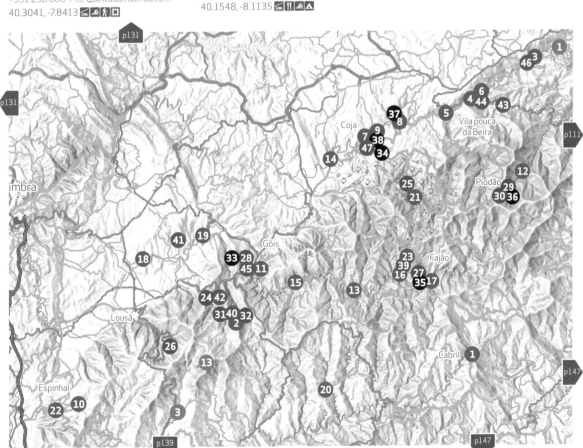

42 CASA DE CAMPO DA COMAREIRA

A lovely retreat in the Serra da Lousã
mountains. "On top of the hills, overlooking
the world" is their slogan and you will feel
quite removed from the world here. Just
remember how bustling this busy farming
community would once have been. Sleeps 6.

→ 3330-231 Comareira, Góis
+351 235 778 644, Lousitanea.org
40.1252, -8.1511

43 QUINTA DA MOENDA

Beautiful 18th century watermill on the
banks of the river Alvôco with five self-
catering apartments. A short stroll takes you
to the river beach with grassy banks.

→ Av. Fronteira, 3400-301 Alvoco das Várzeas
+351 238 666 443, Quintadamoenda.com
40.3041, -7.8413

WILDER CAMPING

44 PARQUE CAMPISMO PONTE DAS TRÊS ENTRADAS

Shady relaxed campsite on the banks of the
river Alva with soft turf pitches, bungalows,
furnished tents or apartments. A beautiful
fluvial beach waits just next door. There
is a wonderful communal kitchen with an
enormous round stone barbecue within.

→ See 4 for directions to Ponte das
Três Entradas. 3400-591 Santa Ovaia,
Oliveira do Hospital +351 238 670 050,
Pontedas3entradas.com
40.3072, -7.8717

45 PARQUE CAMPISMO, GÓIS

The municipal campsite with river swims in
the nearby Ceira and some extraordinary
wooden bungalows. Trans Serrano will
organise activities from here (see 28).

→ Parque do Castelo, 3330-309 Góis
+351 961 401 859, Goiscamping.com
40.1548, -8.1135

46 PARQUE CAMPISMO, SÃO GIÃO

A shady camping site with river swims in the
deep green Alva and a traditional, dark little
restaurant over an old mill. Children and
dogs are made very welcome here.

→ Fundação Albino Mendes da Silva,
3400-570 São Gião +351 238 691 154,
Parquesaogiao.blogspot.pt
40.3460, -7.8081

47 PARQUE CAMPISMO DE CÔJA

This is a heavenly campsite, by the peaceful
banks of the river Alva, with steps down to
the river beach.

→ Prego do Soito, 3305-096 Côja
+351 235 729 666, Fcmportugal.com
40.2670, -7.9954

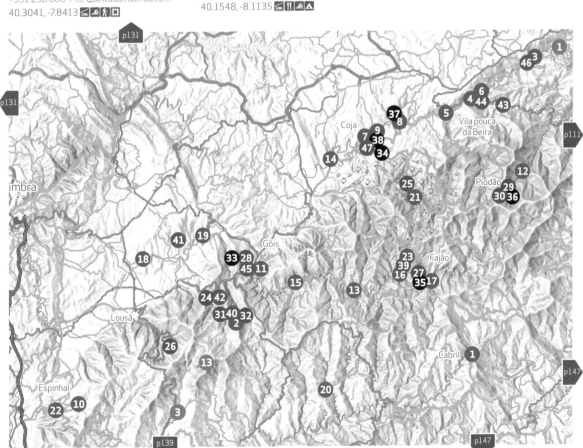

LEIRIA

Our perfect weekend

→ **Catch** sight of eagles wheeling overhead on the banks of the Zêzere river

→ **Open** your eyes underwater to a subaquatic kingdom of rocks at Fragas de São Simão

→ **Picnic** on the mountains under shady pine trees at the old Santo António da Neve ice-houses

→ **Explore** the labyrinthine caves at Grutas de Alvados

→ **Leap** and tumble down Portugal's biggest sand dune at Salir do Porto beach

→ **Climb** up the Fórnea plateau to find your own wild cave at Cova da Velha

→ **Windsurf** over the golden lagoon at Lagoa de Óbidos as coastal winds fill your sails

→ **Feast** on freshwater fish on the veranda overlooking the calm River Zêzere at Restaurante O Barqueiro

→ **Daydream** in a hammock at Casal de São Simão surrounded by wooded hills and distant craggy outcrops

→ **Wander** along riverbanks past old watermills, mossy bridges and wild woodland on the Casal de São Simão walking trail

The history of human settlement in Leiria province dates back hundreds of thousands of years. It is a land, bordered by the sea on the west and the mountains to the east, which continues to enchant those who visit. One of the most fascinating and evocative discoveries here was of a 25,000-year-old skeleton in a cliff-side cave. The child, known as the Lapedo Child, had been buried with a red shawl, dyeing the surrounding earth red, a shell necklace and a deer-tooth headdress. The skeleton is of considerable importance in the understanding of human evolution.

At Foz de Alge the mouth of the great Zêzere river opens up, offering deep and calm swims while eagles wheel in the air above. Further inland, at Fragas de São Simão, the Alge has carved a dramatic gorge with cliffs of limestone and quartz. The river below flows as clear as crystal.

Known as "the kingdom of stone", Leiria is home to the great limestone plateau of Serras de Aire e Candeeiros. Here the rivers plunge their channels underground and have created a network of subterranean caverns. Outcrops of quartz, limestone and granite, encircling the limestone massif, are only the tips of a subterranean wonderland, as the sinkholes, ravines and depressions testify to a glittering dark-stone underworld.

At Grutas de Mira de Aire, with conjoining caverns reaching 112m underground, you can explore the Octopus Gallery, the Fountain of Pearl, the Black River, the Organ and the Pulpit. The initial cavern, a great calcified cathedral, was discovered by men looking for water in the dry summer of 1947. Swinging into the vaulted darkness on ropes, they had only their voices and dropped stones to gauge the abyss beyond their dim gas lamps.

The less visited caves of Grutas de Alvados drip with stalactites which form a natural parapet over a 70m drop to fathomless darkness. Ancient rocks, ossified into shrouded figures, throng the shadowy passages. A stalactite Madonna looms from one recess, and these calcified statues are older than 24,000 years. Time itself is encased within the damp walls here in a dark-bellied system, deep underground, the seat of creation, the wild womb of Earth itself.

RIVERS & WATERFALLS

1 FRAGAS DE SÃO SIMÃO

A towering gorge over crystalline water. Further downstream, the water forms a large green pool with jumping rocks and a fallen tree across. There are several waterfalls before the river disappears into woodland.

➜ From Aldeia de Ana de Aviz, take N237 dir Bacelo for 3km. Turn R onto M525, follow signs to Fragas de S. Simão. Park before bridge and walk up past old mill-houses. Pass café and green pool and scramble up rocky path to gorge.

5 mins, 39.9155, -8.3195 🍴🧍‍♀️👨‍👩‍👧⛺🏕🏊

2 PRAIA FLUVIAL, ANA DE AVIS

A small riverbank with a grassy area, a little close to main road and fairly manicured. But it does have a library.

➜ Just off the N237, turn off at signs for Aldeia de Ana de Avis. Parking.

2 mins, 39.9185, -8.2846 🏊‍♂️♿️🅱🍴

3 PRAIA FLUVIAL DO POÇO DE CORGA

Three tiers of bathing pools filled by the River Pêra: one shallow, deeper and then a sandy pool below. Great picnic spot and huge rocks for drying off. Old oil olive press museum upstream.

➜ From Castanheira de Pera take N236 N and follow brown signs to Poço Corga.

2 mins, 40.0250, -8.1902 🏊🧍‍♀️♿️🍴

4 PRAIA FLUVIAL DO MOSTEIRO

A small, lively picnic spot with two cafés by a lawn and a water slide into the Ribeira de Pêra.

➜ From Pedrógão Grande take the IC8 W and turn off for Cacilhas. From Cacilhas follow signs to Praia Fluvial Mosteiro. Parking.

2 mins, 39.9357, -8.1861 🏕🍴♿️🅱

5 PRAIA FLUVIAL DE MEGA FUNDEIRA

Large stone steps lead down to the shallow Ribeira da Mega, a stream which locals claim has healing properties. A good small bar serves beer and snails in summer. A 3km walking trail, Trilho de Mega Fundeira, passes here.

➜ From the N2 between Pedrógão Grande and Louriceira, turn off at signs for Mega Fundeira and follow signs to the Praia Fluvial. Park just up the lane and walk down.

2 mins, 39.9855, -8.1216 🏕🍴🏊

DUNES & LAGOONS

6 SALIR DO PORTO SAND DUNES

This is Portugal's biggest sand dune. Climb up its sides and, weak in the knees, fill up your lungs over a view across the coastline. Then run all the way back down.

➜ Salir do Porto; parking after Dunas Café.

5 mins, 39.5020, -9.1518 🏊

7 LAGOA DE ÓBIDOS

A lagoon protected from the sea by dunes which act as a barrier. The water is warm and salty and has an average depth of 2m. It's a perfect place to learn to windsurf, sail, kitesurf, paddleboard or canoe.

➜ Call Escola de Vela da Lagoa for activities +351 262 978 592, Escoladeveladalagoa.com

2 mins, 39.4097, -9.2020 🏊♿️🍴🏄

8 PRAIA DA BOAVISTA

A beautifully deserted beach but the tide comes in fast so be careful.

➜ Park in Boavista and take the track down to the beach.

10 mins, 39.4758, -9.1906 🏊⛰🏊🌀

9 PRAIA DO SALGADO

A quiet beach, even quieter if you walk away from café area. Sandy with crashing waves.

➜ From Venda Nova exit towards Casal do

Pias and take the Rua do Praia do Salgado on your L and follow track down to the beach.
2 mins, 39.5475, -9.1114 🏖🍴

10 FOZ DO ARELHO

The gentle Óbidos lagoon flows across the dune barrier to create a shallow stream over the beach – great paddling or warmer dips. Deserted off-season but popular in summer.
➜ Take the N360 into Foz do Arelho and park up at the sea front. Walk down to the beach.
5 mins, 39.4336, -9.2280 🏖🅱🏖

11 PRAIA DO BOM SUCESSO

The beach on the S side of Foz do Arelho (see 10), this is a perfect place to watch the sunset over the sand dunes of this beautiful curling coastline.
➜ From Vau take the M573 all the way N to the coast and follow signs to 'Bom Sucesso'.
5 mins, 39.4262, -9.2386 🅱🏖🏖🏖

PARKS & PICNICS

12 SENSORY ECO-PARK DA PIA DO URSO

Set in the beautiful rich forest of Batalha, this is a unique wild park offering new experiences and sensations to the visually impaired. There are trails, sounds, smells and shapes through which you can discover the region's history. Hidden along the woodland paths are structures for climbing and wild play: a wooden planetarium, a watermill, a Jurassic climbing frame, a music station and a creative station. Also picnic tables, old windmills and wonderfully shaped rocks. The trail passes the park's namesake sinkholes, the Pia do Urso (bears' watering holes).
➜ From Barreiro Grande take main road N for 500m, follow signs on L. Portela das Cruzes, 2495-031 São Mamede +351 244 769 110
2 mins, 39.5982, -8.7166 🏖🏕🚶🏖🍴

13 SANTO ANTÓNIO DA NEVE ICE-HOUSES

On the ancient hilltop of Cabeço de Pereiro stand several small ice-houses. Once used for collecting the snow to make ice for the King of Lisbon. Now, at high summer, a perfect place for a picnic under pine trees.
➜ From Coentral follow signs for St. António da Neve N up the hill.
5 mins, 40.0788, -8.1610 🏞🏕🏕

ROCKS & CAVES

14 PEGADAS DE DINOSSÁURIO

In the Serras de Aire e Candeeiros Natural

Park you can see the most beautifully preserved footprints of the world's greatest animals: 20 tracks of enormous sauropods left 175 million years ago imprinted onto a limestone slab. These animals were quadruped herbivores with long necks and short tails. There is an interactive centre with a film introduction and after that you are free to wander. Tuesdays–Sundays.

→ Estr. de Fátima, 2490-216 Ourém +351 249 530 160, Pegadasdedinossaurios.org
5 mins, 39.5728, -8.5888 ♿B⇄🚻€

15 GRUTAS DE ALVADOS

A cave network discovered by shepherds. Sparkling stalactites over 24,000 years old throng the walls of this subterranean cathedral. This lesser-known cave network takes much smaller tour groups, even individual tours, and the natural lighting allows your imagination to run wild.

→ Grutas de Alvados, 2480-034 Alvados, +351 244 441 274 Grutasalvados.com
2 mins, 39.5392, -8.7525 🅿️🍴€

16 GRUTAS DE MIRA DE AIRE

Explore a hidden world in these networks of subterranean caves 112m deep: explore the Octopus Gallery, Pulpit and Black River.

A guide will tell you of their discovery and history. €6.50 for an adult ticket.

→ Signed off the N243 into Mira de Aire. Parking. Av. Dr. Luciano Justo Ramos 470, 2485-050 Mira de Aire
+351 244 440 322, Grutasmiradaire.com
1 hr, 39.5403, -8.7040 🅿️€

17 PENEDO FURADO

Bring some good luck and follow tradition by running under this 'stone with holes', a massive weathered rock incongruous with the calm lagoon.

→ From Foz do Arelho continue around Lagoa de Óbidos on the coast road.
1 min, 39.4274, -9.2121 ♿🚻

18 COVA DA VELHA

Discover your own cave, or the Old Woman's Cave as it's known, hidden in the limestone hills of Fórnea. Dry in summer, in winter the cave becomes a mouth springing with bubbling water.

→ A trail passes here (22) or access from N243 from Alcaria: follow signs for 'Fórnea', take dirt track through olive groves. Park in clearing and walk the 2km pedestrian route up to the cave.
30 mins, 39.5572, -8.8047 📷⛰️🅿️✿

19 CASAL DE SÃO SIMÃO WALKING TRAIL

A beautiful 5km circular walk past the rivers Alge and Fato, past wild swimming spots under the Fragas de São Simão (see 1), old watermills, ancient bridges and wild dense woodland.

→ Signed from Fragas de São Simão (see 1).
1.5 hrs, 39.9155, -8.3195 ▦▦◐⚐▲▲◢

20 MEGA FUNDEIRA WALKING TRAIL

A 3km signed trail following the course of the stream.

→ Leads from the Praia Fluvial da Mega Fundeira (see 5).
1 hr, 39.9855, -8.1216 ⟰◢

21 PRAIA DA VIEIRA WALKING TRAIL

Beginning at the mouth of the River Lis this 11km circular boardwalk explores the river, dunes and pine forests of Leiria and Pedrógão.

→ Leaving Marinha Grande follow EM242-2 towards Praia da Vieira, then L at final roundabout (with a boat in the middle).
3 hrs, 39.8795, -8.9684 ⟰◢

22 FÓRNEA – ALCARIA WALKING TRAIL

This 11km trail will take you up over the magnificent natural amphitheatre known as Fórnea, formed by the limestone plateau as it drops away to form a sweeping curve. In spring, a waterfall cascades out of the Cova da Velha cave hidden in the side of this amphitheatre and rushes through the valley. In summer, when the source has dried, you can explore this cave.

→ Begin/end at Café da Bica, Alcaria, on N243.
3 hrs, 39.5689, -8.7946 ▲▭▦⟰▐▐◢

23 CAMPO ARQUEOLÓGICO DE VALE DO LAPEDO

Explore the enchanting Lapedo valley with its river, wild hillsides and strange limestone formations. It was also where they found the Lapedo child, of great significance as this 25,000-year-old skeleton revealed that the child was progeny of Neanderthal and human interbreeding. You can discover more in the small interpretation centre or follow a short signed walk from here.

→ From Leiria take the N350 E for 9km, into Carrasqueira, continue until the Café Paisagem de Lapedo by the carpark. Park here. Call ahead to book a visit on +351 244 839 677 or museudeleiria@cm-leiria.pt. Centro de Interpretação Abrigo do Lagar Velho - Lapedo, Carrasqueira 2414-006 Santa Eufémia
1 hr, 39.7580, -8.7313 ⟰♻▲

24 RESTAURANTE O TERREIRO DO LAGAR, CABEÇA REDONDA

A rural restaurant opposite olive groves, the locals come here to eat. The portions are very generous with typical Portuguese dishes made with fresh local produce. Specialities include *bacalhau à lagareiro, polvo à lagareiro* and *medalhões de lombo recheados* (stuffed tenderloin medallions.)

→ From Maxial take the M560 NE for 1km. Cabeça Redonda, 3230-012 Ansiao
+351 236 677 226
39.9321, -8.4067 ▦▐▐

25 COGUMELOS DA SERRA DA LUA, VALVERDE

A colourful array of fresh mushrooms for sale, gathered that morning at this organic mushroom farm: frilled, hooded, pinks and ochres. Also has great recipe suggestions.

→ Just off the N362 in Cabeça Veada, to your R if entering from Valverde. Travessa Lagar Velho 7, Valverde, 2025-240 Alcanede
+351 927 521 274, Serradalua.pt
39.4787, -8.8568 ▐

26 FESTIVAL DO CHÍCHARO, ALVAIÁZERE

A festival in Alvaiázere to celebrate the green pulse traditionally grown in this area. There's dancing, music and wonderful local gastronomy – perhaps try a slice of the deliciously sweet *tarte de chícharo*. Mid June.

→ Alvaiázere, Alvaiazerecapitaldochicharo.pt
39.8245, -8.3820 ▐▐▐

27 RESTAURANTE O BARQUEIRO

This fishermen-run family restaurant is the only building on this promontory. The catch of the day is served on the long terrace overlooking the Zêzere.

→ From Foz de Alge take the road N along the River Alge, cross at the first bridge on your R, turn R again and follow down. Rua Cova da Eira, Fóz de Alge, 3260-090 Figueiró dos Vinhos +351 236 551 647
39.8308, -8.2770 ▦▐▐▐▭

28 RESTAURANTE SOLAR, FIGUEIRÓ DOS VINHOS

A hall in the town square hung with hunting paraphernalia and with dramatic soaps running on the television. Great dishes at good prices. Ask for the *dorada* fish.

→ Praça Município 9/13, 3260-408 Figueiró dos Vinhos
39.9028, -8.2758 ▐▐▐

29 RESTAURANTE NACO NA PEDRA, SALIR DO PORTO

Have your steak cooked on a hot rock, or a smooth hot stone: it seems an appropriate dish for Leiria, the Kingdom of Stone.

→ Rua do Casal 5, 2500-680 Salir do Porto +351 936 069 473
39.4931, -9.1569 🍴

30 ADEGA DO LUÍS, LIVRAMENTO

This is a rustic hideout, with the only giveaway being the smell of wood smoke and cooking coming from their chimney. Try devilish grilled meats or stews from the wood oven, and all the cakes are baked onsite.

→ Rua Principal 650, Livramento, 2480-162 Porto de Mós +351 964 103 287
39.5880, -8.8121 🍴♿🍴

31 VINHOS CORTÉM

An organic vineyard set in a valley just E of Caldas da Rainha. It's a protected area and very quiet. At night wild pigs come down the hills to settle in the vineyards. Stay in their self-catering guest suites with a pool and garden. Chris and Helga have planted many different varieties and their wine lots are small and won't be found in any supermarket. You'll have to visit them for a tasting!

→ Rua Joao Alves 37- 39, Cortém, 2500-741 Vidais +351 262 930 027, Vinhoscortem.com
39.3786, -9.0681 🍴♿

RURAL RETREATS

32 CASAL DE SÃO SIMÃO

A couple of pretty traditional little houses in the schist village of Casal de São Simão. Casa Amarela and Casa a Lura are two idyllic cottage escapes with logfires, hammocks and views to the wooded crags of São Simão.

→ Casal de São Simão, Figueiró dos Vinhos +351 917 279 176, Casaldesaosimao.com
39.9163, -8.3226 🍴♿

33 CASA DO VALE DO PAPO, VALE

A drystone house in the village of Vale surrounded by the rural hills of Serra do Sicó. A cosy house with a number of walks to caves, rivers and strange rocks signed nearby. Sleeps one to six.

→ Aldeia do Vale, 3100-000 Pombal +351 236 217 633, Casadovale.pt
39.8998, -8.5724 ♿

34 COOKING & NATURE EMOTIONAL HOTEL

Tranquil modern architecture with views across Serras de Aire e Candeeiros.

Cooking lessons with regional and seasonal ingredients, overseen by chef Nuno Barros. A balancing and healing retreat to bring you back into harmony with nature.

→ Rua Asseguia das Lages 181, 2480-032 Alvados +351 244 447 000, Cookinghotel.com
39.5486, -8.7734 ♿

WILDER CAMPING

35 CAMPING FOZ DE ALGE

Sleep beneath pine trees and watch the eagles circling above the River Zêzere. Simple and hearty Portuguese cooking in their restaurant. Paths lead down to the river for a swim.

→ Foz de Alge, 3260-090 Arega, Figueiró dos Vinhos +351 236 641 108, Pcampismofozalge.eu5.org
39.8267, -8.2739 ♿

36 CAMPING O MOINHO, BOLO

A small campsite with access to the gentle River Pêra and Praia Fluvial Poço da Corga. A baker comes in the mornings July/August.

→ See 3 for directions to Poço da Corga. Bolo, Poço da Corga, 3280-113 Castanheira de Pêra +351 236 438 762
40.0253, -8.1897 ♿

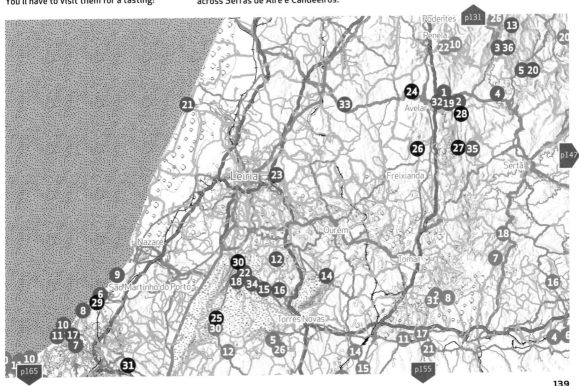

CASTELO BRANCO

Our perfect weekend

→ **Perch** high on a rock above Monsanto, be silent, and let the porous stones speak

→ **Leap** into the cool water at Fonte do Pego surrounded by wild hills

→ **Skinny-dip** by the reedy banks of the River Ocreza

→ **Hold** your breath as eagles whirl over their sky-scraping nests along the wild River Erges

→ **Watch** for wild Iberian lynx in the hills of Serra da Malcata

→ **Bivvy** down on the banks of Barragem Marechal Carmona canopied by dark sky studded with stars

→ **Share** a heaped plate of deliciously salty *migas de peixe*

→ **Marvel** at the 600 million year old 'painted snakes' in the Penha Garcia ravines

→ **Play** hide and seek in the woods outside Alvito da Beira

The rocks and hills of the Castelo Branco district, where central Portugal borders Spain, hold geological secrets many thousands of years old. The towns of Penha Garcia, Idanha-a-Velha and Monsanto crown ravines of granite and quartz, 600 million years old, some with snaking fossils holding memories of an ancient ocean. At the river beach in Penha Garcia you can discover trilobites writhing on the ocean floor, one ancient moment caught forever and thrust up to the mountains.

In Monsanto, tiny stone houses are built haphazardly around great boulders scattered like marbles over the hilltop; its narrow streets smell of wine cellars, crypts and old books. Stone houses, chapels and bread ovens are built wedged between boulders acting as roof here and a ceiling there: a balance between the man-made and natural. Look out for the *marafona* – or rag-doll – weavers who sit in doorways with their baskets of colourful wares.

A path leads from Monsanto to its Templar castle. A stone arch of a long-gone chapel remains, Ozymandias-like, to frame the wild sun-bleached hills beneath. The hills lie enveloped in a seemingly perpetual silence, while below murmur the legends, myths and songs of the land.

This weathered and primeval landscape continues further into the Raiana area before the frontier with Spain. Salvaterra do Extremo, a village on the extremities of Portugal, is lost in a landscape composed of extremes: beyond the vast open plains of Idanha-a-Nova the granite ravines rip up out of the flats to form towering stone chasms. Hundreds of birds of prey nest along the gorges through which the wild River Erges flows. The landscape is overwhelming and, if you take one of the nearby walks, you can lose all sense of scale.

This immensity feeds into the Raiana mindset, in the words of local artist and poet Nunes Pereira: "The little that God gave me/ Fits in a closed hand/ A little with God is everything/ A lot without God is nothing".

To the north, the Serra da Malcata nature reserve is home to the Iberian lynx, while if you follow the Ocreza, Pônsul and Aravil rivers flowing south-west into the Tejo, griffon vultures, black storks, golden eagles and Egyptian vultures are the guardians of the upper reaches of this river. See this wildlife on foot following any number of walks, plenty of which have opportunities for a dip in a wild river along the way.

LAKES & RIVER BEACHES

1 BARRAGEM MARECHAL CARMONA
Constructed in 1946, this reservoir is a haven for wildlife with its sandy shores, trees and flora. A beautiful stargazing spot.
→ From Idanha-a-Nova, along the N354 or N332 there are various tracks leading off with signs to the Barragem Marechal Carmona.
10 mins, 39.9468, -7.1967 ⛰️📷⛺🚻🛍️🐕🚣

2 PRAIA FLUVIAL DA TABERNA SECA
Steep slopes with olive trees fall down on the one side of the River Ocreza, with a shingle beach on the other.
→ From Taberna Seca take the N233 W to cross the river Ocreza, then follow signs L.
1 min, 39.8388, -7.5941 ♨️🍴🏊

3 PRAIA FLUVIAL DO SESMO
By the schist village of Sesmo, this river beach is surrounded by hills. Formed by a dam in a small tributary to the river Ocreza, it has built-up sides but deep and wide water.
→ From Pomar take the main road S for 1.5km, turn R down narrow cobbled road, keep R and follow road down 500m to beach. Parking.
1 min, 39.8596, -7.7426, 🏊🅱️🍴⛲

4 PRAIA FLUVIAL DE ALMACEDA
A small river beach in the village of Almaceda with built-up banks but deep green water. There is an old olive press you can visit, which was once river-powered.
→ Take the M525 into Almaceda and park near the bridge.
1 min, 40.0072, -7.6611 🏊🅱️

5 PRAIA FLUVIAL DO MALHADAL
Green, deep lake surrounded by olive groves. There's a high diving platform that's perfect for a thrilling leap.
→ From the CM1172 follow signs for Praia Fluvial Malhadal.
1 min, 39.7966, -7.9527 ⛲🏊🍴🅱️🌊

6 PRAIA FLUVIAL CEREJEIRA
A wide and deep shingle-bottom river beach, dark green water. Lawns and shade.
→ From Sarzedas take the N233 S for 10km, after bridge take sharp R at signs to Cerejeira. Follow signs S to 'Praia Fluvial' from Cerejeira.
2 mins, 39.8099, -7.7531 ⛲🏊🍴🅱️🌊

7 PRAIA FLUVIAL DA FRÓIA
Built-up banks and ladders lead down into deep, green fresh water. Picnic tables.

→ From Sobreira Formosa, head N along the EN233 to the village centre, then follow signs to the river beach.
3 mins, 39.7894, -7.8385 ⛲🏊🍽️

8 RIBEIRA DO ALVITO
Olive groves and a deep swim by a small waterfall just outside Alvito da Beira.
→ Walk straight down from the village.
1 min, 39.8242, -7.7984 ⛲🏊🍴🌊

WATERFALLS & SKINNY DIPS

9 FONTE DO PEGO
A man-made but gorgeous waterfall cascades into a rock pool. Follow a path up to see rocks teeming with fossils like a mass of eels. They are trace fossils, known locally as 'painted snakes' and thought to be 490 million years old.
→ From Penha Garcia follow signs for Praia Fluvial de Pego. Park on the cobbled street and walk down the hill, L at the houses and along the river.
5 mins, 40.0438, -7.0143 🏊🚶👓🌊

10 RIO OCREZA
Pass the deserted watermill and the smoky

greenish-yellow water widens and deepens. Tall grasses run down along the river banks until a large smooth stone allows for a jumping entrance. Secluded and perfect for a skinny-dip.

→ Along the N233 heading towards Taberna Seca. Just after the bridge over the River Ocreza park and take the path on the upstream side.
5 mins, 39.8418, -7.5923 ⬛⬛⬛⬛⬛

11 MEANDROS DO RIO OCREZA

A wild place for a dip in the Ocreza, surrounded by wooded hills.

→ From Bugios take M546 S for 2km, turn R down the dirt track before the bridge crosses the Ocreza.
2 mins, 39.7324, -7.7171 ⬛⬛

12 RIO ERGES

Following the border with Spain for most of its journey, this is one of Portugal's wildest rivers. The granite, limestone and schist rock has been reworked by the eddying river into strange formations. Eagles, vultures and storks nest in the ravines. The river is cool and slow between Salvaterra and Segura. A 10km signed walking trail along the river, discovering old mines, begins/ends here.

→ Park in Segura and follow the red/yellow walking signs from the Igreja da Misericórdia (39.8251, -6.9772) to the river and upstream.
30 mins, 39.8250, -6.9652 ⬛⬛⬛⬛⬛⬛

MOUNTAIN VILLAGES

13 ÁLVARO

A tiny slate-built hillside village overlooking the River Zêzere. It has a complicated religious history: there are 15 temples here, with a rich and strange collection of sacred art. A 7km signed and circular walking trail begins at Igreja Matriz de São Tiago, passing chapels, rivers, streams and olive groves.

→ From Pampilhosa da Serra take the N344 then N351 S for 17km in total until Álvaro.
2 hrs, 39.9758, -7.9662 ⬛⬛⬛⬛

14 PEDREIRA VILLAGE

A cluster of schist houses on the banks of the river. Once a major centre for flour milling, now empty; the river still runs under the old bridge.

→ From Cunqueiros take the EM1309-1 then N351 S for 3km, turn L at signs for Pedreira.
2 mins, 39.7902, -7.8546 ⬛⬛

15 IDANHA-A-VELHA

This small village on the banks of the Pônsul river was built in the 1st century BC under Emperor Augustus, when its name was Civitas Igaedinorum. It was conquered by Visigoths in the 6th century, later becoming an important Episcopal seat. This was once a busy town along an important trade route between Coimbra and Mérida. Now its quiet cobbled streets, storks nesting in ancient monastery towers and a heavy wide Roman bridge lend charm to a village marooned by fields. There is a collection of 86 Roman epigraphs, the largest in Europe, exhibited in the Museu Epigráfico Egitaniense (near the

Lagar de Varas olive oil press, see 18).

→ From Penamacor take the N332 S for 23km. Park outside and walk in.

5 mins, 39.9960, -7.1444 ⊞🎿🍴

16 SARZEDAS WALKING TRAIL

A 14km signed, circular route which begins in the quaint schist village of Sarzedas and follows its old Roman pavement out into cork oak woodland, passing old wolfram mines.

→ The walk begins at the Capela de Santo António. From Castelo Branco take the N233 W for 20km until Sarzedas.

3.5 hrs, 39.8502, -7.6848 🚶🏔⊞

17 MONSANTO

A village like no other: tiny houses built among great boulders which serve as roofs and walls. Ruins, trails and strange rocks characterise the hill above. A Templar castle is reached along a path winding up the mountain from the village. It crowns the mountain with its battlements and if you clamber up its walls you can enjoy earth-shattering views across the Raiana plains and out to Spain.

→ From Monsanto take the Pé Calvo track uphill to the castle. Information boards in town.

10 mins, 40.0363, -7.1133 🏔🚶🎿⊞✶

18 LAGAR DE VARAS, IDANHA-A-VELHA

Great massy oaks are used as levers in this once donkey-powered traditional olive press.

→ See Idanha-a-Velha. Head to the cathedral.

5 mins, 39.9958, -7.1446 ⊞

HIKING TRAILS

19 BOULDERS WALKING TRAIL, MONSANTO

Marvel at the ancient boulders and tors scattered over Monsanto's hills along this 4.5km circular walking trail. The way leads under the Joined Rocks, passes the ruined medieval chapel and reaches the Templar castle with views across to Spain.

→ Begins/ends opposite the Posto do Turismo Monsanto. See also 17.

1.5 hrs, 40.0392, -7.1142 🚶🏔📷🎿✝

20 ROTA DOS FÓSSEIS, PENHA GARCIA

See the 600-million-year-old snaking fossils in the rocks of Penha Garcia, dip into the cool Pônsul river, see the old traditional water mills and the silent, silver reservoir, all along this 3km circular walking trail.

→ Begins/ends at Largo do Chão da Igreja, Penha Garcia.

1 hr, 40.0417, -7.0184 🚶📷🍴🏔🏊

21 PORTAS DE ALMOURÃO

Jagged quartzite rocks fall away into the Ocreza river forming what looks like two doors opening to let the river in. A nesting place for vultures. The Grifo walking trail passes here (see 22 below).

→ Can be seen from the road leading E from Foz do Cobrão or follow the first part of the Grifo walking trail (see 22).

20 mins, 39.7349, -7.7488 📷🔺🚩

22 VOO DO GRIFO WALKING TRAIL

See the old water mills along the meandering

145

Ocreza river, 500 million-year-old geological wonders from an ancient ocean and the Portas do Almourão, all along this 11km circular walking trail.

→ Begins/ends at the Igreja da Foz do Cobrão. 4 hrs, 39.7319, -7.7593

23 PATHS OF ENCHANTMENTS AND HIDDEN CORNERS

This 11km circular walk begins in Alvito da Beira river beach (see 8). It's an ancient wooded path which links the old schist villages of the valley; it follows the river and passes abandoned water mills, with various spots for a dip along the way. The walk's magical name may be due to a legendary sack of gold buried in an ox-skin somewhere between Pereiro and Nogueira villages.

→ Begins at Alvito da Beira river beach (see 8). 3 hrs, 39.8242, -7.7984

WILDLIFE WONDERS

24 SERRA DA MALCATA

This nature reserve covering over 16,000 hectares of shale hills and wild woodland is shot through with the rivers Meimoa, Côa and Bezágueda. It was created to preserve the Iberian lynx. You might catch a glimpse of these rare feline creatures hunting for hares. It's more likely, though, that you'll see black vultures. There is a 9km, circular walking trail signed from the Meimoa reservoir.

→ Begin/end at the N332 as it meets the Meimoa reservoir from S. 2 hrs, 40.2556, -7.1168

25 ROTA DOS ABUTRES, SALVATERRA DO EXTREMO

Discover the wild Raiano landscape on this 10km signed, circular walking route. Look out for vultures, eagles and black storks. There is a bird hide en route with views out to Spanish border castles before the trail dips down to the wild River Erges.

→ Begins and ends at Igreja Matriz Salvaterra do Extremo. 4 hrs, 39.8836, -6.9145

LOCAL FOOD

26 RESTAURANTE PETISCOS & GRANITOS, MONSANTO

A restaurant hidden under enormous granite boulders. The doorway is small and squat, as though shortened under the great stone weight. Inside João will cook you the region's typical *migas*, fried bread with garlic, herbs and fish or *peixe de água doce*, mountain

river catch. For pudding there's *papas de carolo*, a regional variation on sweet rice.

→ Rua da Pracinha 16, Monsanto, 6060-087 Idanha-a-Nova +351 277 314 029 40.0385, -7.1149

27 CAFÉ RESTAURANTE DA AMOREIRA, IDANHA-A-VELHA

Named after the mulberry tree in the town square, this is the social hub of sleepy Idanha-a-Velha. Traditional and hearty dishes are served in its dark bar.

→ Rua da Amoreira, Idanha-a-Velha, 6060-041 Castelo Branco +351 277 914 180 39.9965, -7.1437

28 O FORNUM DU VIRIATO, MONSANTO

A cosy venue wedged in between the granite stones of Monsanto (see 17) where you can enjoy the views out over the wild hillside with a glass of wine and a choice of cheeses, hams, sausages, jams, honeys and breads as well as meads. The place is a tribute to its Lusitanian or Celtic heritage, and has occasional Celtic music nights with Portuguese bagpipes and *adufe* drums.

→ R. do Castelo 19, 6060-091 Monsanto +351 277 314 009, Tavernalusitana.com 40.0374, -7.1144

29 RESTAURANTE VALE MOURÃO

A restaurant with bare stone walls and views over the Ocreza river. Try the *cabrita à moda da aldeia* or fish from the river. There are regional Mourão dishes and wines, and they do a mean *pudim de ovos com suspiro*.

→ R. da Capela 13, Foz do Cobrão +351 272 543 012, Valemourao.blogspot.pt 39.7317, -7.7594

30 FESTA DE MIGAS, SEGURA

A festival to celebrate the local dish *migas de peixe* – a delicious recipe of fried bread with oils, herbs, garlic and river fish, of which there are hundreds of variations. Sometimes there are donkey parades. Mid June.

→ In the village square in Segura. 39.8265, -6.9780

31 RESTAURANTE O RATO, ALFRÍVIDA

This is the place to try *migas de peixe* – fish migas. It's a simple restaurant, popular with locals. Try the wild boar – *javali de caldeirada* and they make *tijelada* for pudding.

→ From Retaxo take the EM533 S for 7km into Alfrívida and it's on your R. 6030-051 Perais +351 272 989 388 39.7188, -7.5369

32 RESTAURANTE BEM-ME-QUER

An artisan cuisine inspired by the flavours of regional ingredients in this tiny schist village. The dishes are healthy, with the inclusion of vegetarian and raw-food recipes. There is a great selection of Portuguese wines. Rural guesthouses available but restaurant is also open to non-residents. Book ahead: by appointment only.

→ Rua da Bica, Martim Branco, 6000-003 Almaceda +351 968 887 857, Xistosentido.pt

39.9458, -7.6258 ⏣❗⏣⏣

RUSTIC RETREATS

33 TAVERNA LUSITANA, MONSANTO

A couple of cosy B&B ensuite rooms hidden above the tavern. A tribute to the wild hills Lusitanian heritage, even the biscuits they make are printed with the Celtic swirl from a granite *stele* found in Idanha-a-Velha. Incredible views.

→ See Fornum du Viriato (28)

40.0377, -7.1144 ⏣❗⏣⏣⏣⏣

34 PARQUE DE CAMPISMO DO FREIXIAL

A campsite on the banks of the River Bazágueda with beautiful shady trees, a children's playground, views out to distant blue mountains and a river beach. It's nearby the Serra da Malcata Natural Park and feels very in tune with nature.

→ Ribeira da Baságueda - Sitio do Freixial, 6090 Penamacor +351 277 385 529, Cm-penamacor.pt

40.1307, -7.0743 ⏣⏣⏣⏣

35 QUINTA DA BAZÁGUEDA

This is a very isolated farm in the heart of the Serra da Malcata mountains, with pigs, chickens, turkeys, geese, ducks and dogs. Fernando, Marta and Daniel keep the ancient traditions alive with their natural building and traditional life in the 16th century houses. Simple accommodation and meals provided in the rustic house or caravan in exchange for farm help for a few weeks.

→ Quinta da Bazágueda, 6090 Penamacor +351 277 394 875

40.1912, -7.0896 ⏣⏣⏣⏣

36 CASA DA TIA PIEDADE, MONSANTO

A cosy stone cottage in the heart of Monsanto with beautiful mountain views. Sleeps five.

→ R. da Azinheira 21, 6060-091 Monsanto +351 966 910 599, Casadatiapiedade.com

40.0390, -7.1133 ⏣⏣⏣⏣⏣⏣

37 CASA DO FORNO, SALVATERRA DO EXTREMO

Simple guest rooms with a garden and pool in a border village. Dry stone walls and cobbled lanes run down to dusty olive groves and the wild river Erges. There are a number of walks nearby and views out to the ruined Spanish border castle of Peñafiel.

→ Rua de S. João, 6060-501 Salvaterra do Extremo +351 277 455 021 Casadoforno.com.pt

39.8819, -6.9135 ⏣⏣⏣⏣

RIBATEJO

Our perfect weekend

→ **Sail** out to the mysterious Almourol castle, its marooned turrets reflected in the River Tejo

→ **Giggle** as enormous tropical butterflies alight on your skin at the Butterfly House in Santa Margarida

→ **Stroke** the noses of the ancient breed of Sorraia horses kept semi-wild at Alpiarça

→ **Cheer** the horsemen as they lead the cattle-blessing of Riachos

→ **Dance** late into the night to traditional *pimba* music at Pereiro

→ **Dive** down into the cool, sweet water of Castelo de Bode reservoir

→ **Swirl** a glass of dry red wine from Cartaxo

→ **Feel** the horses' hooves thunder and kick up the sand at Colete Encarnado, Vila Franca da Xira

→ **Jump** over the waterfall at the hidden pool, Pego da Rainha

→ **Watch** for hoopoes - or *poupa* - darting from their nests at Reserva Boquilobo

→ **Feast** on *ensopado de enguias* at Valada, a rich stew made from eels caught in the Tejo

Ribatejo is a beautiful region running from Lisbon along the north side of the River Tejo – the Tagus – until it is joined by the winding River Ocreza. Beyond this lie the wild hills of Castelo Branco and, further still, Spain. This is a land of low-lying fields of maize or tomato, growing along the Tejo. In winter the Tejo floods its banks; in spring, eels swim upstream to mate; and in summer, arid heat hangs over cowboys and bullfights.

Even in summer, as the air boils and the sun beats down, you're never too far from a refreshing plunge into a river. Villages appear lethargic in the heat, life slows to a rhythmic pace. Despite this, the small-scale farms, vineyards and stables still achieve great renown. Golegã is known as the 'capital of the horse', and Cartaxo, the 'capital of wine'. Add to this their renowned bullfights and it's a potent mix.

During the summertime *festas*, this is a land of raised pulses. In Golegã, Riachos and Vila Franca de Xira, cobblestones are buried beneath sand as horsemen and women saunter in and charge back to dusty bullfights and feats of daring. In Golegã, during the annual horse fair, horses are ridden into bars, even discotheques. The wild invades the town. But not all *festas* are so frenzied: in Pereiro the cobbles are strewn with flowers and hung with garlands one year in the making. The whole village celebrates its saint and home-comings for three days, with wines, dancing, street food and open doors.

River beaches line the banks of the steady, wide Tejo, offering dips in waters pleasantly cool, but significantly warmer than the sea. At Ortiga you can take a canoe and explore the wooded green river banks opposite. Or travel north to the reservoir at Castelo de Bode filled by the Zêzere river, pine-covered hills sloping down to meet its banks. Nearby, the Ocreza river valley holds some of the world's most ancient rock carvings, some 20,000 years old.

In the evening, remind yourself you are in one of Portugal's oldest wine-growing regions and relax with a glass of the DOC do Tejo from Cartaxo. If you are there in springtime, when the eels are in season, try *ensopado de enguias*, slow-cooked rice with eels in broth or *açorda de sável* made with the fatty local fish. These unique flavours will immerse you in the place.

WATER ADVENTURES

1 RIVER PARK, VALADA
Valada is a small village on the banks of the Tejo. The path to Santiago de Compostela passes by. Valada's high flood walls testify to past winters when the Tejo would burst its banks. While there is no longer such dramatic flooding, be wary of winter currents and stay within the buoyed area. In summer the water is surprisingly warm. Canoes for hire: +351 966 675 554.

➔ From Azambuja take N3-3 E into Valada. At crossroads with N3-2 turn R, then L, and follow with flood wall on your R. At end of flood wall, turn R to the river and park. Walk along the river, downstream, past picnic area to the River Park.
4 mins, 39.0777, -8.7611 ⚓🏕️🅱️🌊🍴⛵

2 PRAIA FLUVIAL, ALVERANGEL
The soft, sweet water of the Castelo de Bode reservoir is the main source of drinking water for Lisbon. You can walk down its banks and slip in under the calm surface. Emerge to watery views across to the opposite banks and pine-covered hills.

➔ From Castelo de Bode, take the N358 N for 2.5km, turn R onto CM1117 and follow signs for Alverangel. At Alverangel follow brown signs down to Praia Fluvial.
2 mins, 39.5477, -8.3078 ⚓🏔️🖼️

3 PRAIA FLUVIAL DE CARVOEIRO
A large stone-built pool. Pine woodland stretches away beyond the waterfall which fills the pool. High-sided but deep enough for a dive, the river water moves gently through but remains warm. Children's river pool, barbecue grill and grassy banks.

➔ From Mação follow brown signs to Praia Fluvial de Carvoeiro.
2 mins, 39.6301, -7.9232 ⚓🍴🌊🅱️

4 PRAIA FLUVIAL DE ORTIGA
A sandy and popular river beach on the wooded banks of the Tejo. A floating pool allows for safe bathing if there are more extensive river currents but usually functions as a diving platform. Canoes for hire.

➔ From Mação follow brown signs to Praia Fluvial Ortiga.
2 mins, 39.4829, -8.0019 🍴🅱️🌊⚓🏕️🖼️

5 PRAIA FLUVIAL, OLHOS DE ÁGUA
Winding, shallow river with shady trees. Very busy at weekends with family picnics but deserted during the week.

➔ From Alcanena take N361; at 2nd roundabout follow signs for Amiais de Baixo; stay on this road until after the river, then follow signs to Praia Fluvial/Olhos.
1 min, 39.4453, -8.7116 ⚓🌊🅱️🌊🍴

6 PRAIA FLUVIAL DO ALAMAL
Chase the ducks across this sandy river beach and follow them into the water. The Tejo here is slow-flowing and wide, with a roped-off swimming area. Belver Castle rises imperiously from the wooded hills above.

➔ From Gavião follow signs for Praia Fluvial Alamal.
2 mins, 39.4880, -7.9675 🅱️🌊⛲🏕️🚶🌊⚓

7 PRAIA FLUVIAL DO PENEDO FURADO
A popular river beach with sparkling clear water and several waterfalls filling the pool. Smooth rocks slope down to the edge and woodland surrounds it. Nearby is the Penedo Furado rock. Just beneath this outcrop is a fossil, the 'Bicha Pintada', thought to be 480 million years old. From here you can see over the wooded hills to the Castelo de Bode reservoir. Myths, tales and legends abound.

➔ From Brêscovo take the road N for 2 km and turn left at brown signs for Penedo Furado.
2 mins, 39.6257, -8.1622 🚶🌊💧👁️🚻🅱️

11

8

9

8 PARQUE NÁUTICO DE ALDEIA DO MATO

This is a very tranquil place for an early evening dip in the calm waters of Castelo de Bode reservoir surrounded by pine forests.

➜ From Aldeia do Mato follow brown signs for Praia Fluvial.

2 mins, 39.5454, -8.2774 🏔🏖🏞

9 PEGO DA RAINHA

An idyllic oasis hidden within the parched and dramatic granite massif of the Vale do Ocreza, which is rich in rock engravings. Shaded by trees, and protected by an enormous rocky outcrop, where eagles and vultures nest. The blue pool is deep enough for a plunge from the top of a low waterfall.

➜ From Zimbreira follow brown signs to Pego da Rianha. Turn down the dirt track, park near the information board and walk 1km down this mountain track (difficult road).

15 mins, 39.5755, -7.8284 🏔🚶🏔🍴🏞

10 ALDEIA PATACÃO

This old fishing village on the banks of the Tejo, now fallen into disrepair, testifies to the ancient fishing culture along this river. You can still see wooden houses built on stilts to survive the winter floods. A little further on is a river beach, unguarded.

➜ From Alpiarça take the road N to Q.ta da Lagualva de Cima and follow to the river bank.

5 mins, 39.2981, -8.5803 🏖🏞

ROMANTIC CASTLES

11 CASTELO DE ALMOUROL

A Knights Templar castle rising from its island on the Tejo. There are as many variations on its legends as waves lapping its shores. Take the small guide boat out to explore.

➜ From Tancos follow signs to the castle. Boats leave every 30 mins.

2 mins, 39.4621, -8.3838 🏞🏖 B 🚴 €

12 CASTELO DE ALCANEDE

A picturesque castle on a hill with beautiful views over wild hills. It's thought to have pre-historic foundations, later to become Roman and then Moorish. It's in great condition with old carvings, passageways and crests to discover.

➜ From Alcanede follow brown signs up the hill.

10 mins, 39.4172, -8.8213 🏞🏔🏖🚶

FESTAS & FAIRS

13 FESTA DO COLETE ENCARNADO

The name translates as the party of the 'red

13

waistcoast' with overtones of 'incarnate' or 'made flesh'. Being one of the biggest bullfights in Ribatejo, the name is apt. The entire town becomes simultaneously a party and a bullring. There is also a procession with costumed riders cantering into town. Later on, revellers with beer and *bifanas* (sandwiches of slow-cooked pork) cover the sandy road but at any point there can be a shout and a scattering of people to the sides as an enraged bull invades the party. Caution needed. Early July.

→ Parking limited. Take train to Vila Franca de Xira from Lisbon. The party is in the whole town.
2 mins, 38.9549, -8.9871

14 FESTA DA BÊNÇÃO DO GADO, RIACHOS

A joyful several-days-long festival in the small town of Riachos. The festival centres around the 'blessing of the cattle' where horses and local horsemen – naturally – lead in the cattle to be blessed. There is also a separate *passeio equestre*, horse parade, with a party, and a *passeio de pasteleiras*, bakers on bikes. Artisan stalls, crafts, folklore and food. Last week of July.

→ Riachos, Torres Novas. Accessible by train from Lisbon to Riachos/Torres Novas/Golegã.
2 mins, 39.4326, -8.5051

15 GOLEGÃ NATIONAL HORSE FAIR

Equestrian culture is ingrained into the life of Golegã and this municipality has some of Portugal's most famous stud farms. This ten-day-long festival every November transforms the town into an even more lively horsey hub. All day and all night the streets are packed with horses – they are everywhere, even in the bars and discos. Narrow streets are filled with stands; try the regional drinks Ginga, Agua-Pé and Abafado, or relax with a glass of wine and watch the spectacle in the square.

→ Main square, Largo do Marquês de Pombal.
2 mins, 39.4022, -8.4825

13

16 FESTAS DO PEREIRO

The small town of Pereiro is bedecked with garlands of flowers, which hang over the streets from wall to wall. For the main procession of Our Lady of Health, the streets are strewn with flowers and herbs. There is dancing to *pimba*, the traditional happy music, late into the night with *bifanas*, *pregos* and endless *minis*, mini-beers, served till dawn. Last weekend of August.

→ From Mação take N244 N for 4km. Park outside and walk in.
30 mins, 39.5875, -8.0130

16

17 FESTA DA NOSSA SENHORA DA BOA VIAGEM, CONSTÂNCIA

The dangers of navigation have always attached themselves to the seafarers and fishermen who lived upriver at Constância. For centuries, Easter Monday has seen the blessing of the boats. Hundreds of traditional fishing boats, colourfully festooned, sail into the harbour for a blessing. Their ceremonial setting sail is a dramatic sight. They return, of course, for a lively party to celebrate their fortune and full nets.

→ Train from Lisbon; the nearest station is Praia do Ribatejo, downstream along the Tejo.
30 mins, 39.4751, -8.3377 🚂🍴🛶🏊

WALKS & WILDLIFE

18 TRILHO DAS BUFAREIRAS

This is a signed 9km linear walking route from Vila de Rei to Penedo Furado river beach. It passes panoramic views, mystical rocks, ancient fossils and waterfalls.

→ Begins at the *pelourinho*, pillory, of Vila de Rei.
1.5 hrs, 39.6735, -8.14661 🥾🏊🚶

19 RESERVA NATURAL DO PAUL DO BOQUILOBO

An inland wetland formed by the Tejo and Almonda rivers; sheltered Montado cork and long dry grasses intersperse the wetlands. There is a signed PR trail here and a couple of bird hides. In summer you might glimpse nesting herons: this is one of their most important nesting sites in Portugal. There are storks and cockatoo'd hoopoes here too.

→ Well signed from Riachos/Torres train station (1st L out of station). Or drive from Azinhaga. Walking trail signed from information centre.
45 mins, 39.4088, -8.5267 🚶🏊🏞

20 RESERVA NATURAL DO CAVALO DO SORRAIA, ALPIARÇA

40ha dedicated to the protection of the *sorraia* horse in Alpiarça – an ancient breed of Iberian horse – rediscovered in 1920, and thought to be the ancestor of the *lusitano* and Spanish Andalusian horse. There are possibly fewer than 200 of these horses worldwide. Their arched necks and convex noses appear in rock drawings in Granada 20,000 years old. See some of these horses here semi-wild as you explore the lakes and woodland. A good restaurant too.

→ From Alpiarça take N118 S until the roundabout, take 2nd exit signed P. Natural and follow brown signs. Rua José Relvas 374, 2090 Alpiarça +351 927 414 247, Cm-alpiarca.pt
1 hr, 39.2421, -8.5760 🍴🚗🐴🚶

21 BUTTERFLY HOUSE AT PARQUE AMBIENTAL DE SANTA MARGARIDA

Many-hued tropical butterflies will land on you at this *borboletário*. Do not underestimate how large a butterfly can be. Explore the pond, fish, flora and wildlife too.

→ Follow signs for Parque Ambiental in Santa Margarida.
15 mins, 39.4462, -8.3180 🚶🚗🏊

22 EVOA, TEJO ESTUARY BIRDWATCHING

The Tejo estuary is the largest wetland area in Portugal and is considered one of the most important in Europe due to the 120,000 migratory birds that rest here. At the Evoa conservation centre there are 5km of walking trails, three lagoons, four bird hides, viewing points and daily guided tours.

→ From Vila Franca de Xira take the N10 over the Tejo and after 3km follow signs R. Evoa.pt
2 mins, 38.8498, -8.9735 👁€🍴🚶

FOOD & WINE

23 RESTAURANTE CASA DAS ENGUIAS

Tucked just behind Valada's old flood wall, beyond the dark café entrance is a sun-trap patio and then a cavernous restaurant. If you want to try the region's speciality – the eels that swim upriver to mate in early summer – then this is the place. The owner and head chef, 'O Toscano', has won the district's Gold Award for his *enguias*. If you're not up for eels, Toscano's *peru* (turkey) steaks with special *molho* are wonderful. The Cartaxo wine here is good.

→ Rua Primeiro de Maio 27, 2070-516 Valada +351 243 749 230
39.0806, -8.7605 🍴🍷

24 O SABOR DA PEDRA, ALVERANGEL

A luxuriously rural place to try the local fish dishes and wines. Sunlight pours in through wide open windows with views out over the deep blue Castelo de Bode reservoir. An elegant place utterly in harmony with the surrounding nature, taking delight in its flavours and harvest. There are log fires in winter and hundreds of wines to taste or drop in to buy.

→ 3km S of Alverangel centre towards the reservoir. Rua do Rio 5, Alverangel, 2300-152 São Pedro de Tomar +351 249 371 750, Osabordapedra.com
39.5486, -8.3089 🍴🍷🚗🏞

25 SANTARÉM GASTRONOMIC FESTIVAL

For the last couple of weeks of October the cobbled streets of Santarém are decked with tables heaving under regional cooking, smoked meats, cheeses and wines. Ancient recipes and their rich flavours are rekindled and brought to life with music and cheer.

→ Casa do Campino, Santarém +351 243 300 900, Festivalnacionaldegastronomia.pt
39.2296, -8.6909 ▦⬛❗️🍴🅿️⬛

26 PENEDAS BAR, MALHOU

A hidden restaurant outside Malhou, not too promising from outside but the food is sublime. Sit in the back garden, with a roaming peacock, and try the cheeses, wines and *moelas*, marinated gizzards.

→ From Malhou take the long straight road W towards Amiais de Baixo. Head practically out of town but before you hit the farms take a tiny road on R signed Penedas Bar. Rua Miguel Bombarda, 2380 Malhou +351 249 881 840
39.4273, -8.6924 ❗️🍴🅿️

27 ADEGA COOPERATIVA DO CARTAXO

You can drop in to this friendly winery and buy the DOC do Tejo and regional wines at remarkably reasonable prices. Wine-tastings if you book ahead.

→ On N365-2 W of Cartaxo centre. 2070-220 Cartaxo +351 243 770 987, Adegacartaxo.pt
39.1553, -8.8095 🅿️

28 ADEGA COOPERATIVA DE ALCANHÕES

A new winery but very old wine. The wine from this region was mentioned in the 15th century *Chronicles of Don Fernando*: the court enjoyed "dancing… wine and fruit of Dalcanhães …". Their DOC do Tejo can be purchased here.

→ 2000-371 Alcanhões +351 243 429 151, Adegaalcanhoes.pt
39.2959, -8.6583 🅿️

RURAL RETREATS

29 MORGADO LUSITANO

A marvellous escape for those seeking an equestrian holiday with views over the Tejo, pine woodland, orchards and the 18th century manor, and only 15 mins from Lisbon airport. The estate was built by the Count of Ribeira Grande after the Great Earthquake of 1755. Now they train the finest *lusitano* horses in dressage. Book an intensive week's riding lessons or simply stay in the estate and enjoy their cuisine and rural paradise.

→ Quinta Da Portela, Cabeço Da Rosa, Alverca do Ribatejo +351 219 936 520, Morgadolusitano.pt
38.9046, -9.0702 🍴🔥⬛❗️🅿️🔥⬛▦

30 O PÁTIO DO JUDEO, VALVERDE

Three self-catered apartments in a 19th century house just within the Serra de Aire e Candeeiros Natural Park.

→ Rua Principal EN362, Valverde, 2025-201 Alcanede +351 243 400 012, Opatiodojudeu.pt
39.4600, -8.8574 ⬛⬛

WILDER CAMPSITES

31 PARQUE DE CAMPISMO DE CASTELO DE BODE, MARTINCHEL

Fall asleep to waters gently lapping at the banks of the Castelo de Bode reservoir. This is a peaceful campsite near several hiking trails. Bungalows available.

→ 2200-638 Martinchel +351 241 849 244, Fcmportugal.com
39.5402, -8.3191 ⬛❗️🧍⬛

32 ECO PARQUE DE ALVERANGEL

A beautiful tiered and grassy camping park under pine trees by the Castelo de Bode reservoir. There is a little gate to a private jetty for a dip in the clear, sweet water.

→ Rua do Rio 5, Alverangel, 2300-152 São Pedro de Tomar +351 249 371 750
39.5487, -8.3089 🍴⬛⬛⬛⬛❗️Y

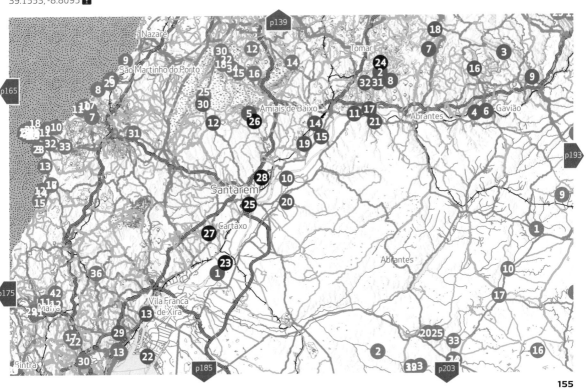

PENICHE &
BERLENGAS

Our perfect weekend

→ **Bounce** over the high seas in a fishing boat to
the mysterious island of Berlenga

→ **Feast** on fresh crab overlooking the sea-
sprayed Rochas da Consolação

→ **Snorkel** through clear water, silvery fishes and
strange semi-precious rocks at Forte de São João

→ **Let** your thoughts soar over the horizon from
wild sea caves

→ **Bask** in sun-soaked sand at Baleal

→ **Surf** the wild waves at Porto das Barcas

→ **Meditate** on the strange split cliffs at Cruz
dos Remédios

→ **Imagine** the dinosaurs who once roamed the
coast at Lourinhã

→ **Bed** down in the 17th century Forte de São João
Baptista

→ **Scramble** up ancient fishermen paths as the
tide surges around peninsular Papoa

→ **Watch** the sun set into sea-drenched splendour
from the wild cliffs at Cabo Carvoeiro

The peninsula of Peniche, a hundred kilometres north of Lisbon, is famous for its waves. Surfers gather here year-round like pilgrims. At any point in the town you can glimpse the sea, and the great thing with Peniche is that if there are no waves on the one side of the peninsula then there will be on the other. As well as the wild Atlantic surf, it also has long sandy beaches, calm coves and limestone cliffs wrought with ravines, crevices and sea caverns worn by the plunging, sucking sea.

The sea dominates everything.

There is a 'lost world' feel to Peniche. Raúl Brandão, journalist and playwright, described the Nau dos Corvos – just off the tip of the peninsula – as "a great rock sunk three hundred metres deep – and perhaps the last remnant of Atlantis, rising up from the blue sea and dripping blue". There are places on this peninsula which are timeless and elemental, whether you are getting in touch with the wild power of the waves or sitting in a smooth sea cave such as the Varanda de Pilatos.

The small and enigmatic Berlenga island lies 12km off the coast. Every morning and evening, passenger boats laden with sacks of onions, potatoes, boxes of cakes and bread bounce over the waves, followed by flocks of screaming gulls. Green hills rise from the waves where seagulls nest everywhere, in grass, caves, beaches, pinnacles and eroded stacks. The question at the port as the boxes are unloaded is inevitably, "Have you been to Earth today?" And with the gulls wheeling and cawing overheard, it certainly feels far removed from the world beyond.

The sea at Berlenga is far warmer than some of the more open Atlantic beaches on the mainland. Gentle and clear like sea-green stained glass, the water offers fantastic diving. An arched bridge zig-zags from the main island to the fortress of São João, built on a marooned rock. Underneath the fort is a shadowy cave but the water lapping inside is lit up by its quartz stone walls. It's like swimming in a dark sapphire.

Returning on the last boat, you'll find that Peniche has no shortage of great seafood restaurants. Along the harbour there are dozens to discover. Our favourite has got to be Sol é Vida. Here you can eat the freshest crab and watch the fishermen below on the Rochas da Consolação, Rocks of Consolation, while sea spray bursts madly up.

6

SEA CAVES & STRANGE ROCKS

1 VARANDA DE PILATOS, PENICHE

A small thinking-place in a sea-carved stone chamber down a ladder in the cliff-side. Let your thoughts soar out across ocean views while sheltered from wild Atlantic winds. Large enough for one or two, depending on the size and scale of your thoughts.

→ A moment N of Cabo Carvoeiro lighthouse: walk up the main coastal road and look for the wooden plaque 'Varanda de Pilatos' before the Cruz dos Remedios.

3 mins, 39.3638, -9.4060

2 GRUTA DA FURNINHA

Explore these natural sea caves worming out from the side of the Peniche cliffs. The sea and sky are framed by wind-pummelled stone mouths. Still used as fishermen's caves, 19th century excavations revealed an exhaustive amount of ancient remains here: Neanderthal man had inhabited the caves for 20,000 years.

→ From Peniche Fort head towards Cabo Carvoeiro; take the most coastal road, pass the wooden plaque to Furnas and park nearby (before the steps at Cova de Dominique). Follow the path down a little way towards the

cliffs and caves. Take great care.

20 mins, 39.3564, -9.4013

3 ROCHAS DA CONSOLAÇÃO

Great stepping stones down to the sea resembling the Giant's Causeway. The stones are said to have healing powers and lying on these rocks while the wild waves crash around does restore some balance. Alternatively head over to the little bar and enjoy fresh crab and chilled wine (Sol é Vida, see 23).

→ From Peniche take the IP6 out and turn R at Casal da Vala. Continue on Rua Principal to Lugar da Estrada, then R to Avenida da Praia straight to the Praia das Rochas car park.

1 min, 39.3239, -9.3615

DIVING & WRECKS

4 TROMBA DO ELEFANTE

These rock formations on the southern tip of the small island of Berlenga resemble an elephant's trunk, *tromba*. It's a favourite spot with divers. The rocks meet the sand 15m underwater and you can see finned gurnards and red mullets. In the distance, you may see conger eels and octopus.

→ Contact AcaSubOeste for diving lessons

and equipment +351 918 393 444, Acuasuboeste.com.

2 hrs, 39.4082, -9.5125

5 THE PRIMAVERA WRECK

An Italian steamer lost on 28 October 1902 after a fire on board, the Primavera is a relatively shallow wreck with a maximum depth of 22m. In addition to the wreck, which is fantastic, the cargo of marble blocks has created a unique underwater environment that attracts such creatures as octopus, lobsters and conger eels, and many gold sea bream.

→ Contact AcaSubOeste for diving (see 4).

2 hrs, 39.4074, -9.5038

6 COVA DO SONHO

This is one of several mysterious caves lit up by aquamarine water along the coast of Berlenga island. Others include Flandres, Blue, Muxinga and Lagosteira Caves. Explore them with a day paddleboarding.

→ Contact SUP Academy for day trips to Berlenga from Peniche +351 962 374 793, Standupportugal.pt

2 hrs, 39.4109, -9.5109

SECRET BEACHES

7 PRAINHA DA BERLENGA

A tiny sandy beach sheltered by the dramatic slopes of Berlenga. The water is aquamarine and there are a couple of caves into which you can easily swim and explore.

→ As the boat docks (see 21), follow the path down into the first cove.

3 mins, 39.4150, -9.5075

8 PRAIA DO PORTINHO DA AREIA SUL, PENICHE

A locals' beach. The water is much colder than in the bays but the sand, quiet and clear water make up for this.

→ From Peniche fort walk through the sun-bleached and sea-washed neighbourhood of Bairro do Visconde, along the coastal side to this small beach.

15 mins, 39.3543, -9.3886

9 PRAIA DO BALEAL (NORTE)

Wander around Baleal until you find a small cove or secret beach. Waves come in gently here, lapping on the sand, having crashed in on larger rocks further out. Perfect for small children with buckets.

→ Park up in Casais do Baleal and walk down to the beaches.

5 mins, 39.3727, -9.3384

10 PRAIA DA ALMAGREIRA

Great big red sand dunes to explore like Portugal's mini Valley of the Kings.

→ From Ferrel follow signs to Praia Almagreira along the coastal tracks to the beach.

10 mins, 39.3792, -9.3138

11 PRAIA DO BALEAL (SUL)

Between Praia do Baleal (Norte) and along the coast SW into Peniche the beach here is sandy and often far emptier.

→ Walk S from Baleal along the coast until quieter.

15 mins, 39.3638, -9.3462

12 PRAIA DO PORTO DAS BARCAS

A quiet sandy beach with some wild surf. If the winds are cold, snuggle down in the sand and let the sun warm you or bring a windbreaker.

→ From Lourinhã head towards Atalaia de Cima and follow 'Praia' signs.

2 mins, 39.2269, -9.3398

10

13 PRAIA DE PAIMOGO

An empty stretch of sandy beach guarded by a 17th century stronghold rising imperiously from the cliffs. In the early '90s about 100 dinosaur eggs were discovered here, some containing embryonic bones. Now the eggs can be found at the Lourinhã museum. Low tide reveals old fishing ponds, testimony to an activity now extinct. Still a popular place with anglers.

➜ From Lourinhã take the N247 towards the coast. After Seixal pass the church and then L at signs to Hotel Dom Lourenço; take the first exit at the roundabout and continue on this road to the coast.

3 mins, 39.2852, -9.3372 🏖🏊

14 PRAIA DO ZIMBRAL

A quieter stretch of sandy beach between Porto Dinheiro and Porto das Barcas.

➜ From Atalaia de Baixo take the road S for 1km, turn R at the Boa Viagem sign and continue until beach.

2 mins, 39.2198, -9.3415 🏖🏊

15 PRAIA DE VALMITÃO

A long stretch of sand bathed by crystal-clear waters. It can be popular due to the healing properties of the water, associated with its high iodine content.

➜ Follow signs for 1km from Ribamar.

2 mins, 39.2030, -9.3459 🏖Ⓑ

DINOSAURS & DUNES

16 MUSEU DA LOURINHÃ

See treasure found along these cliffs: huge razor-edged dinosaur teeth, skulls, dinosaur eggs and even a fossilised dinosaur nest at this lively little museum. "The museum gives to Lourinhã not only the fossils but their identity," says local palaeontologist Octavio Mateus. "People see in dinosaurs part of themselves." The centre is colourful and imaginative, perfect for engaging children.

➜ Rua João Luis de Moura 95, 2530-158 Lourinhã +351 261 414 003, Museulourinha.org

1 min, 39.2419, -9.3132 🏖🏠♿€

17 ROTA DOS DINOSSAUROS, LOURINHÃ

The small town of Lourinhã is known as the 'land of the dinosaurs' due to the excavation of teeth the size of daggers, nests of fossilised dinosaur eggs and skulls of enormous wild beasts that once roamed this coast. See this wild coast along a 10km signed Rota dos Dinossauros.

13

11

18

17

19

→ Starts next to the Lourinhã museum and finishes at Paimogo fort.
1.5 hrs, 39.2420, -9.3128 🚶🗺️🏊

CLIFFTOP HIGHS

18 PAPOA

A small peninsula off the Peniche peninsula. The rocks jut up to form a disintegrating battlement, along which you can carefully tread its sandy spine and spread your arms like a seagull to catch the wind.
→ N side of Peniche, signed off N114.
1 min, 39.3745, -9.3780 📷🏔️🖼️

19 CABO CARVOEIRO

A spot once contested as being the 'most westerly tip of Europe', until this title was given to Cabo da Roca. Wild winds rip and roar up the craggy cliffs and the views out across to the mystical island of Berlenga are stunning. Waves crash on rocks beneath. Inevitably there will be a wily fisherman on the rocks below, and probably therefore a bit further west than you.
→ From Peniche fort take the Estrada Marginal Sul W and follow signs to Cabo Carvoeiro.
2 mins, 39.3592, -9.4087 🍴📷🖼️

20 CRUZ DOS REMÉDIOS, PENICHE PENINSULA

The cliffs are split into surreal shapes as though after the convulsions of an earthquake. Their layers of limestone form giant towers teetering over the slap and pull of the sea sucking beneath. Crawl up, and stick your head over the edge to breathe in the darkness between the rocks: crypts, old libraries, cellars, mould and death.
→ From Cabo Carvoeiro walk 300m N along the coastal road. Cruz dos Remédios is signed.
5 mins, 39.3626, -9.4067 🅅📷🖼️

WILD ISLANDS

21 BERLENGAS ARCHIPELAGO

The Berlengas archipelago is composed of three islands, the largest of which is Berlenga at 1.5km long. Pink rock and green grass slope down to the emerald water. Hundreds of seagulls wheel and caw overhead; the whole island is their home and is richly perfumed by damp feathers and *guano*. Look out for loud chicks nesting in the grass and prepare to be pelted if you stray from the path. There are a couple of beautiful small beaches here for a swim, and caves can be reached by swimming or kayak.

22

There is one good but expensive restaurant and a hut selling coffee and *bola de berlin*. Bring cash or a picnic to the island and leave it clean. For diving call Berlenga Sub +351 965 107 728.

→ Boats leave every morning and evening from Peniche harbour: call Viamar +351 262 785 646.

1 day, 39.4149, -9.5075 🌊🚤🏊🚶🏕️🏠🍴€

22 FORTE DE SÃO JOÃO BAPTISTA

The 17th century fortress of São João is built on monastic remains on an island off Berlenga. It can be reached by a bridge zig-zagging out over rocks and lapping waves, or by a short swim. If you choose the latter, be aware of small boats chugging into caves and bring a snorkel: the water is surprisingly warm with semi-precious rocks and caves to explore, and colourful fish. For diving contact Berlenga Sub: +351 965 107 728

→ From Peniche take the boat to Berlenga (see 21) and follow the walkway up and into the island. Eventually you will see the fort.

15 mins, 39.4113, -9.5101 🏯🚤🏠📷🚤

23 SNACK BAR SOL É VIDA, CONSOLAÇÃO

'Sun and Life' offered on these Rocks of Consolation. Great fish, very fresh crab. Eat out on the veranda with the salt wind in your hair. Watch fishermen on the rocks below while you console yourself with dressed crab and a sparkling dry white.

→ Largo Nossa Sra. da Consolação 9 +351 963 708 840

39.3239, -9.3616 🍴🍷📷

24 RESTAURANTE O BACALHAU

A sign in the window of this unassuming restaurant offers a "walk on the wild side". Although by all outward appearances shut, walk on in and discover their vine-decked patio garden, grilled fish and pub tables. Try their fried *jaquinzinhos* and tomato rice. Very cheap.

→ Rua Dom Luís de Atayde 114, 2520-408 Peniche +351 914 324 011

39.3593, -9.3794 🍴🍷

25 BAR SÃO PEDRO

Seashells decorate the walls in this happy colourful little *cervejaria* and restaurant. Set back from the main parade of seafood

20

21

haunts. Simple great local dishes.
→ Rua José Estêvão 97, 2520-467 Peniche +351 262789658
39.3553, -9.3793 🍴❗

26 RESTAURANTE DO PARQUE

If you are in Peniche, the dish to try is *caldeirada*. A rich fish stew made in a large pot for sharing, it usually has big prawns, octopus, monkfish, conger eels, dogfish, sea bass and skate. It's excellent here. These are hundreds of fresh fish to see and choose; they will grill and fry to local recipes. An absolute haven for fish lovers.
→ Parque do Baluarte, Av. 25 de Abril, 2520-202 Peniche +351 262 789 251, Restaurantedoparqu.wix.com
39.3641, -9.3783 🍴❗

27 RESTAURANTE MARISQUEIRA DOS CORTIÇAIS

A restaurant right by the sea with a beautiful view for sunset. They make excellent *caldeirada* here. Other specialities include *lagosta suada*, lobster cooked in a clay pot with parsley, bay leaves and wine.
→ Porto D Areia Sul, 2520-244 Peniche +351 262 787 262, Doscorticais.com
39.3538, -9.3868 🍴❗📷

28 MERCADO MUNICIPAL DE PENICHE

A noisy and colourful market, popular with locals, with heaps of mouthwatering seasonal fruit and vegetables, fresh fish, local meats, regional cheeses, breads and local cakes. Open daily, closed Mondays. Arts & crafts fair every second weekend.
→ R. António Conceição Bento 23A, 2520-294, Peniche
39.3603, -9.3800 🍴

WILDER CAMPSITES

29 CAMPING BERLENGAS

Berlenga is a protected island and so, of course, camping numbers are limited. However, staying on this wild island is still possible and a magical experience. Fall asleep to the slap and the pull of the sea and wake up to the most spectacular dawns.
→ Camping reservations can be made at the Peniche Touristic Point +351 262 789 571, Turismo@cm-peniche.pt
39.4148, -9.5063 🔺🎪🚻🚿

30 PENICHE PRAIA CAMPING

A camping field on the Peniche clifftops by the Remédios rocks. There are pretty

bungalows to choose from and the campsite is sheltered. A nice bar, with snacks, and a pool.
→ Estr. Marginal Norte, 2520-605 Peniche +351 262 783 460, Penichepraia.pt
39.3692, -9.3922 🔺🎪🍴🔺

WILD HAVENS

31 FORTE DE SÃO JOÃO BAPTISTA, BERLENGA

You can stay in this 17th century fortress on the tiny island. Monks used to provide shelter here for seafaring people. The rooms have views across the sea and its inherent solitude still holds an ascetic appeal. There is, however, a communal kitchen and bar in the courtyard.
→ Reservations through the Associação Amigos das Berlengas +351 912 631 426, Berlengareservasforte@gmail.com
39.4113, -9.5101 🌊🛶🚤🚻🍴❗

32 CASA DO CASTELO, PENICHE

A luxurious guesthouse transformed in the 19th century from the old walls of a Moorish castle. Rich history meets you at every step as you explore its corridors with stained glass windows, cornices and balustrades. Surrounded by a beautiful garden and the green hills inland from Peniche.
→ Estr. Naçional 114 16, 2525-023 Atouguia da Baleia, Peniche +351 262 750 647, Casacastelo.com
39.3399, -9.3256 🍴🚶❗❄️🌸

33 JANGA SURF MANSION

Forget the packed dorms and bunk beds of other surf camps, this 19th century retreat combines big comfy beds and antique bedrooms with hectares of communal space, a pool and views out to the flaming sunsets over Berlenga Island. Take it easy in nature and meet other surfers. A Janga surf van makes trips to and from the house.
→ Estr. Naçional 114, 2525-801 Serra d'El Rei +351 262 003 100, Quintadojuncal.pt
39.3351, -9.2789 🍴🚶❗❄️🌊

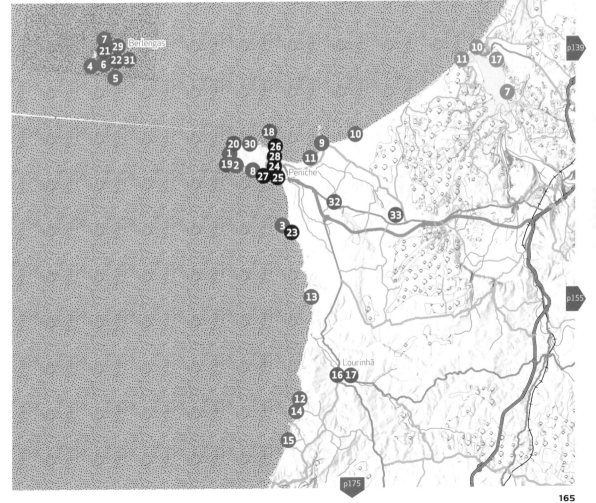

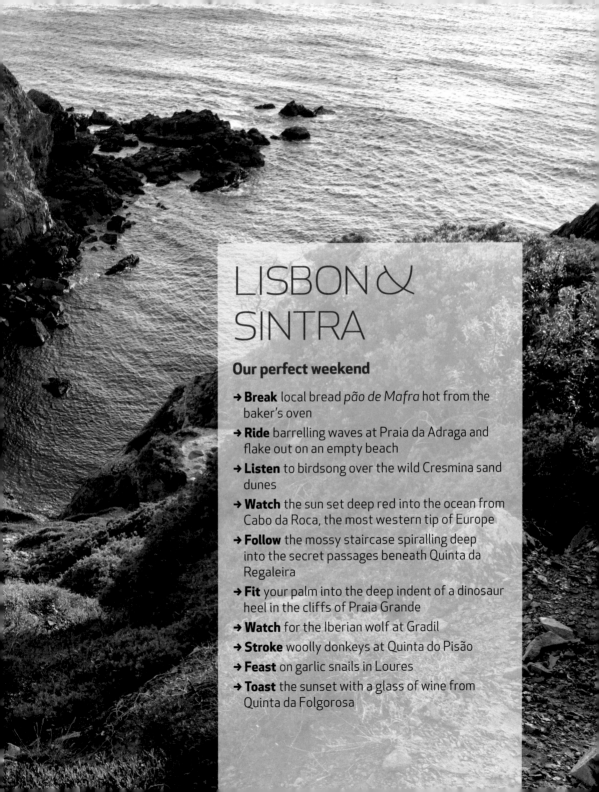

LISBON & SINTRA

Our perfect weekend

→ **Break** local bread *pão de Mafra* hot from the baker's oven

→ **Ride** barrelling waves at Praia da Adraga and flake out on an empty beach

→ **Listen** to birdsong over the wild Cresmina sand dunes

→ **Watch** the sun set deep red into the ocean from Cabo da Roca, the most western tip of Europe

→ **Follow** the mossy staircase spiralling deep into the secret passages beneath Quinta da Regaleira

→ **Fit** your palm into the deep indent of a dinosaur heel in the cliffs of Praia Grande

→ **Watch** for the Iberian wolf at Gradil

→ **Stroke** woolly donkeys at Quinta do Pisão

→ **Feast** on garlic snails in Loures

→ **Toast** the sunset with a glass of wine from Quinta da Folgorosa

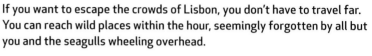

If you want to escape the crowds of Lisbon, you don't have to travel far. You can reach wild places within the hour, seemingly forgotten by all but you and the seagulls wheeling overhead.

The Sintra hills are considered a place of enchantment, with caves, Moorish castles, princely palaces and wild ancient woodland. Along its coast are secret beaches with significantly fewer towels and pitched parasols than the popular Costa da Caparica to the south of Lisbon.

Follow the sandy Guincho footpath through dusty myrtle until you reach the quieter beaches at Abano and its wild cliffs. North from here the rocks of the Sintra massif erupt into great Jurassic crests veined with ancient cooled lava. Sun-warmed igneous rock curves to form front-row seats for sunset with a clear view of the red sun as it slips under the Atlantic horizon.

Exposed to strong sea winds, the Sintra hills are often shrouded in fog, the odd grey turret or pinnacle peeking out over woodland. These misty hills, immersed in myth and legend, are perhaps best understood as a place where things are thrown into different perspectives. "Where the land ends and the sea begins" was how Camões described Cabo da Roca in his sea-flecked epic poem 'Os Lusíadas'. Down the ages it came to be a place representing not simply the most western point of Europe – or the edge of the then-known world – but represented the departure to new lands, new discoveries… the New World.

Pilgrims flocked to chapels here, sailors departed and returned and Neolithic communities left their marks in caves that you can still explore around the hills of Lousa. Now surfers make an annual pilgrimage to the Ericeira World Surfing Reserve, an 8km stretch of coastline with sandy bays and barrelling waves. But there are other footprints, much deeper, stamped on these rocks. At Praia Grande, enormous footprints were left on the earth by a weight-bearing heel, ten times larger than that of a human. Dinosaur prints in soft mud have lithified over the course of 125 million years.

This landscape tells a noisy tale, with many narratives crossing ways and clamouring for attention. Head back to the beach after sunset – the waves crash on in darkness and stars pierce the sky with surprising intensity.

SECRET BEACHES

1 DUNA DA CRESMINA

Dramatic beaches along the 66ha of dunes which are part of the Sintra-Cascais Natural Park. The beaches have views over to Cabo da Roca and the Sintra hills. Rich in wildlife; look out for stonechats, wagtails and lizards. Wooden walkway down to the beaches.

→ By car: from Lisbon take N6 following N247 toward Guincho. By train: CP trains connect Cascais with Cais do Sodre station in Lisbon. Scotturb buses (404-415) connect Centre Cascais to Guincho. Bike path from Cascais.

2 mins, 38.7265, -9.4689

2 PRAIA DO ABANO

A hidden cove, a stone's throw from the Cresmina dunes (see 1), and overlooked by the imposing 17th century Guincho fort. The Abano cliffs rise up on the other side.

→ From Charneca take N247 to Guincho, and continue for 500m until signs L for Praia. After Bar Guincho parking, follow white dirt road for 700m. Park by the fort. Walk 100m down to R.

2 mins, 38.7414, -9.4727

3 PRAIA DA ADRAGA

The cliffs slope down to form a sandy beach.

At one side the rocks arch into the sea forming a shape like an elephant's trunk. There is shade under here and a small cave. Part of the World Surfing Reserve. A walking trail continues along here until Cabo da Roca (see 23).

→ From Almoçageme follow the road to the coast. Parking.

5 mins, 38.8035, -9.4854

4 PRAIA DE RIBEIRA D'ILHAS

A sandy beach with a stream forming a warm, wide paddling pool before it meets the sea. Popular with surfers. There is an easy hike up the cliffs from here.

→ From Ericeira take the N247 N for 3km. Turn L at brown sign for Ribeira das Ilhas. Parking

10 mins, 38.9877, -9.4194

5 PRAIA DO MAGOITO

The cove is sheltered by beautiful layers of stone in the curved cliffs. It can be busy in summer, but walk 5 mins in either direction to be alone. You can see the distant shape of the Ursa rock from here. Part of the World Surfing Reserve.

→ Signed from Magoito.

2 mins, 38.8632, -9.4494

6 LAGOA AZUL

Shady trees surround this lake, the perfect spot for a dip or a picnic. Also popular with mountain bikers as several tracks through the Sintra hills begin here.

→ Take the N9-1 into Penha Longa and follow signs to Lagoa Azul.

1 min, 38.7676, -9.3969

FISHING VILLAGES

7 AZENHAS DO MAR

Perched on a cliff, this town is built as close to the sea as a town can be. Its tiled roofs ramble down to the rocky shore. The town merges gradually into the sea as three natural rock-sided swimming pools fill with the rising tide. There is no beach but a brook babbles down past a grassy picnic area; further up, old watermills turn.

→ 10km NW of Sintra

15 mins, 38.8394, -9.4609

8 ELÉCTRICO DE SINTRA

The classic 1930s Brill tram connects Sintra with the pretty coastal town of Praia das Maças. It follows a beautiful winding route of 13km between mountains and sea. It runs in summer only.

11

10

→ Tram departs from outside the Museum of Arts in Sintra. €3

40 mins, 38.8031, -9.3816 🚹 Ⓑ 🔧

9 PRAIA DOS PESCADORES

Watch for flamingos from this picnicking area along the Tejo and its salt-marsh banks. There are a few kilometres of boardwalk with bird hides along this stretch and a fishing museum by the old harbour. Little boats moor here along ancient spindly wooden jetties.

→ From Póvoa train station cross the tracks to the side out of town and walk along the road

to the river. From here follow the river trail upstream.

15 mins, 38.8580, -9.0604 🍴 🎋 🚹 🍴

PARKS & WILDLIFE

10 QUINTA DA REGALEIRA, SINTRA

The Regaleira palace is an exuberantly Gothic palace with turrets, decorative columns, lancet windows and gargoyles that reach up to the misty hills as though they grew from the encroaching forest. Built by the eccentric 19th century architect Luigi Manini, the grounds are riddled with alcoves, secrets tunnels, caves, underground waterfalls and a well with a twisting Gothic staircase. A wild garden perfect for explorations and hidden picnics.

→ 2710-567 Sintra +351 219 106 650, Regaleira.pt

2 hrs, 38.7962, -9.3960 🔧 🎋 🚶 ♿ 🍴 €

11 PARQUE NACIONAL DE MAFRA

18th century hunting grounds, eight square kilometres of which are bounded by the old wall. Inside is a rich and protected biodiversity open for hiking, biking, horse riding, archery and crossbow activities. Look out for polecats, weasels, red deer and

fallow deer, red foxes and eagles.

→ Portão do Codeçal, 2640-602 Mafra +351 261 814 240, Tapadademafra.pt

2 hrs, 38.9641, -9.3035 ✈ ♿ €

12 IBERIAN WOLF RECOVERY CENTRE, GRADIL

This centre was established in 1987 as a sanctuary for wolves which can no longer live in the wild. This is a large sanctuary so you'll have to keep your eyes peeled. Visits must be booked ahead.

→ Quinta da Murta, Picão, 2665-150 Gradil, Mafra +351 261 785 037, Lobo.fc.ul.pt

1 min, 38.9607, -9.2715 🏔 ✈ €

13 QUINTA DA PIEDADE, PÓVOA

A tiny park with a pretty cafe in the old palace of Póvoa, owned by the same family from the mid-14th century until 1916. There is a chapel with beautiful *azulejos*, glazed ceramic tile decoration, hidden in the gardens and a little farm with chickens and ducks running around the donkeys, goats and sheep.

→ From the station walk into town and up the hill. Signed off the N10 in Póvoa.

30 mins, 38.8635, -9.0696 🔧 🍴 🎋 🚹

17

14 PARQUE FLORESTAL DE MONSANTO

The hills here were re-forested in 1930s with the aim of being Lisbon's 'green lung'. The 1,000 ha of green hills with hiking trails, bike tracks and picnic spots do indeed provide a breath of fresh air.

→ Buses to Monsanto leave from Rossio train station. The park is signed from the A5.
1 hr, 38.7366, -9.1946 🚶🚲🍴🏖🌳🚻

15 QUINTA DO PISÃO, SINTRA-CASCAIS

A 450ha park in the foothills of Sintra where you can visit woolly donkeys and explore a network of woodland trails. Listen out for barn owls and larks.

→ Signed off the N9-1 in the Sintra-Cascais Natural Park. Parking.
30 mins, 38.7588, -9.4191 🐾🌳🚶

16 PEDRA AMARELA BASE CAMP

Located on the south slopes of the Sintra-Cascais Natural Park. Pedra Amarela Campo Base organises outdoor activities and adventure programmes within the park. Activities include tree climbing, high ropes, rock climbing, rappel, zip line, archery, hikes, treasure hunts and workshops in conservation and soil bioengineering.

→ From Malveira da Serra take the N9-1 E for 2.5km until signs for Pedra Amarela. Estrada da Serra, Parque Natural de Sintra-Cascais +351 211 388 398, Cascaisambiente.pt
2 mins, 38.7666, -9.4333 🏕🐾🌳

17 ANTA DE CARCAVELOS

This is an elevated and mysterious area, and very wild. There are several megalithic dolmens and burial sites across these hills. It is entirely possible that the dolmen may be overgrown. However, it is still an eerily beautiful spot.

→ Note: this is not the coastal Carcavelos near Cascais but inland, near Lousa. From Carcavelos village follow Rua das Antas until the end and walk 50m.
2 mins, 38.8858, -9.2166 🐾🖼🏔

18 SANTUÁRIO DA PENINHA

If walking the Guincho Trail (see 25) your eye might be caught by a mysterious squat building crowning the hill to the east. This is the semi-wild Santuário da Peninha, a 16th century sanctuary built at the highest point of the Sintra National Park. It serves as a shrine to a local mute shepherdess whose voice

16

returned in full force having seen Our Lady appear on these rocks. A site of pilgrimage for many years after, those who walked these paths left hundreds of inscriptions on the church pulpit, successive generations of inscribed names and messages. Sailors' wives used to pray and watch from here. Outside is the Fonte dos Romeiros – Travellers' Fountain – where pilgrims could bathe their feet in cool running water.

→ From Almoçageme take the N247 S for 5km, turn L at brown signs for Reserva da Peninha and follow for 3km.
2 mins, 38.7684, -9.4606 🏛🖼✝

CLIFFS & CAVES

19 PRAIA GRANDE DO RODÍZIO

Set in the side of these cliffs are the footsteps of dinosaurs, so large that it will take you a while to see them. It's as though they just ran by yesterday but, in fact, it was 125 million years ago in the Early Cretaceous era. Their footprints have fossilised, convulsed and been thrust high up the sides of the limestone cliff. The wind cuts sharply down the stairs as you pass the now-vertical tracks.

→ Travel from Colares to Rodízio, then follow signs to Praia Grande; continue until the end of the road and park. Take the narrow steps down between the cliffs.
10 mins, 38.8097, -9.4797 🌊

20 PEDRA DA URSA

Approach this clifftop view along the windy track. With each step closer, the white Pedra da Ursa rocks rise up from the sea and the roar of the ocean grows steadily louder. Below is the westernmost beach in Europe and a local legend tells how these rocks got their name. When the earth was just a massive ball of ice, a bear lived here with her children. When the earth began to thaw, the gods ordered the bear to move but she

refused and, enraged, the gods turned her to stone. The rock, called Ursa (bear), remains.

→ Exit the N247 at Ulgueira and follow signs. Park and walk down the track to view rocks. Access to the beach is dangerous.
2 mins, 38.7899, -9.4914 🌊🏖️☀️🍴🏞️📷▽

21 GRUTA DE SALEMAS

This forgotten cave is set high up on the hillside, a dark portal above the wooded slope reaching to some ancient dark recess. Inside its sides are so black you'll emerge with black palms from feeling your way in the dark. Archaeological excavations revealed a village occupied from Neolithic times until the Middle Ages. Little is left today. Perch on a stone and survey the hills of Loures.

→ From Lousa take the road to Salemas; before the bridge over the A8, take the dirt track to the R. Park at the fork and walk downhill. The cave will emerge to your R.
3 mins, 38.8758, -9.2030 🏔️🏞️🍴🏕️🐾

22 FALÉSIAS DO ABANO

The Abano cliffs are formed of veined Jurassic rock and cooled lava. Their west-facing sun-warmed stone makes a perfect sunset spot.

→ Follow the footpath up the cliffs from Praia do Abano (see 2) N for 800m.
15 mins, 38.7448, -9.4721 🚶🌊📷

WILD WALKS

23 CABO DA ROCA

The most westerly tip of continental Europe, known as Promontorium Magnum to the Romans. On the one side you have misty Celtic hills with greens and yellows, on the other brilliant blue sea. A 5km walking route winds its way along the cliffs and continues through pine woods and sand dunes, to Adraga beach (see 3). Plenty of smooth dips in the rocks to cradle you as you contemplate the sea.

→ From Malveira da Serra take the N247 N, after 5km turn L at blue signs for Cabo da Roca, follow for 3km. Parking. For the walk follow PR7 walking signs.
3 mins, 38.7803, -9.4989 🚶📷🎯

24 SANTA MARIA TRAIL

This 2km circular walking trail ascends two of the most striking peaks of Sintra: the wooded summit around Castelo dos Mouros and the tree-knotted hillside at Palácio da Pena. The trail mainly follows paved paths through the forest, with a gentle slope.

→ Start in Largo Rainha D. Amélia (opposite the National Palace) in Sintra historical centre.
1 hr, 38.7973, -9.3904 🚶🎯💬🏛

25 GUINCHO WALKING TRAIL

A signed and circular 9km walking route along the Abano cliffs and its secret beaches, turning inland along rivers through woodland and chapels. It makes use of the older pilgrim trail to the 16th century Santuário da Peninha (see 18), a hilltop sanctuary.

→ Begins and ends at Forte do Guincho.
3 hrs, 38.7398, -9.4727 🚶🏊🚣🍴⛪🚻📷

26 SETEAIS WALKING TRAIL

This 3.5km circular walking trail follows a stretch of the most beautiful road in Sintra, and then continues along a forest trail with vistas over the slope of the hill overlooking the historical centre. It passes Palácio da Pena and Castelo dos Mouros.

→ See Santa Maria Trail (24) for the start.
1 hr, 38.7974, -9.3904 🚶💬🎯🎯

FAIRS & FESTAS

27 FESTA DO OURIÇO DO MAR, ERICEIRA

15 restaurants across Ericeira participate in

173

this festival celebrating the sea urchin. Each year you can try imaginative entries such as a *ouriço-do-mar* risotto with shrimp and asparagus, sea urchin sushi with seaweed, soup, pasta or simply grilled with lemon, even *ouriço do mar* cocktails! Early April.

→ Câmera Municipal de Mafra, 2644-001 Mafra +351 261 810 100
38.9711, -9.4165

28 FESTIVAL DO PÃO EM MAFRA

Mafra is proud of its bread and has every right to be. Windmills are scattered over its hills and the bread itself is slightly sweet, with a soft crumb and tough crust. In mid-July Mafra hosts the bread festival with numerous local bakeries taking part.

→ Câmera Municipal de Mafra, 2644-001 Mafra +351 261 810 100
38.9409, -9.3317

29 FESTA DO CARACOL SALOIO, LOURES

Snail pilgrims travel from far and wide to celebrate the land-hugging mollusc, the snail, in Loures. You can linger over a snail *feijoada* (bean stew), or try snail *empadas*, snail pizza, snail *patanisca* or even, and this is only for the brave, snail custard tart, *pastel de nata*. But nothing beats the simple plate of *caracois* (little snails cooked in garlic and beer) with a cool *cerveja*. Most of July.

→ 2670 Loures +351 211 150 352
38.8316, -9.1727

30 NOSSA SENHORA DA BOA VIAGEM

This festival is to celebrate safe journeys of Ericeira's local fishermen. The boats are processed through the town and at night they are illuminated on the water. Mid-August.

→ Ericeira
38.9653, -9.4186

31 FESTA DO VINHO E VINDIMAS, BUCELAS

Visit Bucelas in the heart of the Loures wine-growing region in mid-October for its festival celebrating the new harvest and ancient wine-production festivities. A must for all oenophiles. With parades, wine-tastings and hundreds of bottles and vintages, they know how to have a good party.
38.9117, -9.1306

FRESH SEAFOOD

32 VIVEIROS DE MARISCO CESAR, ERICEIRA

A seafood shop decorated like a mermaid's cave with water tanks of *sapateira*, crabs and *ouriços do mar*, sea urchins, under fountains.

→ On the national road just S of Ericeira. N247 - Edifício César, 2655-319 Ericeira
+351 261 864 378
38.9589, -9.4145

33 CANTINHO DA AMIZADE, ALMOÇAGEME

This is an old men drinking cups of wine together kind of café or *tasca* in the tiny village of Almoçageme, near Colares. It's a good place for lunch just inland from the coast; have whatever dish they are cooking. The *bachalau espiritual* is heavenly, but every day is different. There is usually a large cake, baked fresh, and ready for sharing.

→ Rua Praia da Adraga 2, Almoçageme, Colares +351 912 706 493
38.7964, -9.4704

BREAD & WINE

34 CANTINHO DA VÁRZEA, COLARES

A *pastelaria* with local artwork and a great selection of regional cakes. Down the road, one minute's walk from the river, is a cheerful fruit and veg store with local produce.

→ Alameda Coronel Linhares Lima 2, Colares +351 309 862 420
38.8036, -9.4493

35 QUINTA DA FOLGOROSA, DOIS PORTOS

A farm with a 300-year history of wine production. The Duke of Wellington appreciated their wines as the vineyard was close to Torres Vedras, the hills used defensively against Napoleon's invading troops. Now you can visit the vineyard and buy wine, take a tour of their old building and technology, or enjoy a wine-tasting. At tastings their wine is paired with food to fully appreciate its flavours.

→ From Dois Portos take the CM1085 for 3km, cross straight over M353, on your R after 200m. 2565-171 Dois Portos
+351 919 902 914, Quintadafolgorosa.pt
39.0413, -9.1540

36 QUINTA DO SANGUINHAL, BOMBARRAL

Fernando Pessoa, one of Portugal's greatest poets, was reported to often stop mid-flow, pick up his hat and leave saying, "I'm off to Abel's." This habit puzzled the poet's coworker, Luiz de Almeida, who only later realised that these visits to Abel's were to the nearest depot of the Abel Pereira da Fonseca shops for a glass of wine. In 1926 Abel Pereira da Fonseca established the Companhia Agrícola do Sanguinhal. Why not announce you're "off to Abel's" and visit the Quinta do Sanguinhal for wine-tastings, walks through the 19th century gardens, and tours of the cellars and brandy distillery.

→ From Bombarral take N361 S for 3km; Quinta is signed on the corner. 2544-909 Bombarral +351 262 609 190, Vinhos-sanguinhal.pt 39.2547, -9.1442 ▣▦

WILDER CAMPING

37 LISBOA CAMPING

A campsite under shady pine trees in Lisbon's Monsanto park, 1,000ha of woodland riddled with paths and trails.

→ Lisboa Camping & Bungalows, Estrada da Circunvalação, 1400-061 Lisboa +351 217 628 200, Lisboacamping.com 38.7236, -9.2080 ▦▯▮▰▲

38 QUINTA DOS SETE NOMES, COLARES

This is an ecologically sustainable farm, just outside Colares in Sintra. The cooperative also runs gardening, handicraft, yoga and meditation classes and offers eco-camping at the farm. Compost toilets, showers and a communal kitchen and lots of delicious fresh fruit and vegetables.

→ Avenida do Atlântico 107B, Banzão,

2705-287 Colares +351 914 634 051, Quinta7nomes.com 38.8127, -9.4597 ▲▮

RURAL RETREATS

39 CASA DE CAMPODA FLORESTA ENCANTADA, MAFRA

A nine-bedroom country house in the old hunting grounds at Mafra. Wake up to birdsong outside your window and enjoy a wander in the woodland before breakfast.

→ Tapada Nacional de Mafra, Portão do Codeçal, 2640-602 Mafra +351 261 817 050, Tapadademafra.pt 38.9385, -9.3254 ▰▯▮▱▮

40 QUINTA DOS MACHADOS COUNTRY HOUSE & SPA, BARRAS

An elegant retreat with 29 guest rooms over two family houses in Mafra farmland. The outdoor pool is surrounded by woodland and there is access to a spa with jacuzzi, sauna and treatments.

→ 500m S of Barras on N8. 2665-006 Barras +351 261 961 279, Quintamachados.com 38.9875, -9.2749 ▮▯▰

41 ALMÁA SINTRA HOSTEL

A retreat and eco-hostel in the heart of the Sintra hills. The property is 12th century with 4ha of garden. Private and shared rooms are available. Spring water supplies the house and the furniture and decor is made with recycled material by local artists.

→ From Sintra take the N247 for 3.5km towards Quinta Grande, turn L at signs for Restaurante down Caminha Castanhais for 1km then R. Caminho dos Frades, Quinta dos Lobos 2710-560 Sintra +351 219 240 008, Almaasintrahostel.com 38.7980, -9.3992 ▮▯▰▱▦

42 ALDEIA DA MATA PEQUENA

A small rural village in Mafra with a dozen houses within the Penedo do Lexim, an extinct volcano. A great place to experience nature as eagles and stealthy foxes inhabit this rich and well-preserved natural landscape.

→ From Mafra take the N9 S for 10km into Cheleiros, turn E following River Lisandro for 600m then take the sharp L, follow for 900m. Rua S. Francisco de Assis, 2640-366 Igreja Nova, Mafra +351 935 141 909, Aldeiadamatapequena.com 38.8956, -9.3200 ▮▯▰▱▲▦

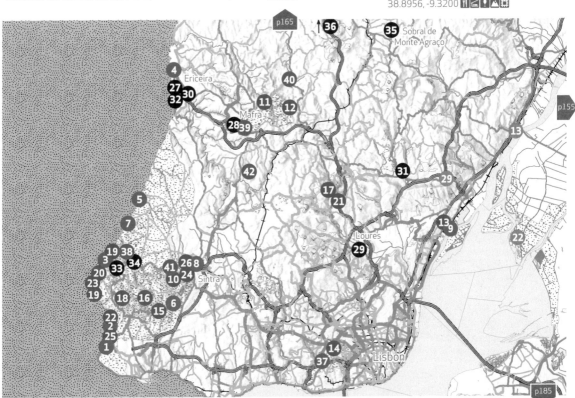

SETÚBAL &
RIO SADO

Our perfect weekend

➜ **Unwind** by the warm coastal lagoons of Lagoas de Santo André

➜ **Skinny** dip at the secret cove Praia da Baleeira

➜ **Dive** down beneath the waves to discover conger eels off Pedra da Anixa

➜ **Watch** for laughing dolphins nosing out of Estuário do Sado Natural Reserve

➜ **Balance** along the precarious jetties at Carrasqueira's ancient fishing harbour

➜ **Discover** 1st century fish-salting vats in Tróia

➜ **Scamper** through sun-dappled woodland by the dunes at Mata dos Medos

➜ **Sing** from the clifftops at Pedra da Mua as seagulls wheel over dinosaur footprints

➜ **Whisper** in the dust of Neolithic burial chambers at Quinta do Anjo

➜ **Feast** on creamy Azeitão cheese, bread and Setúbal wine

➜ **Bunk** down in a cosy wooden lodge in the foothills of Serra da Arrábida

The Setúbal coastline, which lies over the River Tejo (Tagus) just south of Lisbon, is known as the Costa Azul. The turquoise, sometimes emerald, sea certainly lives up to its name.

This is especially true of the Serra da Arrábida coast where the limestone peaks and pine forests fall quickly away to searingly blue sea edged by sandy beaches. The whole stretch of coast is riddled with caves and grottoes. While the area is a popular getaway from Lisbon, it is nonetheless possible to find a deserted cove, such as the forgotten Praia da Baleeira.

The Serra da Arrábida hills are ideal for trekking, biking and climbing. You might spot a Bonelli's eagle circling in the wind overhead. The limestone continues under the sea where crevices and platforms protect hundreds of fish, conger eels and crabs. Pedra da Anixa is one of these rocks, encircled by sea, just 200m off the coast, a great spot for first-time divers.

Hans Christian Andersen visited these hills in 1866, and its most mysterious coastal cave, Lapa de Santa Margarida. This grotto has seen a strange history: sea monsters, the Madonna and pirates have all crossed its watery line of vision. Inside the cave "is a veritable church hewn out of the living rock" wrote Andersen, and there really is a 17th century chapel hidden in this cave, "with a fantastic vault, organ pipes, columns, and altars".

Further west is Cabo Espichel, its sanctuary to Our Lady perched on the cliff-edge, looking out over the sea. Up the smooth cliff-side, bending their path towards the church, run the footprints of dinosaurs left 145 million years ago, in the Late Jurassic era. Thought once to be the footsteps of a donkey bearing the Madonna up the cliff, the site became a place of medieval pilgrimage. Follow the cliff track to Pedra da Mua at sunset to view these tracks.

Further south in the Sado estuary, by the Tróia peninsula, there is a bottlenose dolphin community. They come here to eat *choco*, the cuttlefish, for which these waters are renowned. You can take a boat ride out to see the dolphins or gorge on the *choco frito*, the Portuguese take on fish and chips, at Setúbal.

End your day with a glass from one of Setúbal's many vineyards – Quinta da Invejosa is our favourite – and a feast from the sea. They do so many seafood dishes well here.

COASTAL LAGOONS

1 LAGOA DE ALBUFEIRA

The Lagoa de Albufeira is formed by two lagoons: Lagoa Pequena and Lagoa Grande. Lagoa Pequena is further inland and by far the wilder of the two. It's surrounded by pine woodland and sandy banks. The shallow water is quickly warmed by the sun and is very still, a good spot for a paddle. Lagoa Grande is also popular with water sports.

➔ Pass Apostiça, driving S on the N377 and take the first brown sign you see for Lagoa Albufeira (just after signs for Lagoa Pequena). 2 mins, 38.5201, -9.1528

2 LAGOAS DE SANTO ANDRÉ E DA SANCHA

While the Sancha coastal lagoon is smaller with a reedy bed and Santo André is larger, both are havens for birdlife and surrounded by dunes and greenery. Geese, lapwings, curlews and cormorants all flock here. Santo André has good windsurfing conditions and is great for a gentle swim or paddle. The beaches along this stretch are quiet and sandy. There is a 4km walk from Praia do Porto das Carretas (38.0806, -8.8084) along Santo André lagoon and dunes. Turn R through the gate immediately before the car park and follow the path N. From the Sancha lagoon there is a 3km walk to the L at the tree nurseries as far as Caracola.

➔ From Sines take the A26-1 N for 20km and turn L after Aldeia de Brescos. Follow signs until the end of the M544. Parking. 2 mins, 38.1130, -8.7970

COASTAL HAVENS

3 PRAIA DOS COELHOS, PORTINHO DA ARRÁBIDA

Beautiful rocks at this beach and down from long sloping steps through Arrábida woodland. It can get busy in high season.

➔ Just off the N379-1 from Portinho da Arrábida E towards Outão. Park at (38.4844, -8.9709) and follow the steps down to beach. 7 mins, 38.4816, -8.9696

4 PRAIA DAS BICAS, ALDEIA DO MECO

A long stretch of sandy beach with naturist areas on the N, where you can also find algae-rich clay in the cliff-side, great for a full body mask. It can get busy but if you turn L before the wooden walkway down to the beach, there are amazing clifftop views and a fishermen's cafe. The path here leads to the next beach, Praia da Foz.

➔ From Aldeia do Meco follow brown signs for Praias and then to Praia das Bicas. Parking. 10 mins, 38.4636, -9.1931

5 PRAIA PORTINHO DA ARRÁBIDA

The strata of the Arrábida hills rise out of the pine forest and fall swiftly into the sea. The beach here is long and sandy and the water, protected by a bay, is slightly warmer and strikingly blue. Beneath the waves there is a particularly rich marine diversity. Pedra da Anixa (see 6), where the Arrábida rock surfaces again, is home to over 70 different aquatic species. It's a great place to snorkel.

➔ From Outão take coastal road W. Parking. 10 mins, 38.4795, -8.9805

6 PEDRA DA ANIXA

Just 250m off the Arrábida coast is this jagged rock formation surrounded by pure blue water and a sandy seabed. Its cracks, cavities and platforms provide shelter for crabs, conger eels and bream, to name but a few. It's a wonderful spot for first-time divers.

➔ Call Vertente Natural for local diving and watersports activities: +351 210 848 919, Vertentenatural.com 2 hrs, 38.4778, -8.9728

7

7

10

SECRET BEACHES

7 PRAIA DA BALEEIRA

This secret cove is protected by cliffs either side and due to lack of sand, small size and steep access it remains unvisited. From the high and steep descent down, the sea appears startlingly blue against the white cliff face. Wild rosemary covers the clifftops. It's perfect for a skinny dip.

→ From Serra da Azoia take Rua da Baleeira at orange signs for the Area Desportivo. Pass the football pitch and park after 500m (38.4240, -9.1857). Walk straight ahead and then always take L until you begin to descend.
20 mins, 38.4166, -9.1898

8 PRAIA DAS AREIAS BRANCAS

The beaches here at White Sands are some of the cleanest in the country and with ideal conditions for windsurfing. Several hiking trails in the dunes lead to the lagoons of Santo André and Sancha (see 2).

→ Located between the lagoons of Santo André and Sancha, turn W off the A26-1 at (38.0388, -8.8009) and follow road towards the coast.
2 mins, 38.0675, -8.8164

9 PRAIA DA FOZ

This is a fantastic beach for wild waves. It's caught between two high cliffs with beautiful rock strata and a sandy beach stretching between.

→ From Aldeia do Meco follow brown signs for Praias, past turn to Praia das Bicas and continue for 1.5km to the sign for Arrábida Nature Reserve. Beach on your R. Parking.
10 mins, 38.4536, -9.1986

ANCIENT & SACRED

10 NOSSA SENHORA DA CABO ESPICHEL

This sanctuary sits as close to the cliff edge as can be. Once a pilgrim destination, long rows of low doors beneath the porticos lead to ancient quarters. 600 years ago a fisherman caught sight of the Madonna riding a donkey up the near-vertical cliff-side here. He followed and found nothing but the mule's footprints set deep in the rock. A sanctuary was built on the site. Years later, in the early 20th century, the footprints were recognised as the tracks of dinosaurs 145 million years old. So the Madonna, it turns out, had not been riding a donkey. From the neighbouring cliff, Pedra da Mua (12) you can still see these tracks as clearly as the fisherman once did.

9

→ From Sesimbra take the N379 W and follow signs towards Cabo Espichel.
2 mins, 38.4200, -9.2158 ⛰️◎✝🎪

11 TRÓIA

Known as the 'Pompeii of Setúbal', a phrase coined by Hans Christian Andersen on a visit here, this was the largest known fish-salting facility in the Roman world. Tróia emerged in 1st century history as an industrial Roman city, whose occupants were engaged in fishing and harvesting all kind of seafood for export across the Roman Empire. It reached the apex of its splendour in the 3rd century AD and began to fall by 400AD. Today you can wander around their fish-salting vats as well as an early Christian basilica, their baths, a residential area and a mausoleum and necropolis.

→ Located on the Tróia peninsula. The turn-off for the site is on the Comporta-Tróia road, about 3km S of the end of the peninsula and about 1.5km NE of the new ferry dock. A 2km dirt road, R, leads to the Roman ruins.
5 mins, 38.4861, -8.8845 €🏕️🐾⛰️

12 PEDRA DA MUA

Wild cliffs accessed by a dirt track from Cabo Espichel. It was from here that the fisherman saw the Madonna climbing the neighbouring cliff. This is the best place to view the dinosaur prints left behind.

→ See Cabo Espichel (10) then follow brown signs for Pedra da Mua; turn and park. The dirt track is signed and leads to the viewing spot on the next clifftop.
15 mins, 38.4253, -9.2153 ◎⛰️🎪

13 THE WHISTLER TREE, ÁGUAS DE MOURA

The oldest cork tree in the world. The Whistler Tree in Águas de Mouras is over 230 years old. Its name is due to all the songbirds that make its twisting boughs home. Harvested since 1820, it has produced corks for millions of wine bottles! Chances are you'll have drunk from one.

→ Entering Águas de Moura from the N on the N5; cross the A2, pass the low houses, first L after the Laranjeira shop. Tree is on L. Parking.
1 min, 38.5864, -8.6909 🍴

CAVES & GROTTOES

14 GRUTAS DA QUINTA DO ANJO

These Neolithic sepulchres were hewn into the soft limestone rock of Arrábida by our ancestors over 4,500 years ago. Four large circular chambers with domed skylights

12

13

can be entered by low tunnels bored into the rock. Excavations in 1876 discovered arrowheads, axes, ceramic vessels, pins and buttons made of bone. They had been used as burial chambers for about 1,000 years. Just 200m outside the village of Quinta do Anjo, the caves are surrounded by the dappled shade of olive trees and, further out, the Arrábida hills.

→ From Quinta do Anjo follow brown signs for Sepulcros Neolíticos. Park by the information board and walk down.
2 mins, 38.5640, -8.9387 🅰♿💤✛

15 LAPA SANTA MARGARIDA
The limestone cliffs of Serra da Arrábida are filled with caves and grottoes, some forgotten, others remembered. This cave has competing mysteries which, down the ages, have accrued on the rock. The womb-like entrance is disturbed only by the lapping waves; further inside the cave is a 17th century chapel with offerings of coins, shells, candles and flowers beneath the images of its saints. Hans Christian Andersen wrote, "It is a veritable church hewn out of the living rock, with a fantastic vault, organ pipes, columns, and altars." The "living rock" is covered with fossils; fishermen left offerings, and Damião

de Góis, Renaissance philosopher recorded sea monsters here. It became a medieval place of pilgrimage after the miraculous rescue of fishermen from pirates.

→ Park on the hill into Portinho da Arrábida (38.4710, -8.9878). Opposite the three-tiered and multi-arched white house is a footpath signed Casal do Meio; follow the wide, shallow steps down to the cave.
7 mins, 38.4699, -8.9867 🌊⬤♿💤✛🎣

SEA VILLAGES & CONVENTS

16 CARRASQUEIRA
An ancient fishing community on the Sado estuary whose harbour is built entirely on wooden stilts. It is a precarious and labyrinthine knot of moorings where fishermen still return with their catch of *choco*, *robalo*, *dourada* or *linguado*. For a tiny town there are also a few good fish restaurants here (see 21).

→ From Alcácer do Sal follow the N253 W and turn R at signs for Carrasqueira. Once in the village continue for 500m until river
2 mins, 38.4127, -8.7565 🍴♿

17 CONVENTO DOS CAPUCHOS
The gardens of this 16th century former

convent are filled with little nooks for quiet moments – picnic tables, hidden statues, ivy-covered doorways and a duck pond. The tiny garden chapel is decorated with complex mosaics of salvaged tiles and sea shells. If you continue on the path further out there is a wonderful view of the whole Fossil Coast of Costa da Caparica.

→ The 174 and 163 bus will take you here from Almada. Or take the N10-1 towards Costa da Caparica and at the Capuchos roundabout follow brown signs to Capuchos. Parking.
5 mins, 38.6451, -9.2216 ♁⛱

WILD WALKS

18 MATA DOS MEDOS, FONTE DE TELHA

Despite its name – Forest of Fear – the only fear here was that of the dunes encroaching onto agricultural land. To inhibit this, João V planted a pine forest here in the 18th century. This is a lovely shady place to go walking. A couple of circular walks begin from the Interpretation Centre. Look out for eagles, foxes and, if you are lucky, falcons.

→ Estrada Florestal da Fonte da Telha, Mata Nacional dos Medos, 2825-494 Fonte de Telha +351 212 918 270
30 mins, 38.5951, -9.1944 🚶⛰🏖🚲➡✛

WILDLIFE WONDERS

19 PRAIA DO CORVO

Known locally as the Beach of the Crow, this is a sandy stretch of the Tejo river beach before the inland marshes. It's a great spot for flamingos. There is a wooden birdwatching observatory on the way to the beach.

→ From Almada to Quinta da Varejeira; take Rua Soeiro Pereira Gomes to the coast. Parking.
5 mins, 38.6543, -9.1267 🚻🏖⛰

20 DOLPHIN BOAT RIDES, SETÚBAL

Watch bottlenose dolphins chasing alongside from the deck of your sailing boat. The guided tour can take you around the Sado estuary or the Arrábida coast.

→ Call +351 265 238 000, Vertigemazul.com. Departures from Setúbal: Edifício Marina Deck, Rua Praia da Saúde 11D 2900-572. Departures from Tróia: Marina Tróia, 7570-789 Carvalhal.
3 hrs, 38.5206, -8.8969 🏔€➡

LOCAL FOOD

21 RESTAURANTE RETIRO DO PESCADOR, CARRASQUEIRA

A downbeat *tasca* with a lazy dog outside and

an unassuming air. However, Carrasqueira is an ancient fishing harbour and this is a great fish restaurant. The *arroz de marisco*, seafood rice, and *ensopado de enguias*, eel stew, or *massa de peixe* are very good. And the house white wine is pretty good too.

→ Avenida dos Pescadores, 7580-613 Alcacer do Sal +351 265 497 172
38.4097, -8.7516

22 RESTAURANTE RETIRO DO MECO, ALDEIA DO MECO

This lively restaurant has lots of tables outside, it's popular with the locals and set back from the road. It specialises in local fish dishes: try the *lulas recheadas*, stuffed squid with a rich sauce.

→ Rua do Comercio 40, Aldeia do Meco, 2970 Setubal +351 212 683 771
38.4714, -9.1710

23 RESTAURANTE A DESCOBERTA, ALCÁCER DO SAL

This is a great place to try the regional dish *arroz de lingueirão*, razor clam which they serve on tables along the Sado riverfront. The *lingueirão* are likely to be from Murta or Carrasqueira fishermen further downriver.

→ Rua João Soares Branco 15, 7580-093 Alcácer do Sal +351 265 612 025
38.3713, -8.5086

24 REI DO MAR, SETÚBAL

Deep-fried cuttlefish with chips is the dish to try in Setúbal. They say this dish was created when a rogue cuttlefish found its way into a chef's *churros* preparation. Almost every restaurant here will serve this speciality. A Portuguese twist on fish and chips.

→ Av. Luísa Todi 50, 2910 Setúbal
+351 918 634 700
38.5227, -8.8862

25 RESTAURANTE SANTUÁRIO DO CABO ESPICHEL

Since the mid-14th century this was a place of pilgrimage. However, this church with its back to the sea and great cloistered square in front, is 17th century. Magnificent views out across the cliffs to Cabo da Roca and the Sintra hills. There is a low-key restaurant here that serves seafood: crab, clams, prawns as well as grilled quails, *codernizes*, and grilled *chouriço*.

→ Take the N379 and follow signs to Cabo Espichel. Just by the car parking area, on one arm of the church square.
38.4202, -9.2152

26 DOÇARIA DE AZEITÃO, SETÚBAL

A little café with a few regional products – biscuits, cheeses and *tortas de azeitão*. Azeitão is home to the famous José Maria da Fonseca winery, Portugal's oldest bottler of red wines. Locals come to this cafe to drink the wine sold by the glass for a few cents.

→ R. Miguel Bombarda, 2925-437 Setúbal
38.5320, -8.9891

27 ADEGA DE FILIPE PALHOÇA, POCEIRÃO

Setúbal wine is world famous, and this 90-hectare family-run vineyard and winery, now in its third generation, produces Setúbal wines with as little chemical as possible. *Vinho tinto*, *branco*, *rosé* and the region's famous Moscatel wines are all produced and matured here from the regional grapes: Castelão, Syrah, Alicante Bouschet, Touriga Nacional, Cabernet Sauvignon, Fernão Pires and Síria. Their Quinta da Invejosa reserva is a glorious mellow vintage and worth every penny. Book in advance for a wine-tasting, vineyard chariot tour or *adega* tour. Drop in to buy the oak-aged Reserva wine or a 'bag in a box' at very reasonable retail prices. Closed Sunday.

→ Along the N5, 2.5km S of Poceirão train station. Estrada Nacional, Quinta da Invejosa, 2965-575 Poceirão + 351 265 995 886, Filipepalhoca.pt
38.6208, -8.7268

28 ALKAZAR GOURMET, ALCÁCER DO SAL

Named after the Moorish castle which still crowns the town, this little shop and café sells all kinds of regional products: local spiced chutneys and honey, cheeses and wines, biscuits, herbs, soaps, craft beers and fresh confectionery. Try the delicious cakes made from pine-nuts, pinhoadas, Alcácer do Sal's sweet speciality. It contains a cornucopia of Setúbal district's produce and famous wines.

→ Rua Machado dos Santos 4, 7580-162 Alcácer do Sal, +351 265 088 739
38.3713, -8.5078

29 CAMPING FETAIS, ALDEIA DO MECO

A simple campsite just outside Aldeia de Meco and close to the naturist beaches around Praia do Meco. Bungalows and tipis are available and there is a swimming pool, bar and aviary.

→ Rua da Fonte 4, Fetais, Aldeia do Meco,

2970-063 Sesimbra +351 212 682 978,
Camping-fetais.com
38.4682, -9.1761 🍴◿Ⓑ⛺

30 ECOPARQUE OUTÃO

A simple caravan and campsite overlooking
the water where the Sado meets the sea. A
stone's throw from the Arrábida beaches.
Wooden bungalows and caravan park.

➜ Rua da Figueirinha, Outão, 2900-182
Setúbal +351 265 238 318

38.5028, -8.9285 ⛺

WILD RETREATS

31 CASAL DO FRADE, ARRÁBIDA NATURAL PARK

A beautiful farmhouse, eco-friendly and
with a 'back-to-nature' feel, but with all the
amenities of a luxurious break.

➜ Quinta Casal do Frade, Rua do Casalinho,
2970-050 Aldeia do Meco, Sesimbra
+351 918 593 007, Casaldofrade.pt

38.4511, -9.1741 🍴◿♀

32 PARQUE AMBIENTAL DO ALAMBRE

Here are eight wooden bungalows,
surrounded by trees, just before the uplands
of Serra da Arrábida. The park has several
small walks which lead out from the grounds
and also has an extensive programme of
outdoor activities: climbing, abseiling,
caving, canoeing and hiking are open for
all to take part. They also run workshops
in medicinal plants, scientific illustration,
permaculture and nature photography.

➜ Estrada Nacional 379-1, 2925-318 Azeitão
+351 212 180 103, En.alambre.ymcasetubal.org

38.4890, -9.0292 🍴🚶♨◿

33 HERDADE DA BARROSINHA

The Barrosinha estate was founded in
1947 and still deals in the production of
wine, cattle, rice, cork and pine. The estate
encompasses two chapels, hills, gardens,
old mills and rice fields along the Sado
estuary. The Barrosinha estate has 15 guest
rooms within walking distance of the river.
The restaurant serves regional cuisine and,
naturally, fine local wines.

➜ Herdade da Barrosinha, 7580-514
Alcácer do Sal +351 265 623 142,
Herdadedabarrosinha.pt

38.3621, -8.4820 🍴◿▦♀

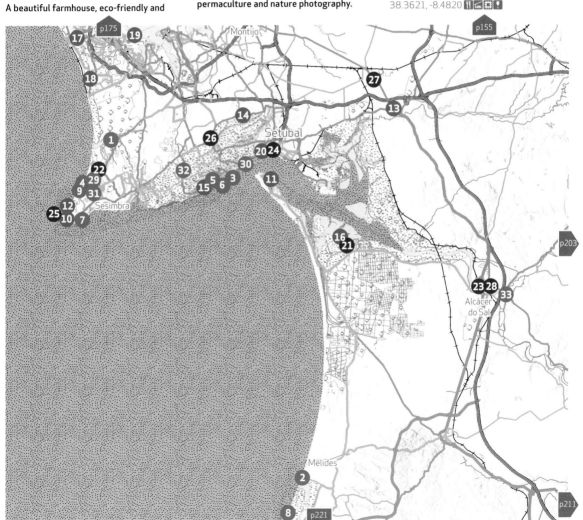

NORTH ALENTEJO: PORTALEGRE

Our perfect weekend

→ **Stargaze** from the wildflower river banks near Ponte da Ribeira Grande

→ **Align** yourself for sunset from Anta do Tapadão and watch as stars pierce the sky

→ **Walk** through chestnut woodlands and along medieval flagstones from Castelo de Vide

→ **See** the wild hills through Neolithic eyes with the Lapa dos Gaivões cave paintings

→ **Catch** the wind in your hair from the rambling battlements of Castelo de Marvão

→ **Feel** the ancient earth energy at Menir da Meada standing stone

→ **Picnic** by the remote Torre do Álamo, a 16th century poet's tower

→ **Dip** in the water under the ancient Roman bridge in Vila Formosa

→ **Feast** on the regional *porco preto*, black pig meats, such as the cured *painho* or *paiola*

Cross the plains of Portalegre, south of the Tejo river, and huge boulders nose out of the undulating hills like whales breaking the surface of the sea. In April, rain runs off them in dark rivulets. Cave paintings, flower-strewn streams, dolmens, menhirs and rambling border castles – Portalegre has a wild beauty charged with history.

High up along the Spanish border along an escarpment, bowed in the middle like a horseback, Marvão castle broods over the Serra de São Mamede mountains. This imposing 13th century defence is a perfect Crusader castle complete with echoing chambers, rambling battlements with twisting staircases, turrets and archers' windows over dizzying views. Alentejo is laid out flat as a map beneath.

Walk from Marvão through farmland, past fountains and forests, to Castelo de Vide where the terrain begins to shift from the gentle hills and plains, to rockier and more dramatic outcrops. Look out for *choças*, the circular, drystone shepherd huts often thatched with branches or straw.

At Coureleiros you can see five megalithic dolmens in neighbouring fields, guarded by curious horses and watchful cows. Granite slabs lean together to form the dolmen, inviting you to step inside and sit in hushed awe in the ancient chamber. Covered in moss, lichen and tiny shards of quartz, your instinct is to touch the stones. These burial places are tactile; reverence was given by offering strings of beads, pots or arrowheads, later excavated here. They are places where the ancients would still be materially connected with the living and, as they still invite your touch, their original use persists. Further south, at Esperança, you can see the land through Neolithic eyes as cave paintings of hunting scenes still survive. Surrounded by the same hills you can be transported back to the artists' world as ochre stains on rock depict boars, hunters, their chiefs and a dragon.

During springtime Alentejo is a riot of wild flowers: poppies, lavender and wild lupins carpet the fields in deep purples and reds. A number of farms here keep the famous Alentejano black pig to range free on their land. Stay at Monte Alto farmhouse where these small pigs are reared for three years: the ultimate in slow food. Try *porco preto* at Os Caçadores in Esperança or *pezinhos de coentrada*, an old and nearly forgotten dish, pigs' feet cooked with coriander sauce at Restuarante O Pedro in Cabeço de Vide.

WILD SWIMS

1 PONTE ROMANA DE VILA FORMOSA

An ancient bridge which once formed part of an important Roman road between Lisbon and Mérida, the ancient capital of pre-Roman Lusitânia, now in Spain. The bridge can be seen from the national road but head down for green banks and deep water. Several legends surround the building of this bridge involving the devil, a black rooster and an unwitting miller. Strong current in spring.

→ From Alter do Chão take the N369 W towards Vale de Açor. After 12km turn L at the brown sign for Pte. Romana. Follow track, park and walk down.

5 mins, 39.2159, -7.7846 🏊🚻🎪🎎

2 PRAIA FLUVIAL PONTE DA RIBEIRA GRANDE

A solid Roman bridge along an ancient military route, under which still runs the Ribeira Grande. Grassy banks slope down to a wide green river. This surrounding area is perfect for stargazing.

→ From Fronteira take the N245 N for 2km and cross the river.

2 mins, 39.0709, -7.6496 🏊⛰️🎎🎪

3 RIBEIRA DA CHOCANAL

A perfect picnic spot by this stream babbling through meadow flowers. Cross the footbridge known, as usual, as the Ponte Romana, but more likely to be medieval.

→ From Crato take the road S towards the train station. After 1km you cross the stream, park after the bridge and follow the small road on your L down to the stream.

2 mins, 39.2795, -7.6415 🎪🐾🎎

STANDING STONES

4 MENIR DO PATALOU

The Menhir of Patalou is a large standing stone that has been moved six metres north. A little granite mark signs the original site. It was first raised over 6,200 years ago.

→ From Nisa take the N359 E towards Montealvão, turn R at sign to Castelo de Vide and follow for 5km. Park and walk down paved track on R.

1 min, 39.4825, -7.5938 🐾⛰️🎎

5 ANTA DE SÃO GENS

A megalithic dolmen (burial chamber) in a quiet, isolated spot. The ruined chapel behind and wind rushing through long grass adds to the eerie atmosphere.

→ From Alpalhão, take the M1176 NW. After 4km you will spot this massive dolmen, R. Park earlier and walk to not disturb the quiet.

5 mins, 39.4480, -7.6762 🐾🎎⛰️

6 MENIR DA MEADA

Standing 7m tall, this is the tallest menhir so far discovered in the Iberian Peninsula. An enormous phallus, still keeping the surrounding land fertile.

→ Well signed from Meada and the M1006. Parking nearby.

2 mins, 39.4959, -7.4455 ⛰️🎎⛰️🎎🐾🏕️

7 COURELEIROS MEGALITHIC PARK

Five megalithic sites across neighbouring fields. They date back to around 3,000 – 4,000BC. Guarded by cattle and a few horses. One great dolmen invites you to step inside, sheltering you like a wild bird. Many archaeological vestiges were found here, such as beads, ceramics, arrowheads and schist plates.

→ From Castelo de Vide take the N246-1 N towards Apalhão; turn R for Meada and follow brown Anta (Dolmen) signs.

10 mins, 39.4440, -7.4701 🐾⛰️🎎🎪

8 ANTA DO SOBRAL

Peacefully alone in its field, this dolmen is an oasis of quiet. Climb inside and listen to the sounds of the world outside.

→ From Portalegre take the N246 N for 14km. The dolmen is L, just off the main road. Park on track after 100m.

2 mins, 39.4001, -7.4905 🚴📷

9 ANTA DO TAPADÃO

One of the most beautiful dolmens in Portugal, it rises up on a gentle incline to survey the sweeping fields. A truly mega dolmen, it opens into a hollow mound with a great stone rolled over its entrance. You can carefully crawl underneath. About 3,000BC.

→ From Aldeia da Mata take the N363 Crato road for 1km. There is a sign to the dolmen and a gate into the paddock. Park by side of road. Walk in, shut the gate for the cattle and follow track.

2 mins, 39.2973, -7.71124 🚴⛰✦📷✦

CAVES & CHAPELS

10 NOSSA SENHORA DE ENTRE-ÁGUAS, BENAVILA

A 15th century church on the shores of the Maranhão reservoir. The name Our Lady Between the Waters evokes pre-Christian goddess worship. There are also myths of the Madonna appearing here where the great olive tree now stands.

→ From Benavila walk over the bridge along the N370 and turn L.

10 mins, 39.1174, -7.8685 ✝🏊

11 LAPA DOS GAIVÕES, ESPERANÇA

Neolithic cave paintings in red and orange pigment decorate the walls of this cave in the hillside. Hunting scenes, wild boars, dancing figures, dragons and captains; let your imagination run wild as you trace out artwork left by our ancestors over five millennia ago. There is a circular 16km signed walking route from the church at Esperança which takes you past the main cave paintings. More information can be found at the Núcleo in Esperança, Rua General Humberto Delgado, 7340-127 Esperança-Arronches +351 245 561 038.

→ Or follow signs from Esperança for Pinturas Rupestres for 2km.

2 mins, 39.1486, -7.1727 ⛰🚴✦🚶‍♂

13

CASTLES & WALKS

12 CASTELO DE OUGUELA

This dusty border castle with Visigothic roots was rebuilt by King Dinis in the 14th century. It surveys its land from its forgotten outpost on a rocky escarpment.

➔ From Campo Maior take the N373 for 8km towards the Spanish border. Castle signed.
2 mins, 39.0790, -7.0315 ▦◰

13 CASTELO DE MARVÃO

This is the first castle you would see when crossing the border from Spain. A marvellous castle with rambling battlements, gleaming turrets, stairways to the sky and echoing chambers below. Stunning views across Alentejo and Spain.

➔ Park outside the walls of Marvão and wander in, following signs for the castle. Small entrance fee.
5 mins, 39.3961, -7.3792 ▦◰◈€◔◰

14 CASTELO DE VIDE – MARVÃO TRAIL

This is an ancient way between two historical towns that passes farms, shepherds' huts, churches, fountains and beautiful chestnut woodland. Some sections of this path are still along medieval flagstones.

➔ Signed, linear trail PR3, 9km. The route begins at the view point in Castelo de Vide on Rua da Circunvalação (39.4172, -7.4544) and ends at Porta de Ródão in Marvão(39.3959, -7.3774).
1.5 hrs, 39.4172, -7.4544 ▲Ⓚ◈▦

WILD PICNICS

15 ELVAS

This is a wild town where wildlife abruptly meets the 13th century walls. Seen from above this walled fortress resembles a many-pointed star. The land falls away into lakes and grassland covered in wild flowers, with the odd goatherd or shepherd. This is a great place for birdwatching.

➔ From Elvas take the N4 for 2km towards Badajoz. Opposite Continent supermarket take the road R and park at the end. Walk uphill through olive groves.
10 mins, 38.8771, -7.1375 ▲◈⍋

14

16 TORRE DO ÁLAMO

A 16th century tower said to have once belonged to the family of the poet Luis de Camões and where he wrote 'Os Lusíadas'. Now a remote and beautiful place for a picnic in the long grass.

16

→ From Cano take the N372 to Sousel, pass the olive tree farm and take the dirt track on your R. Continue 4km along track and park.
2 mins, 38.9285, -7.7576 🏕🏕🏕

REGIONAL DISHES

17 CAFÉ COZINHA ALENTEJANA, AVIS

Try simple, regional and cheap dishes here with a great selection of local wines. Orange trees drop their fruit on the street outside.

→ Avenida da Liberdade 17, 7480-103 Avis +351 242 412 377
39.0534, -7.8912 🍴🍷🏕

18 RESTAURANTE O MIGUEL

Traditional dishes cooked for the locals with steps down from the narrow street to a cosy restaurant. The rabbit, *coelho*, is delicious with round-cut chips. Good house wine.

→ Rua Almeida Sarzedas 32, 7320-115 Castelo de Vide +351 245 901 882
39.4156, -7.4544 🍴🍷🏕

19 CAFÉ RESTAURANTE OS CAÇADORES, ESPERANÇA

This is where the locals go. A humble and friendly café with great *porco preto*, the regional black pig speciality. This is rich, dark and tender meat, strong and delicious, as the pigs have been allowed to roam freely for three years. The owner, Lara Evangelista, is an expert on rural farming here and how to rear and cook the ultimate in slow food.

→ Largo 25 de Abril 1, 7340-111 Esperança +351 245 561 042
39.1576, -7.1923 🏕🍴🍷

20 RESTAURANTE O PEDRO

Regional dishes at this simple, cosy restaurant. Generous portions at good prices. This is the place to try the Alentejana *pezinhos de coentrada*, pigs' feet cooked in a coriander sauce, a lamentably forgotten dish now.

→ Avenida da Libertação, 7460-002 Cabeço de Vide +351 245 634 224
39.1315, -7.5893 🍴🍷🏕

21 PASTELARIA SOL NASCENTE

Many regional and traditional dishes to try in this cosy café. If they have baked a slab of *boleima de maça*, try a piece of this unleavened pastry made with honey, apple, cinnamon and burnt sugar.

→ R. de Olivença 31, 7430-000 Castelo de Vide +351 245 901 789
39.4146, -7.4549 🍴🍷🏕

RUSTIC HAVENS

22 MONTE ALTO, CAMPO MAIOR

Curl up by a log fire in this luxurious country house with panoramic views across undulating farmland. A peaceful haven of luxury and rest but also deeply in touch with its agricultural heritage. Black pigs roam free-range around olive groves, oak orchards, cork *montados* and an allotment. Due to four lambing seasons there are often lambs here too. Ask to visit the *santuário*, fallow fields left wild with views over the reservoir, perfect for a picnic.

→ Herdade do Monte Alto, Degolados, 7370-191 Campo Maior +351 268 688 176, Montealto.com.pt
39.0787, -7.1236 🍴🍷🏕🏕🏕

23 HORTA DO MURO OLIVE OIL FARM

Stay in the old farmhouse surrounded by 7ha of olive groves with horses, bicycles and an outdoor pool. The DOP Biocampo olive oil is produced here.

→ Horta do Muro, 7370 Campo Maior +351 268 688 431, Hortadomuro.com.pt
39.0189, -7.0234 🍴🍷🏕🏕🏕

24 MONTE DA TORRE, ELVAS

An elegant guesthouse surrounded by 210 hectares of working farmland. This is a peaceful retreat and natural haven.

→ N from Elvas on N246; pass junction with A6, continue for 4km, then R on dirt road. Monte da Torre, S.Vicente, Elvas +351 964 044 459, Montedatorre.pt
38.9399, -7.1854 🏕🍴🏕🏕

WILDER CAMPSITES

25 PARQUE DE CAMPISMO DA QUINTA DO POMARINHO, CASTELO DE VIDE

A peaceful and small campsite in the hills of Serra de São Mamede Natural Park. On the site of a former farm, camp among olive trees with no electric light at night.

→ Quinta do Pomarinho N246 km16.5, 7320-421 Castelo de Vide +351 965 755 341, Pomarinho.com
39.4007, -7.4866 🍴🏕🍷🏕🏕🏕

26 CAMPING OS ANJOS, CAMPO MAIOR

A small and jolly rural campsite with a pool and beautiful views.

→ Estrada da Senhora da Saude, 7370-150 Campo Maior +351 268 688 138 Campingosanjos.com
39.0082, -7.0478 🍴🏕🏕🏕

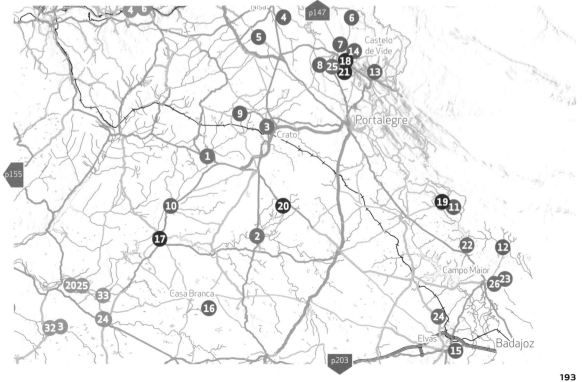

CENTRAL ALENTEJO: ÉVORA

Our perfect weekend

→ **Walk** through wild woodland, guided by the Lucefécit river until Rocha da Mina

→ **Run** along the watchtower at the ruined Fortaleza de Juromenha

→ **Pay** homage to Aldeia da Luz, a village sunk under dark Alqueva waters

→ **Watch** the sunset in Portugal's most ancient olive grove surrounding Anta do Olival da Pega

→ **Lay** along the fallen stones at Anta Grande do Zambujeiro, waiting for moonrise

→ **Cast** your wish at Rocha dos Namorados standing stone

→ **Picnic** by the wild flowers at Cromeleque do Xerez

→ **Feast** on mouthwatering *bochechas de porco assada* within the castle walls of Monsaraz

→ **Toast** the star-speckled night sky with a glass of oak-aged Conde d'Ervideira

Évora is famous for wine-making and abundant springtime flowers, but is as rich in history as it is rooted in viniculture. This is the district for dolmens, disputed borders, wild castles and forgotten shrines but it is also veined with rivers, riddled with vineyards and towns so far apart the lack of electric light reveals a dark sky bright with stars worth the journey alone.

Camp wild and toast the heavens with Borba wine, produce of the surrounding land. At Anta da Olival near Monsaraz you can watch the sunset in one of Portugal's oldest olive groves. As the sunlight catches the long grass you can crawl inside these gnarled trees like curled dragons, some two thousand years old, themselves surrounding a sleepy megalithic dolmen. Or watch the moonrise from Anta Grande do Zambujeiro, one of the largest dolmens in Iberia. Its monumental flint-knapped stones make it feel like a great Egyptian tomb. The damp grass at dusk is home to leaping hares, and a stream slips along nearby.

If you visit in spring, take a dip in the streams matted with star-like crowsfoot blossom, tendrils streaming in the current. There are luxurious tipis at Azenhas de Seda in secluded spots along the banks of Ribeira da Raia, a river which stays deep enough for a dip all year.

At Juromenha, the fortress' contested history continues today. Due to its strategic position along the Guadiana river and frontier, it has been attacked down the ages, successively under Portuguese then Spanish possession. Abandoned in 1920, you can stare out through the ruined 17th century fortress walls at Spain. This 25km stretch of border line will not be defined in bold on your Portuguese map as, while it was waiting to be redrawn, the disputed territory of Olivenza/Olivença was designated a bicultural town.

The Alqueva reservoir acts as another permeable border between the Évora and Beja districts. Monsaraz crowns this blue Avalon with its Templar castle rising up out of the watery scape. The terrace at Os Templários is our favourite place to dine and watch the sunset over the Alentejo panorama.

Buried beneath the waters of the Alqueva is Aldeia da Luz, the poignantly named Village of Light, flooded in 2003. The road to the submerged town leaves from the new; take it to the water's edge. From there it continues down to where, it's said, church bells chime underwater.

WILD SWIMS

1 ALDEIA DA LUZ, BARRAGEM DE ALQUEVA

Stare out over the untroubled surface of Alqueva reservoir under whose dark waters Aldeia da Luz, the Village of Light, remains. The village was flooded in 2003, and a new village was built on the shores with a museum you can visit. The old village had Neolithic and Palaeolithic origins and a fountain which was said to have spouted miraculous waters. Now, at least, the healing waters are mixed with those of one of the largest reservoirs in Western Europe.

➔ From Aldeia de Luz take the road towards the old village, turning R before the museum. Park and walk to the water's edge.
2 mins, 38.3436, -7.3858 ▣◪▲✛

2 RIBEIRA DO DIVOR

This is a large cork *montada* or plantation that slopes down the river. You can walk in and wander but close the gates behind you. In spring there is water deep enough for a dip.

➔ From Mora take the N2 S towards Brotas. After the second roundabout continue on N2 for 500m, turning R at brown sign for Ribeira do Divor. Continue for 10km as far as the river crossing. Park and walk to river bank.
5 mins, 38.9030, -8.2607 ◪▲✛

CASTLES & TOWERS

3 TORRE DAS ÁGUIAS, BROTAS

Eagles' Tower is a deserted 16th century edifice. The eagles have left and only swallows dart in and out from its turrets. The outhouses are abandoned. It's on private property but has public access as it is a national monument.

➔ From Brotas village follow signs for Torre das Águias. This is on private farmland but access is allowed as it is a national monument. Open and close the farm gate securely behind you. Park by the outhouses.
5 mins, 38.8750, -8.1265 ✛▲✛▣

4 CASTELO DE NOUDAR, BARRANCOS

The battlements, staircases and vaulted interior of this border castle crowning the wild hills are medieval, but human occupation of this site dates back to prehistoric times. One of the legends that surround this mysterious place is that inside the castle dwells a serpent. Thought to be an enchanted Moorish princess, it only comes out at night.

➔ From Barrancos take the N258 away from Spain then follow signs to your R to Castelo de Noudar.
5 mins, 38.1781, -7.0628 ▦♨◈⊷

5 FORTALEZA DE JUROMENHA

A ruined fortress on the still-disputed border before Olivença. Wild flowers have overgrown this 9th century fortress and its colourful history. Now you can ramble around battlements looking down to the Guadiana and Spain or peek into abandoned crypts.

➔ From Alandroal take the N373 for 16km turning R at signs for Juromenha. Continue straight through the town following signs for Fortaleza. Parking. No entrance fee.
15 mins, 38.7380, -7.2402 ▦▲◻🚶

ANCIENT & SACRED

6 GRUTAS DO ESCOURAL, SANTIAGO DO ESCOURAL

Discovered by accident in 1963, these caves contain Palaeolithic rock art some 10 – 40,000 years old. The earliest traces of human occupation in these caves date back 50,000 years.

➔ Book an appointment to visit the caves at Centro Interpretativo do Escoural

10

9

8

+351 266 857 000. Closed Sunday, Monday.
1 hr, 38.5444, -8.1376 ▣↩☆€

7 CAPELA DOS OSSOS, ÉVORA

This 16th century chapel decorated with
bones is in the less wild location of Évora
town centre. But only step inside its
shadowy hollows to feel a wild and mortal
connection with the earth. The inscription
over the door reads: "We bones that are here,
waiting for yours" reflects the mindset of
Franciscan monks. Built in order to remind us
we are part of a wild cycle: made from earth,
we will return to it.

→ Follow signs to Jardim Público de Évora,
turn L onto Rua da República for 100m.
2 mins, 38.5689, -7.9082 ✣✝

8 SEPULTURAS MEDIEVAIS, ROSÁRIO

Five or six deep-cut clefts in the rock formed
medieval graves which are now filled with
obsidian-black water and surrounded by
olive trees. An impenetrable aura remains.
An 8km circular and signed walking route
begins in nearby Rosário village.

→ From Rósario follow brown signs for
Sepulturas Medievais for 250m down the track.
2 mins, 38.6264, -7.3475 ✣🏔☆

DOLMENS & STONE CIRCLES

9 ANTA DO LIVRAMENTO, NOGUEIRINHA

Just off the roadside, this dolmen has been
made into a church, because stones that
have stood for around 5,000 years clearly
need buttresses. Nevertheless it is a sweet
union of cultures and times in a sacred place.

→ From São Brissos take the CM1079 towards
Santiago do Escoural. After Nogueirinha the
chapel is on your left. Call +351 266 857
637/128/183 to open the chapel.
2 mins, 38.5248, -8.1292 ✝🏔✣☆⛩

10 ANTA GRANDE DO ZAMBUJEIRO, ÉVORA

Watch the moonrise at dusk perfectly
aligned with the portal of this massive
dolmen. These enormous stones are flint-
knapped flat, covered with ancient marks,
their mega weight resting on each other to
create a dark chapel. You cannot enter but
you can peer in from the mound behind. A
sacred space built in about 4000 BC and
thought to be the largest in Iberia.

→ From Évora take the N380 then CM1079
to Valverde and follow brown signs for Anta.
Follow dirt track for 850m and park. Walk over
the footbridge and up path.
5 mins, 38.5391, -8.0143 ☆🏔✣

11 CROMELEQUE DOS ALMENDRES, ÉVORA

One of the largest groups of standing menhirs in Europe, 96 stones watch from a clearing in the cork oak woodland out over the plains of Nossa Senhora da Guadalupe. Some have swirling designs. Visit out of season for some peace with the stones as, though never busy, this is a popular circle.

→ From Évora take the N114 towards Montemor-o-Novo but after 18km turn left at brown sign to Cromeleque. Follow signs.

10 mins, 38.5575, -8.0611 🅰️✥❀♻️🅱️

12 ANTA DE SÃO DINIS, PAVIA

This dolmen was Christianised in the 17th century when an altar was constructed under its solid stones. Swallows dart in and out of the latticed doorway. You can buy beer and peanuts from Café Dolmen opposite. It's less wild but it is a typical, sleepy Alentejo village with long streets, large chimneys and locals chatting on the corner in thickening evening light. The dolmen feels it's been swept into the corner of the square, perfectly harmonised, always present.

→ Take the N251 into Pavia and follow signs for Centro Historico.

1 min, 38.8942, -8.0170 ♻️▦

13 ROCHA DOS NAMORADOS

Lovers' Rock is a standing menhir in the olive fields by the village of Corval. Legend and locals tell of a strange custom: if you stand on top of the smaller stone and face away from the menhir aiming a pebble, left-handed, towards the menhir, you will determine the number of years to your marriage by the number of your attempts to hit the rock. The menhir is littered with thrown stones. Some must have endured longer than the marriages.

→ From Reguengos de Monsaraz take the M514 to Corval. Continue straight past and the rock is after the roundabout on your L. Parking.

1 min, 38.4450, -7.4755 ♻️▦🖼️

14 MENIR DA BULHOA

Discovered fallen and broken in the late 1960s, this standing stone dates back to perhaps 5000BC. Now re-erected you can, depending on the light, see its sun motifs and the swirling lines that decorate its tall body. Just off the main road, it has a dramatic paved path leading up to it. The menhir stands tall in its flat fields.

→ From Monsaraz take the M514 and follow signs for Reguengos de Monsaraz. At the 2nd

roundabout, take the 1st exit and follow for
1km. Menhir is signed on L.
1 min, 38.4621, -7.3829

15 ANTA DO OLIVAL DA PEGA

Surrounded by Portugal's most ancient olive
grove is this 5,000-year-old dolmen. Further
funerary structures in the nearby fields are
disguised by olive roots. A beautiful place
for sunset through the long grass.
→ From Monsaraz take the M514 towards
Corval, and after about 3km look for a brown
Anta sign to R and follow.
2 mins, 38.4514, -7.3989

16 CROMELEQUE DO XEREZ

This stone circle with a prominent phallic
central stone is a moving monument, in
both senses. The stones were originally re-
erected in 1969 and then moved once again
in 2004 at the construction of the Alqueva
dam. Now they look out over an amazing view
and remain fairly unvisited.
→ From Monsaraz take the M514 to Ferragudo.
At the menhir roundabout take the 1st exit for
the Conjunto Megalithico. Follow signs for the
Convento and park before it. Take the R track
and follow the cement path to the stones.
5 mins, 38.4533, -7.3709

17 SANTUÁRIO DE ENDOVÉLICO DE ROCHA DA MINA

A great rock juts up from the river Lucefécit
and towers over the tree tops. This is Rocha
da Mina, the site of the Lusitanian sanctuary
to the pre-Roman god of healing, Endovélico.
Climb the age-old rock steps up to the sacred
place. Ribbons tied to a tree declare it still to
be a place of worship.
→ From Alandroal take the N373 towards
Redondo. After 7km turn L onto the dirt track
for 2km. Park and walk along the path for 1km.
Cross the footbridge.
20 mins, 38.6626, -7.4751

18 ANTA DA CANDEEIRA

In the hillside of Serra d'Ossa sheltered by
cork trees sits this dolmen, one of the very
few to have a port-hole window or a 'soul hole'.
→ From Redondo take the N381 N towards
Estremoz. After 7km turn R at brown signs for
Anta. Follow signs 1km down dirt track.
5 mins, 38.7039, -7.5527

WALKS & VILLAGES

19 BROTAS

Brotas is a small village with a beautiful
fresh fountain dating from 1699. Here the

18

Madonna healed a cow in the 16th century and it has been a site of pilgrimage ever since, by horse and by foot. The pilgrimage takes place on the second Sunday of August.

→ Take the N2 into Brotas and park just outside. Walk in to find the church, fountains and cafés.

10 mins, 38.8708, -8.1536 ⊞🍴⛵📍✝

20 GAMEIRO RIVER ROUTES, MORA

Walk the river way or forest path through the Ecological Park of Gameiro: each is about a 2km circular walk. There is also a river beach.

→ Signed off the N2 N of Mora. Ecological Park of Gameiro, 7490-909 Cabeção +351 266 448 130

30 mins, 38.9544, -8.1073 🚶🏕️⊞🛶🔻🔄

REGIONAL DISHES

21 RESTAURANTE PORFÍRIO'S, REDONDO

Dine around dark wood tavern tables under the arches of this family-run restaurant. Try the *feijão, bacalhau e poejos* soup: a rich broth with cod, beans and the pennyroyal mint popular here. The wine selection is extensive, naturally, and the *borrego no forno* is beautiful – slow roast lamb with fried potatoes from the garden. The *encharcada*, a regional conventual cake, made with egg yolk, sugar, almonds and cinnamon, is heaven.

→ Rua de Montoito 59-61, 7170-040 Redondo +351 266 909 737. Closed Mondays

38.6474, -7.5445 🍴📍

22 CASA DE PETISCOS O CHOUPAL, ALANDROAL

This unassuming House of Snacks is a great place to try regional dishes: *carne de porco à Alentejana* or *barbo frito*, the river fish for which this area is renowned. The portions are big enough for two.

→ Travessa da Fonte 11, 7250-125 Alandroal +351 962 064 835

38.7026, -7.4024 🍴📍

23 RESTAURANTE OS TEMPLÁRIOS, MONSARAZ

Dine on the terrace of Os Templários and look out from the walls of the ancient Templar castle at Monsaraz. Hidden behind the town's oldest gate, the restaurant commands views out across the Alqueva dam, Beja and Spain. Naturally, the wine cellars are well-stocked at this restaurant in the heart of Alentejo's wine region. Swirl a glass from Carmim, a world-renowned Monsaraz winery, and try

21

23

the gooey baked goat's cheese with olive oil, oregano and Alentejano bread to dip. *Sopa de cação* is a broth made with dogfish, worth a try, but the king of the dishes here is *bochechas de porco assada*, roast pig cheeks with potatoes and pumpkin. With the panoramic views, history, joy taken in the cooking and wines, this is a feast for eyes as well as your appetite.

➔ Rua Direita 22, 7200-175 Monsaraz +351 266 557 166
38.4436, -7.3802

24 RESTAURANTE O FORNO, PAVIA

The owner confidently claims his is *Arroz de cabidela*, rice cooked in pig or chicken's blood, is unlike any you've had in your life! He is not wrong.

➔ Rua 25 de Abril 2, 7490-448 Pavia +351 266 457 579
38.8950, -8.0219

25 RESTAURANTE SOLAR DA VILA, MORA

This is the place to try *migas de espargos com carne de Alguidar*: the Alentejana style *migas* (fried bread) with asparagus and marinated pork.

➔ Rua da Esperança 17, 7490-072 Mora +351 933 818 943
38.9552, -8.0788

26 RESTAURANTE BARBAS, VALVERDE

A cosy restaurant with an enormous cowbell hanging from the curtains. Try the *feijoada*, a hearty bean stew with *chouriço*, beef on the bone and vegetables.

➔ Rua 25 de Abril 23, Valverde +351 965 656 455
38.5330, -8.0212

REGIONAL SWEETS

27 PADARIA GALVÃO, BORBA

This tiny bakery in the old walls of Borba castle has barely space enough for the locals who drop by for one its many cakes. Try the local biscuit *bolo da gema* made with fresh egg yolks.

➔ Avenida Povo, 7150-103 Borba +351 268 890 606
38.8054, -7.4562

28 PASTELARIA LANDROAL, ALANDROAL

Here they make the traditional Portuguese custard-tart, *pastel de nata*, with a wild twist: acorn or *bolota* flour. The acorn flour is very light. A beautiful little *pastelaria* that also has a few guest rooms above.

➔ Rua António José de Almeida 7, 7250-138 Alandroal +351 268 449 662, Landroalresidencial.com
38.7028, -7.4037

29 PASTELARIA CISTERNA, MONSARAZ

Built over Monsaraz castle's medieval stone water reservoir, this dark little *pastelaria* does excellent *empadas de galinha*, small chicken pies, to have with a beer.

➔ R. Direita 24A, 7200-175 Monsaraz
38.4437, -7.3802

WINE & VINES

30 ADEGA COOPERATIVA DE BORBA

The Borba wine shop where you can buy all the winemakers' produce at retail prices. Wine-tastings and olive oil tours can be arranged.

➔ Largo Gago Coutinho e Sacadura Cabral, 7151-913 Borba. To book a tasting call +351 268 891 660 or e-mail geral@adegaborba.pt.
38.8070, -7.4627

31 ERVIDEIRA WINE SHOP

This is the winery that buried cases of their oak-aged Conde d'Ervideira under the Alqueva dam. Here it matures with the darkness and regular temperature unachievable elsewhere. Indulge in a wine tasting and try their *Invisível*, a white wine made with a red grape: each grape is squeezed for a single drop, untouched by the reddening skins.

➔ Rua da Porta de Alcova, 7200-175 Monsaraz +351 266 557 099 ervideirawineshopmonsaraz@gmail.com
38.4429, -7.3807

RURAL STAYS

32 CASAS DE ROMARIA, BROTAS

A number of quaint holiday rentals in the traditional houses of Brotas village. Confraria de Palmela is one of the houses, built in 1678; it sleeps two and is hidden up some steps between walls adjoining the church.

➔ Rua da Igreja 30, 7490-017 Brotas +351 966 948 643, Casasderomaria.com
38.8709, -8.1534

WILDER CAMPSITES

33 AZENHAS DA SEDA AQUATURISMO

This is wild luxury, all the comforts of a rural retreat while sleeping out under the stars. Secluded tipis and tents by the River Raia as it tumbles by the old watermill. This river never runs dry, even in the arid Alentejo summers. The campsite excels in canyoning, canoeing, hike and swim trips, and picnics with local produce.

→ Signed off N251 between Mora and Pavia. +351 266 448 036, Azenhasdaseda.com
38.9394, -8.0245

34 CAMPING ROSÁRIO

Wake up to endless views across Alentejo hills at this campsite near the Alqueva dam.

→ From N273 E of Alandroal, exit for Rosário. Follow signs with blue arrow and red caravan. Monte das Mimosas, 7250-203 Rosário - Alandroal +351 268 459 566, Campingrosario.com
38.6069, -7.3466

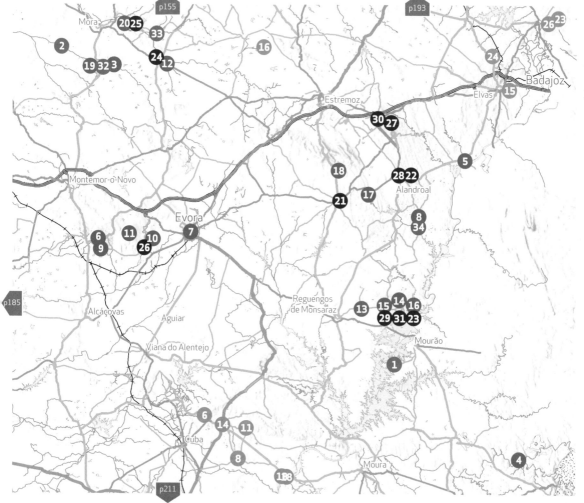

SOUTH ALENTEJO: BEJA

Our perfect weekend

→ **Paddle** in the clear mountain waters at Pego da Cascalheira

→ **Doze** among the wild flowers at Ribeira do Morgadinho

→ **Gaze** across the hushed and haunted fields from São Pedro das Cabeças

→ **Discover** hills inhabited only by wildlife at the hilltop settlements of Castro da Cola

→ **Watch** for eagles from the wild tumbling river at Cascata do Pulo do Lobo

→ **Bivvy** down at night by Anta das Pias and listen to the earth breathe

→ **Indulge** in a *tosta mista*, ham and cheese melted inside buttered, crusty Alentejo bread

→ **Eat** with the locals in the lively Café O Bombeiro with chalked-up daily specials

→ **Stroke** the rare Miranda do Douro donkeys at Alqueva Rural Camping in Pedrogão

Beja is a land of orange trees, colourful washing lines and bullfighting posters curling in the sun. Walk into any village and there will be low white houses and old men drinking outside the café. At Pedrógão, when the rich evening sun falls over the square, children run between café tables and race bicycles across the square. This is old Portugal, where everyone knows everybody.

Life runs at a leisurely pace as if, through a surfeit of ancient sites, some timelessness has rubbed off on the people who live here.

At Pulo do Lobo, the Guadiana gushes through a rocky gorge so narrow it came to be known as the 'wolf's leap'. The legendary wolf leapt to safety onto the other side. It escaped its hunter and that is how it feels to arrive here, deep within the endless stretches of Alentejo. In the words of Nobel Prize-winning novelist José Saramago, Pulo do Lobo "… is not Portugal, it is something from another world… The waters roar, surge, beat, swirl around and gnaw away perhaps a millimetre every century, or every thousand years, a mere nothing in this eternity: the world will come to an end before the water has completed its task."

Further south, as the Alentejo flatlands break into the hills of northern Algarve, is the Pego da Cascalheira. If you take the mountain road from Santa Cruz to get here you will pass idyllic farmhouses, thatched huts and hills strewn with rock roses. Julieta of Santa Cruz, who years ago used to wash clothes in this stream, told us that the water was once as clear as she was once beautiful. The water at this river is still clear and laughs, as much as her, as it babbles over the rocks.

The best Alentejana bread is to be found in the south. *Pão Alentejana* has air bubbles like ciabatta but a heavier crumb and thicker crust. Restaurante O Bombeiro at Castro Verde's fire station is a busy, jovial canteen with baskets of this wonderful bread and regional dishes that make for a good lunch stop.

Finally, climb back up from Pulo do Lobo to discover Anta das Pias. Steeped in time yet impervious to its ravages, this part-buried dolmen survives to greet each dawn. On a little hill rising above the Guadiana, it endures all changes. Rest there the night and it'll be not only your breath rising and falling but that of the earth gently breathing too.

RIVER SWIMS

1 PONTE ROMANA, ALMODÔVAR

Built in the late 12th century this bridge, set just out of town, has Roman origins as Almodôvar was a strategic point along the trade road linking Beja to the Algarve. This is a place for a swim only in spring as Ribeira de Cobres will dry up in summer.

→ Coming from the S, this bridge is just off the N2 on your R as you enter town.
2 mins, 37.5118, -8.0547 🏞🏊🏕

2 PEGO DA CASCALHEIRA, SANTA CRUZ

Here the terrain begins to shift from the flat plains of south Alentejo into the beginning of inland Algarve's wild mountainous region of Serra do Caldeirão. There is water all year round at this swim spot in the Ribeira do Vascão, flooding the road and making a ford crossing. Deep enough for a swim, cradled by mountains.

→ From Almodôvar head south on N2, turn L after Dogueno at signs for Santa Cruz; follow this road for 2km, turn R at sign for Cascalheira (37.4322, -7.9545) and follow for 6km along mountain road.
5 mins, 37.4088, -7.9178 🚶🏊🏕🏞

3 RIBEIRA DO MORGADINHO

Where the Ribeira de Oeiras widens its curves, the shallow water is warmed in the sun. A slow current here but a beautiful swim among the white crowsfoot flowers that grow star-like in scattered webs on the surface. This is a beautiful spot for stargazing.

→ From Almodôvar this spot is 6km S on the N2. After crossing the stream, and passing two curves, look out for a dirt track off the N2 at (37.4765, -8.0200) and slowly follow the track down to its end (very short). Park and walk down to the river.
2 mins, 37.4750, -8.0193 🏊🏕🏞🏞

4 CASCATA DO PULO DO LOBO

Known as the Wolf's Leap, this 16m cascade is in the Vale do Guadiana Natural Park. You might catch glimpse of a black stork or eagle owl or golden eagle circling above this ancient river.

→ See Anta das Pias (see 5) and follow track down to the river. Or if you want to take the car continue into Pias and follow road to the river.
20 mins, 37.8041, -7.6334 🏞🏊🚶🏕

ANCIENT & SACRED

5 ANTA DAS PIAS, VALE DO GUADIANA NATURAL PARK

This is a forgotten dolmen, partially buried and located on top of a small summit with views across the Guadiana valley and the vast horizon. Although not considered a national monument, its strategic placing in the landscape and east-west orientation should be explored further. Aligned perfectly for watching the sunset and moonrise.

→ From Corte Gafo de Cima take the road N towards Pias. After 14km there is a sun-bleached information plaque and a gravel path L. Park here. The Anta is hidden through bushes, on a slight hill, 11 o'clock, as you enter.
2 mins, 37.8153, -7.6504 🏞🏞🚶🏞

6 RUÍNAS ROMANAS DE SÃO CUCUFATE

Wander around Roman ruins dedicated to the martyred Spanish Saint Cucufate. The beginnings of the convent were laid down in the 1st century and abandoned for the first time in the 5th century AD, then again in the 17th century. One hermit monk then remained. Now you can see remains of hot baths, two-storey ruins and medieval wall paintings.

→ From Vidigueira take the N258 W for 4km towards Vila Alva, turn R at brown signs for São Cucufate. +351 284 441 113

1 hr, 38.2236, -7.8453 €❖☰♨

7 CASTRO DA COLA ARCHAEOLOGICAL CIRCUIT

An Iron Age necropolis from about 1,100BC crowns this hill circled by the River Mira. The walk here is through woodland – rock roses, wild thyme, lavender, holm oak and cork – and a very wild stretch of river with no roads nearby. The Celtic settlement was later reinforced during the Arab occupation of Portugal and controlled a principal route of passage to the Algarve. The linear walk around here today is about 35km, signed and on a beaten earth track. There are 14 other archaeological sites – some dating from the Bronze Age – but the wild herbs obscure much of this to the untrained eye. Soak up the wild flora, fauna and timeless views instead.

→ From Ourique take the IC1 6km S until a brown sign R for Castro da Cola. Follow the signs through the villages, and park. Walk begins here.

1 day, 37.5787, -8.3004 ☰♨❖☰

8 PONTE ROMANA DE SELMES

On the outskirts of the village Selmes, where the allotments run down to the stream's edge, is this possibly 16th century bridge.

→ From the main square at Selmes walk down Rua da Ponte.

2 mins, 38.1457, -7.7568 ☰☰

9 CASTELO DE MÉRTOLA

Mértola Castle crowns a rocky hill surveying the Guadiana river and surrounding natural park. The medieval castle in the centre of this quaint town has Islamic origins. The church was originally a mosque and retains a mihrab pointing to Mecca.

→ From the N122 into town, park in the covered parking area and walk up the hill into town, as far as the castle.

10 mins, 37.6389, -7.6636 ❖☰♨

RURAL TOWNS

10 PEDROGÃO

Orange blossom in the square and children running about in the evening, skidding past café tables. A couple of good cafés and a restaurant in the square. This is a quiet village by all appearances, but if you stop by to ask directions, by the end of the day the

12

whole town will know you.

→ A little S of the Alqueva dam. From Moura take the N258 W.

2 mins, 38.1177, -7.6473 ⊞ 🍴 ◁ 📍

SUNSET HILLTOPS

11 MIRADOURO ALCARIA DA SERRA

In the tiny village of Alcaria da Serra is this unlikely hill with beautiful views across all the flat plains of Barranco do Vale da Serra and beyond into Beja. Breathe in the views, with only the birdsong, wind in the trees and tinkling of distant cowbells. Look out for wild deer on the road between Marmelar and Alcaria. The farm used to breed them but now they run wild.

→ Enter Alcaria on the road from Marmelar, continue in and turn R at the end of town into Rua da Boavista; continue up hill, park and walk up to the white round tank.

5 mins, 38.2047, -7.7421 🖼️🖼️

12 SÃO PEDRO DAS CABEÇAS, CASTRO VERDE

This 15th century chapel sits on top of a hill looking out over the legendary site of the Battle of Ourique. In July 1139 Dom Afonso Henriques defeated five Moorish kings and so formed Portugal, which remains one of Europe's oldest countries. After Afonso's success, myths of his miraculous vision of Jesus Christ over this field began to spread and were used down the years to bolster borders threatened by Spain. Now the chapel is a pilgrimage site and a peaceful place to contemplate the endless views over Alentejo.

→ From Castro Verde take the N123, turning R towards Geraldos and follow brown signs for the Igreja.

2 mins, 37.6777, -8.0362 ⊞🧍☩🖼️✝

WINE & DINE

13 RESTAURANTE CHARRUA, PEDRÓGÃO

A locals' restaurant, using fresh ingredients to make regional dishes and puddings. Good wine and Alentejo *migas*.

→ Praça da República 13, 7960-026 Pedrógão +351 284 455 153

38.1178, -7.6470 🍴📍

14 ADEGA COOPERATIVA DE VIDIGUEIRA

This *adega* was founded in 1960 but its history extends beyond as its roots are tangled with the history of the town Vidigueira itself. The name is derived from 'videira' meaning vine, referring to this

9

13

abundant land. The explorer Vasco da Gama was made the first Count of Vidigueira in 1519.

→ Bairro Industrial, 7960-305 Vidigueira +351 284 437 240, Adegavidigueira.com.pt. Closed lunchtime
38.2080, -7.7995 🏨🎫

15 RESTAURANTE CAFÉ O BOMBEIRO, CASTRO VERDE

This is a restaurant in the fire station but, as these are run voluntarily, they are often the centres of the community. This is a lively restaurant with many tables crammed close, and a welcoming atmosphere. They do excellent lunches with hearty portions of traditional dishes. This is the place to get a basket of the real crusty Alentejana bread.

→ Rua da Seara Nova 4, 7780-163 Castro Verde +351 286 327 168
37.7035, -8.0845 🏨🍴

16 RESTAURANTE O MOINHO, ALMODÔVAR

A rustic restaurant, decorated with old farming tools. Wooden chairs and chequered tablecloths. The menu is based on dishes of the day, all regional dishes with homely variations. The grilled Alentejo pork *abanicos* or *secretos*, with chips, rice and salad, is a good choice, or try the stewed wild boar. Try the *paio* sausages to start. Great desserts and local Alentejo wines.

→ Rua do Arco 38B, 7700-055 Almodôvar +351 286 400 156, Restaurantemoinho.pt
37.5118, -8.0595 🍴🏨🎫

17 RESTAURANTE O BRASILEIRO, MÉRTOLA

Despite its name, this restaurant focuses on local produce to cook regional dishes. The menu is seasonal and includes wild asparagus with *migas* and pork ribs, wild partridge (*perdiz açorda*) and slow-cooked wild boar stew. For pudding try *sopa dourada* or the *torrão real*. The wines are local and excellent.

→ Cerro de São Luís, 7750-296 Mértola +351 286 612 660
37.6432, -7.6581 🏨🍴🎫

WILDER CAMPSITES

18 ALQUEVA RURAL CAMPING, PEDROGÃO

As the Guadiana river continues its course south after the Alqueva dam, there is this farm with a camping and caravan park. Baby goats gambol under rare Miranda do Douro donkeys. Horses and llamas, black pigs, rabbits, ducks and peacocks all bring a happy energy to this small but vital farm. You can visit just to see the animals or stay the night,

waking up to a cockerel calling dawn across the hills. Don't forget to visit Solomon's Throne, a natural seat in some of the giant rocks that litter the farmland.

→ SE of Pedrogão, off the N258. 7960 Pedrogão do Alentejo +351 213 552 070, Dosdin.pt
38.1173, -7.6352 🍴🏨🏔🎫🏕

19 CAMPING BARRAGEM MONTE DA ROCHA

This is a jolly and basic campsite but it does have amazing sunsets over the reservoir, stunning Elysian views and swimming access to the water.

→ Situated off the N261-4, W of the reservoir. Barragem Monte da Rocha, Ourique +351 962 064 323
37.7173, -8.3021 🍴🏨🎫🏕

LUXURY HAVENS

20 MONTE DA CORTE LIGEIRA

An exquisite and luxurious guesthouse on an ancient Alentejo farm. Encircled by 250ha with cork oak *montados*, you can fish in several dams on the estate, hunt, taste the local wines, take a pony ride or a refreshing dip in the pool.

→ 7800-631 Cabeça Gorda, Beja +351 284 947 216
37.9024, -7.8268 🏊🍴🎫🏨

21 HERDADE DOS GROUS

A magnificent county estate hotel with olive groves, cork oak forests and vineyards. They make wine, olive oil and keep seven horses for guests. There is very little they don't do – there is even a lake in the grounds.

→ Take IP2/E802 N from Albernoa; 2km after crossing the river, follow signs L for Turismo Rural. 7800-601 Albernoa, Beja +351 284 960 000, Herdade-dos-grous.com
37.8790, -7.9410 🚶🏊🍴🏨🎫

22 MONTE GOIS COUNTRY HOUSE & SPA

Hidden in the Serra do Mú is this exquisite retreat. A typical Alentejo house has been renovated with plenty of hammocks, daybeds, a pool, colourful gardens and a spa. They serve glorious breakfasts with fruits, cakes, hams and cheeses, honeys and local breads. This is a zen environment. Come to be in touch with nature.

→ From Almodôvar head S for 13km, turn R just before Fonte Ferrenhas de Cima, follow dirt track keeping L for 3km. Monte Gois 212, 7700 Almodôvar +351 967 064 146, Montegois.com
37.4323, -8.0940 🏊🍴🎫🏔🏨🎫

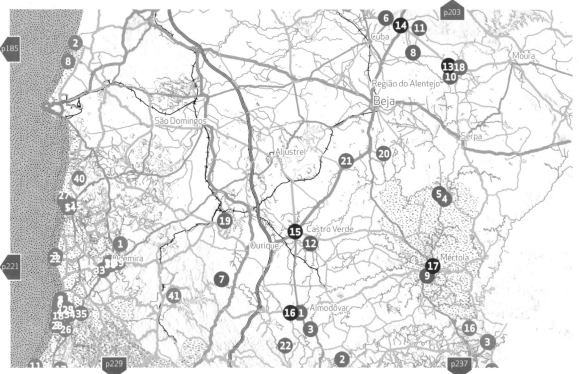

COSTA VICENTINA

Our perfect weekend

- → **Sail** down the winding Mira river and watch for kingfishers and kestrels
- → **Slow** your pace as you go donkey-trekking along the Rota Vicentina
- → **Follow** ancient sailors' steps down to deep sea behind Fortaleza de Belixe
- → **Dash** under the waterfall at the secret beach Praia da Amália
- → **Bunk** down under old eaves in the timeless rural village of Pedralva
- → **Jump** from a rope swing into the deep green river at Pego das Pias
- → **Watch** for baby storks in nests on the wind-torn cliffs of Cabo Sardão
- → **Skinny** dip in the Santa Clara lake with water so clear you can see your toes in the moonlight
- → **Feast** on fresh fish at Porto das Barcas and watch the boats come into harbour
- → **Unwind** by gentle fountains at Cerro da Borrega country house

It is said that to get to know Portugal "you must feel the earth under your feet". Walking the Rota Vicentina, a 400km signed walking route from Cabo de São Vicente along the Alentejo coast up to Santiago de Cacém, is one way to do this. The route comprises old fishermen's trails and smugglers' tracks which, by their very nature, follow this coastline. Pass secret beaches, accessible only at low tide or by steep tracks running down. Perilous paths fork away from the advised Rota, too risky for any but the fisherman's dog.

Praia da Amália is one of these beaches accessible only from a narrow track. Portugal's most famous rags-to-riches figure, the orange-seller turned Fado singer Amália, would escape from Lisbon to this beach. Her house is still hidden above what used to be her private cove where she learnt to swim. A freshwater cascade tumbles onto the sand from the hills, offering a natural shower after a salty swim.

Slightly further north along the Rota Vicentina is Praia do Alvorião, with daunting access down narrow fishermen's steps. Praias Machado and Carvalhal offer further wild blue sea coves along the trail. Slow the pace further and take a donkey-trek along this wild coast; with your supplies packed in panniers, you can go for a few days. Attune yourself to your peaceful donkey and see the coast as ancient people before.

Inhabited since prehistory and protohistory, Costa Vicentina has retained the interest of curious and adventurous people down the ages. This borderland is fraught with the past, the most south-westerly peninsular of Europe, the last shape sailors could see as they departed for foreign lands, and the first emerging on their return. From behind cliff-top Fortaleza de Belixe, follow the ghostly way of long-gone sailors down rocky steps to a silent cove. Waves lap against the last step. Here is water deep enough for a heavy ship to drop anchor.

Moorish castles and Christian fortresses line this coast, and far-flung monasteries, built by those who survived the sea, are now themselves falling into the sea. There is a constant battle between the land and sea, a slap and pull of the tide but also the thundering, elemental clamour for survival. In the midst of all this, at Cabo Sardão atop a cliff rock, a stork has its nest, withstanding the 150kph wind.

WILD SWIMS

1 PEGO DAS PIAS

Large sculptural rocks plunge into a green, slow river. A wild place off-season, with rope swings the only sign of human intervention.

→ From Odemira take N120 for São Luís. At Reguengo Pequeno, R and follow track for 200m following signs to Pego das Pias. Park at the fork.

10 mins, 37.6452, -8.6187

2 RIO MIRA

A sleepy riverbank with a boardwalk out from Odemira. At the steps to the river, a boat once passed twice daily. Folklore tells of the *modas* or plaintive love songs sung over the river on days no boat passed.

→ Enter Odemira by N120; park by petrol station at the roundabout. Walk to the riverbank and follow the wooden walkway L.

2 mins, 37.5980, -8.6452

SECRET BEACHES

3 PRAIA DE CAVALEIRO

A secret sandy cove with crashing waves and dramatic rock strata in wet charcoal greys. The Rota Vicentina passes by here, a lovely spot for a dip in the clear blue sea.

→ From Porto das Barcas take the CM1158 N for 7km, turn L at signs for Cabo Sardão and follow to lighthouse. Park and walk 1km down dirt track to R until wooden rail and track down to the beach.

3 mins, 37.6057, -8.8158

4 PRAIA DA AMÁLIA, BREJÃO

The famous Fado singer Amália had her retreat here: a secret beach where she could learn to swim. Shower in the fresh waterfall after a salty swim. Accessible by a small track or hike on Rota Vicentina (see 16).

→ From Brejão take the coast road towards Azenha do Mar. At the yellow flower sign turn R down track though raspberry fields. Park outside Amália's house. L downhill and follow the track to the beach.

5 mins, 37.4828, -8.7941

5 PRAIA DA FRANQUIA, VILA NOVA DE MILFONTES

Next to the old town by the river mouth is a sandy beach, protected by the curve of the Mira, hidden from the sea waves.

→ From Forte in Vila Nova de Milfontes take the coastal road in the direction of Praia do Farol. Parking near the beach bar.

5 mins, 37.7220, -8.7879

6 PRAIA DO MACHADO, CARVALHAL

A secret sandy cove known only to locals. The rock promontory is known as Castelo-a-Velha, popular with fishermen. Try the small sweet white gorse berries, eaten raw in autumn, known as *camarinhas*. Access from cliffs is difficult.

→ From Brejão go to Carvalhal, L opposite the camping park, pass the greenhouses, through the tunnel, park after R turn. Follow Rota Vicentina signs to first cove.

5 mins, 37.4927, -8.7934

7 PRAIA DO CARVALHAL

A hidden cove with a sandy beach when the tide is out. Great cliffs shelter you from larger waves.

→ From Praia do Machado (see 6) walk N along Rota Vicentina to next cove.

10 mins, 37.4998, -8.7925

8 PRAIA DO ALVORIÃO, CARVALHAL

Quiet and secluded beach as access is hard. Sandy, rocks underwater. There is a fishermen's route via some steps on the south. Take care.

10

14

12

→ See Praia do Machado (6), and follow Rota Vicentina signs N to 3rd cove.

15 mins, 37.5035, -8.7918

SURF & SAIL

9 PRAIA DE ODECEIXE

A beach bordered on three sides by water as river meets sea. Even on stormy days you can find calm water here if you follow inland to the river beach.

→ From Odeceixe follow signs towards Praia. Parking at the beach.

5 mins, 37.4419, -8.7967

10 PRAIA DA ARRIFANA

Five sandstone cliffs like orange giants slope down to this sheltered cove. A good restaurant before the long steps down. Popular in summer. Deserted from autumn.

→ From Aljezur take the N120 S, R at the brown sign to Arrifana. Follow to beach.

10 mins, 37.2942, -8.8657

11 PRAIA DO MONTE CLÉRIGO, ALJEZUR

Long beach when tide is out. Good for surfers and strong swimmers. A few restaurants and snack bars for a beer

nearby. Easy access to Rota Vicentina up the cliffs.

→ From Aljezur take N120 south and R at brown sign to Mte Clérigo. Follow signs.

5 mins, 37.3409, -8.8538

12 PRAIA DO CASTELEJO, VILA DO BISPO

A cove at the end of a valley. A popular surfing spot on one side of the massive rock which rises out of the water like a Henry Moore sculpture. A couple of fishermen stationed on it. Beach deserted beyond this rock.

→ From Vila do Bispo follow signs at the roundabout for Castelejo.

10 mins, 37.1003, -8.9451

13 PRAIA DA BORDEIRA

A good family beach with a river and 4km of dunes. Busy in summer.

→ From Vila do Bispo take N268 N towards Aljezur. After 14km, L at the brown sign for Bordeira and follow to beach.

5 mins, 37.1998, -8.9010

14 DUCA BOAT RIDES

Take a boat inland to Odemira from the coast and you will follow the Mira river, the cleanest in Portugal, as rich in history as in

wildlife. Trace the ancient trading path and look out for osprey, herons and kingfishers.

→ Pickup at the harbour in Vila Nova de Milfontes. Call Rui: +351 969 372 176, Duca.pt
2 hrs, 37.7231, -8.7801 🐦🏊

15 SURF MILFONTES
Get to grips with the board and the wild ocean with Felipe and Pedro. Passionate, patient and wave-wise teachers. Also calmer canoeing trips along the River Mira.

→ Rua Custódio Brás Pacheco 38A, Vila Nova de Milfontes +351 914 732 652, Surfmilfontes.com
2.5 hrs, 37.7278, -8.7783 🏄🐟🐚🏊

WILD WALKS

16 ROTA VICENTINA
Explore secret beaches, wild cliffs and smugglers' routes along this 400km signed coastal walking route along the Alentejo coast. It begins in Cabo São Vicente and splits into the inland Historical Way and the coastal Fishermen's Way, ending in Porto Covo or Santiago de Cacém. Strap on your pilgrim boots to walk part or the whole stretch. Contact Casas Brancas (19) for top quality rural accommodation, donkey walks

or great restaurants along the way.

→ The way is signed from Cabo São Vicente: green/blue for Fishermen's Way and red/white for Historical Way. Rotavicentina.com
14 days, 37.0245, -8.9942 🚶🌀✴️🏕🏞

17 BURROS E ARTES, ALJEZUR
Slow the pace and adjust your rhythm to the donkey's peaceful mood. Sofia leads donkey treks along the coastal paths of Aljezur with a picnic stop along the way. Long walks for 2-7 days can also be organised, you with your donkey, in full communion with nature. Elsa leads workshops in local arts and crafts, pottery, bread-making and weaving.

→ Vale das Amoreiras, Aljezur +351 967 145 306, Burros-artes.blogspot.com
2 days, 37.3380, -8.7775 🚶🌲♨️🎲🏞🐫🐴

HARBOURS & HOSPITALITY

18 AZENHA DO MAR
A tiny cove where the fishing boats come in. Good crab at Restaurante Azenha do Mar. Near to the shore are two great rocks which locals say look like fighting animals. Behind Bar Palinhas, in their garden, is a lovers' seat looking out over these rocks and the sea. Perfect for a sunset.

→ Signs to Azenha do Mar from Brejão.
2 mins, 37.4645, -8.7958 ⊞🍴

19 CASAS BRANCAS

This association, formed by locals, picks the best of the region's rural houses, farms, traditional restaurants and adventure activities. Ask here for donkey walks, bread-making workshops or an excellent surfing school. This is thoughtful tourism caring for the region's culture and nature.

→ Travessa do Botequim 6, 7630-185 Odemira. Casasbrancas.pt
1 min, 37.5987, -8.6449 🍴⛵🏄♀🏕🐴

WINDSWEPT WALKS

20 ECOVIA DO LITORAL

This is a 214km cycle route which links Cabo de São Vicente in west Algarve with Vila Real de Santo António on the border with Spain. The signed way makes use of existing cycle paths and traffic-calm roads. About half the route is on unpaved and gravel trails, passing coastal nature reserves and small villages.

→ Ciclovia.pt
2 days, 37.0233, -8.9954 🚴🏔

21 VIA ALGARVIANA

The Via Algarviana is a 300km long-distance walking route, starting at Alcoutim in the north-eastern Algarve, and ending at the south-western tip at Cabo de São Vicente. There are several places you can join this route between Cabo de São Vicente and Alte in western Algarve. It will take you through the Monchique mountains and inland villages away from the bustle of the coast.

→ Maps and info at Viaalgarviana.org.
10 days, 37.0258, -8.9901 ⊞🏔🚶

CLIFFTOP HIGHS

22 CABO SARDÃO

The most westerly point of the Alentejo coast. High winds, tumultuous waves beating the sheer cliffs and, in the midst of chaos, storks building their nests. In spring look out for their young.

→ From Odemira take N393 towards the coast then CM1124 until you see the lighthouse. Park and walk along Rota Vicentina.
2 mins, 37.5986, -8.8170 🚶📷🏔⊞

23 FORTALEZA DE BELIXE, SÃO VICENTE

Over 100 rock-hewn steps lead down, behind the fort, to the deep blue sea. The last step

24

is water – there is no beach – deep enough to put down anchor. Take a moment and contemplate the cliffs, stillness and birds. Imagine sailors' first shaky steps back on land.

→ From Sagres take coast road W towards Cabo de São Vicente. Just before São Vicente pass the fort on L. Park and walk down steps. 2 mins, 37.0270, -8.9821 ⛰️⭐🏕️

24 TORRE DE ASPA, VILA DO BISPO

Part of an ancient defensive network and the highest point along the Algarve coastline, the Torre de Aspa controlled navigation and helped repel coastal attacks. From this point the alert would be given, with a chain of torches to warn the population. You can see Cabo São Vicente and Sagres from here.

→ From Vila do Bispo take the road running up to the L behind Restaurante A Eira do Mel and follow for 4km following signs to Torre de Aspa. Park by the empty house. 5 mins, 37.0855, -8.9518 ♣⛰️✂️

FRESH FISH

25 CAFÉ CENTRAL, BREJÃO

The best *salada de polvo* in Portugal or, at least, a great example of the Alentejo way that octopus can be served, with parsley, salt, onion and virgin olive oil. Mouthwatering local fish dishes and steaks are cooked on the charcoal grill at the back of the restaurant.

→ Brejão, 7630-569 Odemira +351 282 947 419 37.4803, -8.7667 🍴🍷

26 TABERNA DO GABÃO, ODECEIXE

Choose your fish from the board. An actual board, that is, piled with the fresh, glossy catch. And try the regional sweet potato cake.

→ Rua do Gabão 9, 8670-320 Odeceixe +351 282 947 549 37.4334, -8.7709 🍴🍷

27 RESTAURANTE PORTO DAS BARCAS, VILA NOVA DE MILFONTES

High up on windswept cliffs, Porto das Barcas specializes in stunning views and great fish. Choose your catch as you enter, fresh from the boats unloading in the harbour below. Try Alentejo cheeses with crisp local wine, octopus salad and fish-rice cooked in a clay pot.

→ Estrada Canal, 7645-000 Vila Nova de Milfontes, Odemira +351 283 997 160 37.7382, -8.8009 🍴🍷

27

25

REGIONAL TREATS

28 ESPLANADA DO MAR, ODECEIXE

A small café overlooking the beach, selling colourful smoothies and cakes.

→ At Praia de Odeceixe, park by beach, walk towards steps to river beach. Café tucked away R. 8670-325 Praia de Odeceixe +351 937 036 426
37.4410, -8.7973 🍴🚻🏖

29 RESTAURANTE MIRAMAR

Typical joyful Portuguese *tasca*: a choice of two dishes. House wine, bread baskets and loads of locals. *Serradura* or sawdust dessert is the mother's invention: a deliciously rich mousse with biscuit crumbs.

→ Next door to Café Central Brejão (see 25)
37.4806, -8.7670 🍴🚻🍽

30 CHOCOLATES DE BEATRIZ

Beatriz has created a small chocolate factory in the hills of Odemira. Inside the house is filled with aromas of dark chocolate. In the garden, nibble on fig, almond or chilli chocolate, looking over golden fields and the river below.

→ Estrada do Cemitério, 7630-999 Odemira +351 283 327 205
37.5950, -8.6438 🍴📷

SLOW FOOD

31 RESTAURANTE A EIRA DO MEL, VILA DO BISPO

An old farmhouse filled with antiques, and a restaurateur who believes slow food is the best way to feed your soul. Everything from Algarve farmers.

→ Estr. do Castelejo, 8651-999 Vila do Bispo +351 282 639 016
37.0834, -8.9139 🍴🚻

32 RESTAURANTE O TARRO, ODEMIRA

A less-than-wild location, opposite Odemira's petrol station. But it's close to the river and a great place to try *amêijoas na cataplana*, clams cooked in a giant copper clam-like pot. A huge array of regional dishes and wines.

→ Estr. da Circunvalação, 7630-130 Odemira +351 283 322 161
37.5989, -8.6451 🍴🚻

33 TASCA DO BERNARDO, ODEMIRA

A candlelit, welcoming restaurant with wine barrels and rustic farming paraphernalia. Try the *porco preto*, grilled pork with pineapple and garlic. *Migas de pão Alentejo* is a local delight. A beautiful place for an evening feast.

→ R. dos Carpinterios 3A, 7630-174 Odemira +351 283 386 476
37.5806, -8.6653 🍴🚻

RUSTIC HAVENS

34 CERRO DA FONTINHA, BREJÃO

Old cottages rebuilt in traditional style, reclaimed mahogany beams and sea stones paving the showers. Visit in winter to enjoy woodburners, logs piled outside and bicycles to ride down to deserted beaches nearby. Just outside the village of Brejão, with a bio-pool in the garden. Fresh eggs, cheeses, fruit and bread left on a little tray by your door for breakfast. A heavenly place.

→ 7630-575 S.Teotónio - Odemira +351 917 802 588, Cerrodafontinha.com
37.4695, -8.7606 🍴🚲🚻♿🛏

35 CERRO DA BORREGA

A new house built in ancient ways: the walls are of rammed earth and there's an elegant courtyard. Enjoy the sensual side of nature with exquisite breakfasts, time-worn cork trees, tinkling fountains at night and *medronho* spirit, a fruit brandy, produced here specially for guests. A lavish haven.

→ Vale Juncal, N120 km120, 7630-675 São Teotónio - Odemira +351 966 043 306, Cerrodaborrega.com
37.4738, -8.7240 🍴🚻🚲🛏

36 MONTE DO ZAMBUJEIRO, VILA NOVA DE MILFONTES

Several guesthouses, all with French windows looking out over sweeping mountain views and the winding River Mira. A swimming pool and a reading hammock in the garden. A beautiful place to open windows in the early morning with dawn mists rising.

→ Herdade do Zambujeiro - Monte do Zambujeiro, 7645 Vila Nova de Milfontes +351 283 386 143, Montedozambujeiro.com
37.7079, -8.7521 🍴🚻📷🛏🚲

37 MUXIMA, ALJEZUR

A luxurious African-inspired interior for this guesthouse, with a secret attic-library. Magical by candlelight. Daybeds on the veranda, a treehouse further down, bio-pool and woodland paths for children to run wild. Try the *medronho* fruit jam for breakfast.

→ Montes Ferreiros 265A, Aljezur 8670-000 +351 916 012 830, Muxima-montesferreiros.com
37.3004, -8.7951 🍴🚲🚻🛏🏊🚶🏔

38 ALDEIA DA PEDRALVA

Unwind and enjoy the village pace in one of these mountain cottages rebuilt by the ebullient owner, António. The loving restoration of this old Portuguese *aldeia* gives a strong sense, with narrow streets, old eaves and chatting on doorsteps, of what life was like in these hilltop villages. Bicycles for hire. Bobby, António's big black dog, will accompany hikers along his stretch of Rota Vicentina for a biscuit.

→ Rua de Baixo, Casa da Pedralva, 8650-401 Vila do Bispo +351 282 639 342, Aldeiadapedralva.com

37.1408, -8.8618 🍴⛵📍🔆⛰🚴

39 QUINTA DO CHOCALHINHO, ALDEIA DA BEMPOSTA

Stately dark-wood farmhouse with suites set in cork forest, and hills riddled with footpaths. Horses, donkeys and goats graze the hills nearby. A long swimming pool sheltered between the houses and hills. Fresh eggs, local cheeses, fruit and breads for breakfast.

→ Estrada N263 km2, Bemposta, 7630-028 Odemira +351 283 327 280, Quintadochocalhinho.com

37.6007, -8.6212 🍴📍⛵

40 TRÊS MARIAS, VILA NOVA DE MILFONTES

A remote house with wide views of dusty Alentejo fields and olive groves: a menagerie of pigs, donkeys and sheep, complete with an ostrich, roam their fields. Relax in a hammock listening to the evening birdsong. Delicious dinners, an honesty bar and a delightful breakfast.

→ Ribeira da Azenha, 7645-909 Vila Nova de Milfontes +351 965 666 231, Tresmarias.pt

37.7929, -8.7575 🍴📍⛵♻

41 QUINTA DO BARRANCO DA ESTRADA

Hidden in the midst of the Alentejo hills is a remote family-run guesthouse overlooking Santa Clara dam. Welcoming and relaxed, with dogs, log fires and a parrot. Rooms look out to a garden running down to the lake. The lake is so clear you can see your toes in the moonlight. Alentejo here is particularly rich in birdlife and Frank, the host, runs birding holidays – for longer periods or day trips – for twitchers and beginners, with infectious enthusiasm.

→ Quinta do Barranco da Estrada, 7665-880 Santa Clara a Velha +351 283 933 065, Paradise-in-portugal.com

37.5322, -8.4425 🍴📍⛵🔆⛰🎿🏊

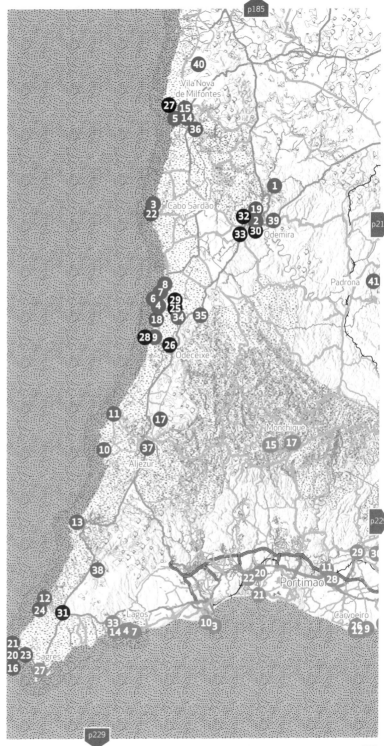

WEST ALGARVE: MONCHIQUE

Our perfect weekend

→ **Plunge** into the cool waters of Queda do Vigário and swim under the pounding waterfall

→ **Kayak** into Benagil sea caves and glide under their vaulted ceilings

→ **Clamber** over the rugged limestone sides of Rocha da Pena's climbing walls

→ **Time-travel** back to the dinosaurs with footprints left in time at Salema beach

→ **Swim** in the azure sea by Carvalho beach and explore cliffs riddled with secret passages

→ **Discover** the secret Convento do Desterro abandoned to the wild, ivy creeps up columns

→ **Taste** the best grilled fish and sample the local *medronho* spirit

→ **Balance** your prayer stone at the summit of Fóia, as the Algarve spreads out like a map below

→ **Stay** in a farm with mango, persimmon and carob trees at Quinta da Figueirinha

Inland from the central Algarve coast, limestone crags rise up from Barrocal, a land wild with olive, carob and myrtle trees. In autumn, folk here still rattle the olive branches, harvesting the olives in nets laid on the ground. Journey inland to discover a peaceful, farming Algarve attuned to seasonal tasks different to the tourism for which the coast is famous.

Rocha da Pena, a hump-backed limestone hill, known here as a *barroca*, rises up from the Barrocal area to brood over the dusty olive groves below. Caves and grottoes are formed in its weather-beaten sides. Try to find the legendary cave, Algar do Mouro, which is said to have given refuge to fugitives down the ages. It's a beautiful spot for a sunset as the last rays catch, turning the rock face orange.

Westward stand the towering Monchique mountains, with Fóia, the peak at 902m, an island emerging from clouds covering the hills below. At this summit, pilgrims leave stones balanced in prayerful columns, *mariolas*, representing a symbolic act of remembrance or unburdening. Lean into the wind, weightless, as your view soars over the Algarve to the dunes marking the border of land and sea.

Time your trip well and you can find the Algarve coast vastly emptied out of season. Benagil cave, a watery Pantheon with sunlight streaming through a hole in its domed ceiling, is accessible only by sea: take a kayak in the early morning for magical solitude. Praia do Carvalho is also riddled with caves; rock-hewn steps lead down a sandy tunnel to the beach with further cliff-carved caves to explore at low tide. At Praia da Salema, head off the tourist track and discover 125 million-year-old dinosaur footsteps imprinted on the rock, whisking you off to a truly wild era.

Follow the coastal walking routes and discover a network of strategically built fortresses. Fortaleza de Almádena is a yellow stone ruin looking out to the blue sea, its staircase leading to the sky. Sit in the open chapel and listen to the thunderous waves beneath. Inland, Paderne castle rises imperial; lit by the late sun, its ruins speak of a distant age, the perfect place for sunset dreams.

1

SEA CAVES

1 PRAIA DO CARVALHO, BENAGIL

A tunnel hewn through rocks leads to the beach. Further up, narrow steps carved into the cliff-side lead to a secret place. Time the tide carefully.

→ Exit N125 on M1154 S, 1.5km W of the Porches junction, and follow signs to Benagil and further W to Carvalho. Parking.

5 mins, 37.0868, -8.4318 🏊🏄⛱️▽

2 BENAGIL CAVES

Take a kayak to explore the Algarve's salty pantheon. Waves lap in on low tide beneath this sun-filled cavern, and blue sky is glimpsed through its high round window. Accessed only by water but you can peer in through the window down from land. Kayaks for hire on beach and in town. Call +351 969 617 828 or find the kiosk at Praia de Benagil.

→ For directions, see Praia do Carvalho (see 1). Park in town and walk down.

5 mins, 37.0870, -8.4238 ⛱️🏄

3 PONTA DA PIEDADE

Steps down to beautiful rock formations: water-filled womb-like caves, arches and pinnacles of red sandstone.

→ N125 to Lagos. Follow signs to Praia Dona Ana and then Ponta da Piedade.

5 mins, 37.0798, -8.6685 🅱️⛱️🏄

SECRET BEACHES

4 PRAIA DA BOCA DO RIO

A quieter beach where wetlands run down to the coast by the river mouth.

→ From Salema follow signs towards Burgau. Turn R at the T junction (Burgau is L), and head to the coast.

3 mins, 37.0664, -8.8092 🏕️⛱️🏊🚶

5 PRAIA DA SENHORA DA ROCHA

A windswept chapel on a promontory above; beneath is a shell-strewn beach with crashing waves. Float on your back, ears underwater, listen to the sand shingling.

→ Exit N125 at Porches and follow signs to Senhora da Rocha. Park in town and walk down to the beach.

5 mins, 37.0973, -8.3857 ⛪️⛱️🚶

6 PRAIA DOS ARRIFES

Beautiful rocks to swim out and explore. A network of rock pools emerges when the tide is out.

→ Turn off N125 at Guia, head towards Albufeira, then follow signs to Praia dos Arrifes.

2 mins, 37.0762, -8.2772 🅱️⛱️🚶

7 PRAIA DAS CABANAS VELHAS, BARRANCÃO

A cove enclosed by beautiful orange sandstone cliffs. This sandy beach is popular with surfers due to its wild crashing waves.

→ From Barrancão follow signs to the beach.

2 mins, 37.0656, -8.7949 ⛱️▽🍴

8 PRAIA DO CASTELO, EVARISTO

Striking, yellow cliffs enclose this sandy cove with deep, blue sea. It can be a popular spot but there are several little rocky coves perfect for exploring.

→ From Albufeira take the M526 W for 6km; turn L at brown signs. Follow for 1km to beach.

2 mins, 37.0731, -8.2986 ⛱️🚶🍴🅱️

9 PRAIA DA MARINHA

Although this beach can get busy in summer, it is snorkelling heaven. There are plenty of nooks and crannies to explore under the clear waves, with countless colourful fish.

→ From Lagoa take the N125 towards Porches, after 2.5km turn R at signs for

12

10

13

Benagil. Follow the M1154 for 3km until a sign for Marinha on your L.

2 mins, 37.0897, -8.4124 🏖️📷🅱️

10 PRAIA DO CANAVIAL, LAGOS

A beautiful sandy, naturist-friendly beach with staggering rocks and a calm, glassy sea. Several secret rocky nooks to explore when the tide is out.

→ From Lagos take the coast road to the Farol da Ponta Piedade Lighthouse (37.0810, -8.6693). Park and walk W along the dirt track.

30 mins, 37.0839, -8.6794 🏖️⛰️

HIDDEN SPRINGS

11 SÍTIO DAS FONTES, ESTÔMBAR

This is a lovely park, about 18ha, with several places to jump into the River Arade. This is marshland and scrub, a few paths and a couple of ancient watermills. One mill dates back to at least the 15th century.

→ From Estômbar train station it's a 30 min walk. Or take the road N to Fontes for 1km, turn L at brown sign.

30 mins, 37.1619, -8.4862 🚶⛰️♿🅿️🚊

12 QUEDA DO VIGÁRIO

The name 'Fall of the Vicar' conjures beguiling nymphs and heady sunlight. The waterfall and pool, with its deep cool water, flowery banks and a hidden cave, certainly creates the requisite Pre-Raphaelite backdrop. Inside the cave, stalactites drip like hundreds of guttering candles in a long-forgotten chapel.

→ From Alte head out along the N124 towards the cemetery; at the roundabout go L and park just by the cemetery. Follow the track downhill until you reach the pool below.

10 mins, 37.2317, -8.1792 🏞️🍴♿🚗

13 ALTE VILLAGE POOLS

A quintessential Algarve mountain town with two old stone swimming pools filled by the rivers Fonte Grande and Fonte Pequena.

→ From Loulé take the M525 N to Salir, head W on the N124 to Alte. Arriving at Alte turn R at the sign for Fontes. Park before the bridge.

2 mins, 37.2375, -8.1732 🏖️🚻🍴🚗

ANCIENT EARTH

14 PEGADAS DOS DINOSSÁURIOS, SALEMA

At Praia da Salema, low tide reveals tracks left by dinosaurs 125 million years ago.

The beach itself is busy but the footsteps, further off E, conjure another, wilder, time.

→ Park uphill to W of Salema beach. Wooden walkway down.

5 mins, 37.0644, -8.8265 🔲🅱

15 FÓIA

At 902m this is the highest point of the Algarve. Watch as clouds skim over the mountain tops below and the land stretches out from hills behind to the southern coastline beyond. Bring a prayer pebble to place on top of the pilgrim stones, *mariolas*, left in tiny balanced towers.

→ From Monchique take the N266-3, following signs for Fóia. Park at the church.

5 mins, 37.3154, -8.5924 🔳🔆🔲✝

16 ROCHA DA PENA

Rocha da Pena is a 497m high, steep cornice of very hard limestone rising up out from the Barrocal hills. Its 2km-long plateau is the highest point of the surrounding area and a perfect place for sunset. Its distinct outline is visible from all the surrounding villages and woodland. With luck you might see indigenous Bonelli's eagles wheeling overhead. Its ravine is about 50m high and, after centuries of erosion, there are

many pockets and caverns. If you want to try climbing there are around 15 climbing sectors linked by a 5km walking trail from the Bar das Grutas in the village of Rocha.

→ Free parking in Rua de Rocha da Pena. From here follow the trail for 1km uphill.

15 mins, 37.2503, -8.0977 🔳🔲🚶

WILD RUINS

17 CONVENTO DE NOSSA SENHORA DO DESTERRO

Abandoned by its sisterhood in the 1755 earthquake, the Convent at Monchique is now a sanctuary for wild things. Spiral staircases lead out into clear air, ivy climbs in, and birds nest in the chancel.

→ In Monchique, park in Largo dos Chorões (37.3180, -8.5566) and walk up the steps to the R side; follow brown signs from the church to the Convento above.

15 mins, 37.3199, -8.5595 ✝🔳🔆🔳

18 FORTALEZA DE ALMÁDENA

Yellow ruins face the blue sea. Arabic arches and perhaps a chapel remain. Sit inside and listen to the birdcall and thunderous waves crashing below.

→ From N125 in Budens, turn S opposite the

227

Restaurante Mira Rio, and follow signs to Praia Cabanas Velhas. Fort is signed just before.
2 mins, 37.0673, -8.8044 🚶🏔️📷

19 CASTELO DE PADERNE

The 12th century castle glows yellow as its sandstone and rammed earth walls catch the last of the evening sunlight. This Barrocal hill has been a dwelling place since Lusitanian times (1st century BC). Now there is a signed 4km walking trail looping around the castle.

➔ From Paderne take the N270 W out of town, pass the church and cross the river and follow signs S to Castelo de Paderne.
2 mins, 37.1570, -8.2005 🚶🏔️➕🏛️📷

20 ABICADA ROMAN RUINS

Forgotten Roman ruins are hidden under thickets in this abandoned farm. The 1st century BC villa must once have been a centre of agricultural production, even with its own quay onto the River Alvor. Once-beautiful mosaics once decorated the floors with goblets, branches, wreaths and stars. Chances are the ruins are overgrown, but it is a lovely spot at sunset and perfect for a picnic or an explore.

➔ Turn off the E-bound N125 after Figueira at (37.1619, -8.5952), turning at brown sign to Abicada. Park by railway track, and follow dirt track to the end.
15 mins, 37.1514, -8.5966 🏔️➕📷🚶⛲🐾

WILDLIFE

21 RESERVA RIA DE ALVOR

This reserve covers an area of 1,500ha around the salt marshes of Alvor. From its boardwalks along the beach you can see hundreds of flamingos and walk along cliffs at Quinta do Rocha, and inland along the Alvor river. The area is a haven for birdlife. Call 'A Rocha Life' (see 22) for birding tours.

➔ From Alvor town follow signs to Praia, then Praia Accessivel. Walks begin here. Parking.
30 mins, 37.1234, -8.5962 🚶🏊🏔️📷

22 A ROCHA LIFE BIRDWATCHING

A small company of birdwatching enthusiasts who give tours in the wilder places of the Algarve: lagoons, rivers, abandoned salt pans, dunes or beautiful cliffs. Tailored to your time/place.

➔ Apartado 41, 8501-903 Mexilhoeira Grande +351 282 968 380, Arochalife.pt
1 day, 37.1444, -8.6079 🐦🏔️🚶

HIKING & BIKING

23 BOCA DO RIO – BURGAU

A 5km walking route along the clifftops from Boca do Rio east to Burgau. It is not wonderfully signed but easy to follow and the tracks along the clifftops dip down to the beaches along the way.

➔ Begins at Praia da Boca do Rio (see 4)
1 hr, 37.0660, -8.8094 🚶🐾🏔️

24 TRILHO DA FÓIA

This 7km signed and circular trail will take you through the Monchique hills past strange stones and beautiful views across the Algarve.

➔ Begins and ends at Fóia mountain (see 15). Follow yellow/red markings.
2 hrs, 37.3148, -8.5962 🚶🏔️

LOCAL FOOD

25 RESTAURANTE A CHARRETE, MONCHIQUE

Ancient and local recipes in this bustling restaurant.

➔ R do Dr Samora Gil 30, 8550-461 Monchique +351 282 912 142
37.3200, -8.5558 🍴🍷

26 RESTAURANTE SUL MAR, BENAGIL

A jolly owner with a traditional coastal restaurant. Today's catch brought over to help you choose. Exquisite local food. Enjoy a beer in the sun outside.

➔ Near Praia de Benagil, S of Lagoa. Estrada de Benagil, Lagoa 8400-427 +351 964 458 647
37.0926, -8.4302 🍴🍷

27 RESTAURANTE ASAGRES

A bare-brick, rustic restaurant in Sagres, Portugal's south-western tip or Land's End. Surrounded by the sea, this restaurant does not disappoint with its culinary celebration of the sea's bounty. Try *massinha do mar*, with fish, clams, shrimp, coriander and a little pasta. Just a light plate of clams is a wonderful treat. Save a space for their lemon mousse or homemade desserts. Along the Ecovia do Litoral cycle path.

➔ Av. Infante D Henrique, Sagres +351 282 624 171, A-sagres.com
37.0082, -8.9447 🍴🍷

28 QUINTA DOS VALES, ESTÔMBAR

A winery and vineyards with beautiful sculptures exhibited throughout their gardens. You are encouraged to enjoy their wines and art together. The guiding principle here is the age-old symbiosis between wine and art. Here, both certainly create a sense of the impossible made possible.

→ From Estômabar take Rua 20 de Junho E under N125 for 1km. Sítio dos Vales, 8400-031 Estômbar +351 282 431 036, Quintadosvales.eu

37.1497, -8.4763 ▨▮◪▯

29 RESTAURANTE TÍPICO PONTE ROMANA, SILVES

A quirky restaurant whose rustic decor and collection of little sewing machines have transformed the space almost to a museum. Overlooks the Roman bridge and Arade river from the south. If they have *açorda de bachalau* on, try this delicious brothy codfish stew with chunks of local bread.

→ Parque Ribeirinho de Silves, 8300-131 Silves +351 282 443 275

37.1863, -8.4375 ▨▮◪▯

RUSTIC HAVENS

30 QUINTA DA FIGUEIRINHA, SILVES

Mango, pomegranate and persimmon trees hang their branches over the terrace. The farmhouse is set in quiet countryside, surrounded by olive and carob groves with several pools. There is an oddly incongruous but fun hippy Irish bar at the end of the garden.

→ Quinta da Figueirinha, 8300-028 Silves +351 282 440 700, Qdf.pt

37.1861, -8.4059 ▮◪◪▯▨

31 QUINTA DO MEL

A farmhouse retreat within shooting distance of the coast at Praia de Falésia, west of Vilamoura. The farm grows and brews an array of teas and herbs. Sweet smells of warm carob bread fill the hall. On the terrace, watch the moon rise beneath twinkling stars, darkness untouched by town lights.

→ Quinta Do Mel, 8201-925 Albufeira +351 289 543 674, Quintadomel.com

37.0981, -8.1626 ▮◪◪▯▨

32 QUINTA DO FREIXO

Stay on a working farm with fig orchards, cork and pine woodland, sheep and barley fields. Jams, honeys and carob bread for breakfast.

→ A little W of Rocha da Pena. R de Quinta do Freixo, Benafim-Loulé, 8100-352 Benafim +351 289 472 185, Quintadofreixo.org

37.2610, -8.1235 ▮◪▨▯

WILDER CAMPSITES

33 SALEMA ECO-CAMP SURF & NATURE

A beautiful, green campsite surrounded by the wildlife and flora of the natural park of south-west Alentejo. This camping park is in a naturist-friendly zone near several beaches. Will organise surfing/kayaking/bike activities here and more.

→ Praia da Salema, 8650-196 Budens +351 282 695 201, Salemaecocamp.com

37.0752, -8.8309 ▨▨▨▩▲▨◪

34 QUINTA DE ODELOUCA

Camp out under the stars in this rural campsite surrounded by the peaceful hills on the Algarve/Alentejo border. The Odelouca river is within walking distance.

→ From São Marcos da Serra take the M542 S for 3.5km. +351 282 361718, Quintaodelouca.com

37.3395, -8.3741 ▲◪◪◪

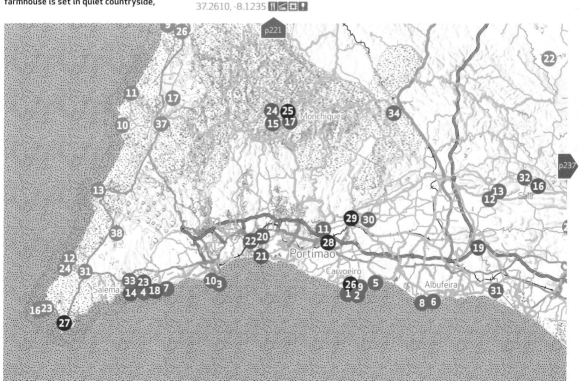

EAST ALGARVE: FARO

Our perfect weekend

→ **Follow** springs, streams and rivers through the lush Benémola woodland

→ **Paint** your bodies with the mineral-rich mud of the Agua Mae salt flats along the Guadiana river

→ **Stand** and wonder at the carved menhirs of Lavajo, set in place on the hills by pre-Celtic ancestors

→ **Watch** for the hundreds of visiting flamingos at the salt marshes of the River Formosa

→ **Run** along the deserted sandy beaches of Ilha da Barreta

→ **Feast** on *caldeirada da patarôxa*, rich dogfish stew, at Olhão harbour

→ **Stargaze** from your tent by the anchor cemetery at Ilha de Tavira

→ **Lace** up your pilgrim boots and trek inland through dusty olive groves along the Via Algarviana

The coastline of the eastern Algarve is characterised by a 50km-long network of sun-drenched dunes and barrier islands which protect the marshes and flooded areas of Ria Formosa from the open sea. Small fishing boats navigate between sea and lagoon through the *barras*, small inlets between the sandy islands.

The region has always depended on coastal and deep-sea fishing, the gathering of molluscs, especially the delicious *amêijoa da ria* or lagoon clam, and salt extraction. Castro Marim with its towering medieval castle, near the Guadiana river mouth, was a Phoenician stopping point and is still surrounded by shimmering salt pans. Roman fish-salting tanks can be found at the forgotten remains of Balsa, near Tavira, a once-heaving port city of the empire.

The migration of birds is particularly visible at the salt pans near the River Formosa, a wonderful place to see hundreds of flamingos. In this area, the frontier between two continents, the lagoons offer birds a stopping point on journeys that for some, like sandpipers, reach as far as the Arctic tundra.

Walk the deserted sands of Ilha Barreta and contemplate the coastline, this meeting point between worlds, with its cycles of sea and land. The chapel, shrines, churches, watchtowers and fortresses that animate the coast, continue inland to wilder reaches of the lesser-known Algarve.

Here the mountainous terrain of Loulé county runs parallel to the Atlantic coastline and reaches its peak in the Serra do Caldeirão mountain range. Cut inland from the coast, and the hills begin to rise with their wild rosemary, cork, olive, carob, oak and chestnut trees.

There are also several springs inland. Fonte Benémola was said to have healing powers and still today miraculously gives water in even the most arid months. Gnarly roots reach the water and, while perhaps not a remedial spring, the water-rich habitat is a haven for kingfishers, moorhens and herons along with frogs, newts and salamanders. The surrounding woodland contains many trails and hidden spots for a river swim or a picnic.

My favourite thing for a picnic is some fresh bread with a smoked sausage, *o chouriço*, from one of the surrounding mountain towns. The *aldeia* Tôr has a festival in January dedicated to smoked meats. It's the perfect amalgam of a land blessed with water, rich vegetation and a love of good food.

RIVERS & WATERFALLS

1 RIBEIRA DE ALGIBRE

In the foothills of Barrocal, just outside the small farming village of Tôr, is this small river crossed by a medieval arched bridge. There is access to a shingle bank and the water is clear, deepening under the bridge.

→ From Aldeia da Tôr take Rua Principal S, turn L on M524 and follow first R until river.

2 mins, 37.1898, -8.0275 🏕🚶🏊⊞

2 FONTE BENÉMOLA, QUERENÇA

Several springs in this natural park flow into the Benémola stream, which was once said to have miraculous healing properties. It is certainly still healing for the surrounding woodland as, even in the hottest, driest months, it gives water to the green vegetation. It remains miraculous in that the spring can produce over four million litres of water an hour. Green light filters through the leaves and gnarly roots bend into the stream. There are several signed walkways through the woods.

→ From Loulé take the N396 to Querença, follow brown signs to Fonte Benémola. Park at the entrance and walk.

30 mins, 37.2086, -8.0092 🏕🚶🏕🏊

3 PRAIA FLUVIAL DO PEGO FUNDO

A beautiful river beach with sandy banks in the meanders of the Cadavais stream just before it joins the widening River Guadiana.

→ Follow brown signs from the centre of Alcoutim. Parking.

5 mins, 37.4721, -7.4768 🏖B🏕🍴🤿

4 PEGO DO INFERNO

A waterfall dashes out between rocks and knotted vegetation into a deep green pool. Formed by the River Asseca before it joins the River Gilão, this swim spot is just inland from the Tavira coast. Several legends surround its depths: that a wagon and rider fell in but their bodies never surfaced, that secret flooded cavities lead to the River Guadiana and that the bottom can never be touched. The place suffered fire damage in 2012 but is gradually recovering.

→ From Asseca take M514-2 for 2km until crossroads. Turn L then R after 10m. Park here, then walk.

2 mins, 37.1553, -7.6960 📷🍴🤿

ISLANDS & HARBOURS

5 ALDEIA DE MARIM

Quiet lapping waves and waterfront with tiny boats and fishermen. Nice for a quiet paddle or swim in shallow water.

→ Turn into the *aldeia* from the N125 (signposted in Marim), head straight down and cross the railway, continue to the water's edge. Park at the small pier.

1 min, 37.0364, -7.7963 🤿

6 ILHA DA FUSETA

A relaxed waterfront with hundreds of small fishing vessels, a bar and sandy walks out to the island at low tide. Sandbanks create shallow swims with warm water, making it perfect for children.

→ From Olhão take the N125 E, and after 7km turn R following signs for Fuseta. Parking.

10 mins, 37.0512, -7.7437 ⛵🤿

7 ILHA DA BARRETA

Also known as Ilha da Deserta, this is one of the wilder islands around the Ria Formosa Natural Reserve. You can gather shells or conches along this 7km coastal strip, also a haven for birdlife. A signed, circular 3km walk begins at the jetty.

→ Easily reached from Faro: regular ferries from Porta Nova pier.

30 mins, 36.9692, -7.9245 🏕🤿🍴🚶🏊

8

10

8 ILHA DE TAVIRA

Sea winds sing through the pine trees lining the edge of a narrow railway track and footpath leading to this island. The wilder side, beyond the anchor graveyard, is Praia do Barril, which is a naturist beach.

→ From Tavira head W on the N125, after 7km turn L at signs for Ilha de Tavira and park along the road. Walk down to the bridge, cross and continue along the track.

15 mins, 37.0842, -7.6659 ⬛🚶🚳

WILD WALKS

9 SETE FONTES WALKING TRAIL

A 9km signed, circular walking trail which, as the name suggests, passes seven springs. A beautiful walk through the dappled green Barrocal hills and into the protected woodland of Benémola. The way passes deep wells, and follows the Menalva stream to Benémola spring. From there it passes Olho waterfall and underground mines supplying water at Cerca Nova. The walk ends with the seventh fountain at Fonte da Silva and mountain views from Corcitos. It passes the Querença hunting grounds, so take care on days when hunting is permitted: Thursdays, Sundays and public holidays.

→ From Loulé head towards Querença until you see a sign to Salir, where you turn R. Pass the village of Corcitos and after 300m walk is signed on your R.

2.5 hrs, 37.2183, -7.9974 🖼🏔🏕🚶🚰

10 VIA ALGARVIANA

The Via Algarviana is a 300km long-distance walking route starting at Alcoutim in the north-eastern Algarve and ending in the south-western tip at Cabo de São Vicente. There are several places you can join this route between Alcoutim and Salir in Eastern Algarve. It will take you along the Guadiana river and into the rugged hills of Loulé, passing the ancient menhirs of Lavajo, magical woodland and traditional villages.

→ Begin at the pier in Alcoutim. Maps and information at Viaalgarviana.org.

10 days, 37.4718, -7.4710 🏕🏔🚶

11 BARRANCO DO VELHO WALKING TRAIL

This 5km signed, circular route takes you through the cork plantations or *montados* that dominate the Serra do Caldeirão mountain range. Enjoy stunning views of this area. There is also a little handicraft shop in the village with gifts based on cork, clay and honey, as well as *medronho* spirit.

→ Take the N124 into Barranco do Velho and park outside Gabinete Técnico Florestal.

2 hrs, 37.2366, -7.9377 🖼🏔🚶🏕🍴

12 GUADIANA ROUTE GR15

This is a 65km signed and linear route that follows the Guadiana from Alcoutim to its mouth at Vila Real de Santo António. Here it connects with the Ecovia do Litoral (see p218). The route takes in the three Algarve terrains of coastal landscape, Barrocal limestone and the northern mountains. It has

many picnic spots, views and river dips along the way.

→ Follow yellow signage from the harbour at V.R de Santo António (37.1967, -7.4145) or from Alcoutim (37.4715, -7.4725).
3 days, 37.4715, -7.4725 🏊🚶🏕⛰🚣

BIRDLIFE & WETLANDS

13 AGUÁ MAE, CASTRO MARIM

You can take a mud bath in the mineral-rich clay of the Guadiana and ancient salt flats within the Marshland Nature Reserve of Castro Marim and Vila Real de Santo António. The traditional *flor de sal*, salt crystals, are gathered here.

→ Salinas de Castro Marim N122, 8950 Castro Marim +351 965 404 888, Aguamae.pt
2 mins, 37.2138, -7.4361 🏖

14 RIA FORMOSA NATURAL PARK

Explore the pine forest and salty wetlands home to egrets, storks, curlews and flamingos, to name but a few. There is also a restored tidal mill and several walking paths to choose.

→ From Olhão take N125 E and turn R after the campsite. Follow brown signs. Parking.
40 mins, 37.0339, -7.8192 🚗🍴🚶

15 BALSA

There is little to be seen here in terms of ruins, but a magic stillness hangs over the air of this once-bustling Roman port now given over to the birdlife of the Ria Formosa lagoons and salt marshes.

→ From Luz de Tavira take the road to the station and park. Cross the tracks carefully and walk down the road opposite for 700m to the riverbank.
15 mins, 37.0830, -7.6970 🚗⛰🍴

STANDING STONES & CASTLES

16 MENIRES DO LAVAJO

Three carved menhirs, dating to around 3,500BC, stand on Lavajo hill just outside Alcoutim. Whether they designate ancient farming territory or sacred space, they command respect.

→ Follow signs from Alcoutim; at signs for the ceramic factory turn L, follow the dirt track, taking the R fork along PR route. Parking.
10 mins, 37.5016, -7.5349 🏖⛰🐾

17 CASTELO DE CASTRO MARIM

This medieval castle was once a marooned island where ships could drop anchor. Now you can explore the ruins, chambers and

battlements with views over the reflective salt flats below. Visit in August for a huge medieval re-enactment festival with street theatre, banquets and music.

→ Follow signs from Castro Marim to the castle; parking outside.
2 mins, 37.2189, -7.4418 🚗🏛🐾

MOUNTAINS & VILLAGES

18 BELICHE DE CIMA

A tiny *aldeia*, typical of the Algarve farming community unchanged for generations. Winding lanes and enduring hills, a perfect

place for a walk in the wild.

→ From Tavira take the N397 N for 20km. Turn onto the M506 after Portela de Corcha and follow for 4.5km.

2 mins, 37.2643, -7.6654 🚻🚶⛰

19 CACELA VELHA

An old fishing village on a hill overlooking the Ria Formosa lagoons. There was once a 10th century Moorish castle here, but the current fortress is 18th century.

→ At the right side of the church, follow the steps down straight into the park. Visit in mid-July for the Noites da Moura Encantada festivities with music, street food and artists paying tribute to its Arabic heritage.

2 mins, 37.1599, -7.5462 🚻🍴

LOCAL FOOD

20 RESTAURANTE DE QUERENÇA

A mix of regional Alentejano and Algarve dishes. Cosy inside, with nooks and small tables. There are local variations on regional dishes such as *galinho cerejada*, chicken stewed with *chouriço*, bacon and parsley, *cherem com fritada de porco preto*, black pig with tortilla, *feijoada de javali*, wild boar stew, as well as a good selection of local wines.

→ Largo da Igreja 1, Querença, Loulé +351 917 368 108

37.1988, -7.9871 🍴🍷

21 RESTAURANTE VISTA FORMOSA, OLHÃO

This is the locals' restaurant where fish is grilled outside in the courtyard as everyone sits at covered tables. Try the *caldeirada da patarôxa*, a brothy dogfish stew; it's delicious. If you're lucky the chef might bring you a bowl of *xerém*, a maize-porridge made with fish stock.

→ Just down the road from the entrance to the Ria Formosa Natural Park (Olhão side) (see 14). Pinheiros de Marim, 8700 Olhão-Marim

37.0329, -7.8221 🍴🍷🐟

22 CANTARINHA DA GUADIANA

A great mix of regional dishes, with the signature Algarve orange and coriander garnishes, at this rural restaurant overlooking the Guadiana river.

→ 9.5km S of Alcoutim. Rua da Laranjeiras 26, 8970-029 Alcoutim +351 281 547 196

37.4031, -7.4579 🍴🍷⛰

23 FESTA DE SÃO LUÍS, TÔR

The ancient village of Tôr, in the foothills of the Barrocal mountains, comes alive for this feast day to the patron saint of animals, São Luís. In true Portuguese spirit, the animals are celebrated with a festival to *chouriço*, smoked sausages. Everyone, visitors and villagers alike, is invited to the open church eucharist and afterwards to try a *chouriço*, drizzled with local wine. Late January.

→ Aldeia da Tôr, Loulé

37.1954, -8.0350 🍴🍷🚻

24 OLHÃO FISH MARKET

A buzzing fish market with hundreds of choices from today's catch, all at a good price. Located at Olhão harbour.

→ Av. 5 de Outubro, 8700-515 Olhão

37.0238, -7.8406 🍴🐟

25 NUNO'S BAR AND GRILL

A simple traditional bar and grill facing the harbour in Fuseta but they do serve an excellent *sopa da pedra* (stone soup).

→ R. Gen. Humberto Delgado C, 8700-011 Fuseta +351 289 791 499

37.0537, -7.7463 🍴📷

RUSTIC HAVENS

26 FAZENDA NOVA

An elegant retreat, 9km north of Fuseta, with a mischievously curated art and design collection. The ten-suite house is surrounded by cleverly designed gardens with secret paths leading to wilder olive groves. This is an upmarket retreat in harmony with nature. The olive oil they produce has an intense flavour and is a real elixir to match the haven they have created.

→ Estiramantens, Santo Estevao, 8800-504 Tavira, +351 281 961 913, Fazendanova.eu

37.1211, -7.7553 🍴🍷⛰🏊

27 CASA DE CAMPO DO VALE DO ASNO

A beautiful family-run farmhouse with ten rooms in the uplands of wilder Algarve, 5km north of Vila Nova de Cacela. Bedroom doors open out to a flower-filled garden with a biological pool and views over the hills.

→ Vila Nova, Vale do Asno-Castro Marim +351 918 778 902, Casacampovaledoasno.pt

37.2068, -7.5295 🍴⛰📷

28 HERDADE DA CORTE

A grand but welcoming country estate, some 15km north-west of Tavira. It has a high-ceilinged hall, fireplaces, swimming pool and terraces complete with elegant daybeds, all surrounded by spectacular views across the wooded valley. Monthly jazz and blues

nights are held here with live bands, popular for locals and guests, but it's also a perfect place for stargazing with a glass of wine.

→ Sitio da Corte, 8800-166 Tavira
+351 281 971 625, Herdadedacorte.com
37.1620, -7.7425 ▦🏔🖼🍴♟☢

FARMS & CAMPING

29 QUINTA DA FORNALHA
A holistic and sustainable eco-farm just outside Castro Marim, run by a family whose ancestors moved here 250 years ago. There are several guesthouses from which to choose, surrounded by orange trees, gardens and farmland. Organic products, fruit, vegetables and homemade food all on offer. A voluntary programme also available in exchange for accommodation with tasks such as building shelter for animals, labelling products or painting.

→ Quinta da Fornalha, 8950-186 Castro Marim
+351 917 107 147, Quinta-da-fornalha.com
37.1986, -7.4832 🏔▦🖼🍴🍃

30 PARQUE DE CAMPISMO DA ILHA DE TAVIRA
A simple campsite surrounded by dunes on this long island stretching away from Ria Formosa. Wake at dawn for a swim and stroll along the deserted sandy beaches.

→ Ilha de Tavira, 8800 Tavira
+351 281 320 580, Cm-tavira.pt
37.1135, -7.6210 🅱️🚤⛵🍴

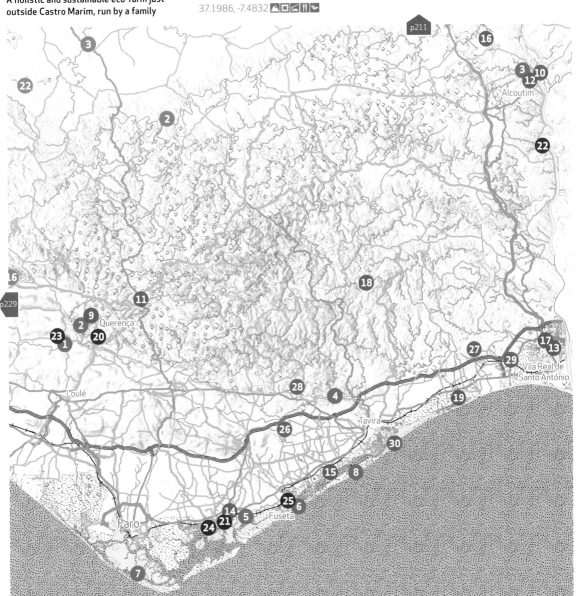

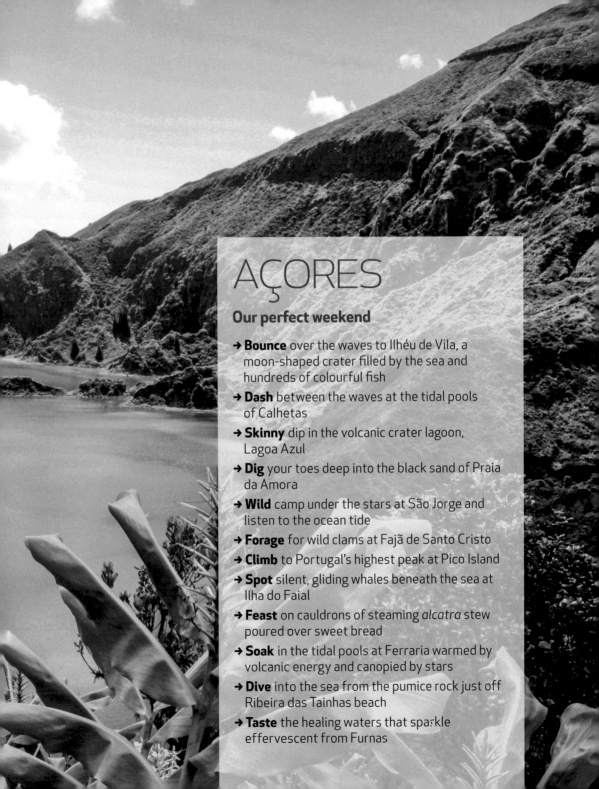

AÇORES

Our perfect weekend

→ **Bounce** over the waves to Ilhéu de Vila, a moon-shaped crater filled by the sea and hundreds of colourful fish

→ **Dash** between the waves at the tidal pools of Calhetas

→ **Skinny** dip in the volcanic crater lagoon, Lagoa Azul

→ **Dig** your toes deep into the black sand of Praia da Amora

→ **Wild** camp under the stars at São Jorge and listen to the ocean tide

→ **Forage** for wild clams at Fajã de Santo Cristo

→ **Climb** to Portugal's highest peak at Pico Island

→ **Spot** silent, gliding whales beneath the sea at Ilha do Faial

→ **Feast** on cauldrons of steaming *alcatra* stew poured over sweet bread

→ **Soak** in the tidal pools at Ferraria warmed by volcanic energy and canopied by stars

→ **Dive** into the sea from the pumice rock just off Ribeira das Tainhas beach

→ **Taste** the healing waters that sparkle effervescent from Furnas

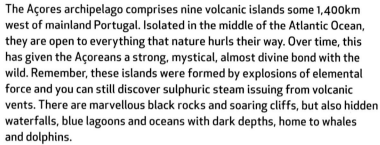

The Açores archipelago comprises nine volcanic islands some 1,400km west of mainland Portugal. Isolated in the middle of the Atlantic Ocean, they are open to everything that nature hurls their way. Over time, this has given the Açoreans a strong, mystical, almost divine bond with the wild. Remember, these islands were formed by explosions of elemental force and you can still discover sulphuric steam issuing from volcanic vents. There are marvellous black rocks and soaring cliffs, but also hidden waterfalls, blue lagoons and oceans with dark depths, home to whales and dolphins.

At Furnas on the island of São Miguel, muddy clay bubbles, pops and hisses within the crater. Locals bury pots of *cozido* stew in the steaming earth which slow-cooks it to perfection in this wild kitchen. Sulphuric fountains, some sparkling and others sweet, spring from the earth and mingle in healing bathing pools. Sit close enough to the steaming Pêro Botelho fumarole and you can hear Earth's heartbeat. The ancient energy of the islands resides in a sense of things bubbling under the surface.

Tidal pools are warmed by volcanic energy on the wild Ferraria coast on São Miguel. Visit at night to swim in a dark pool under the stars, warm as a bath, and feel the tug and give of the ocean. This submerged energy surfaces in Açorean legends. Some claim the Açores as the location for the lost island of Atlantis, others that the beautiful lagoon of Sete Cidades and its crowning peaks are all that survive of a flooded kingdom. Perhaps such myths took root with the brief emergence of a tenth island, Sabrina, along with immense clouds of smoke, in 1811. A Union Jack flag was hoisted, the island's ownership was disputed and, after two months, arguments were resolved as it sunk back into the sea.

Even the food resembles volcanoes, from the delicious barnacles and limpets like fresh, salty craters, and *alcatra* stews bubbling in earthen pots, to the *cozido* stew tasting of sulphur. On the island of Pico, Verdelho grapes are ripened under walls of volcanic stone. At sunset, relax with a glass of white wine and look out across your island, resembling a sleeping dragon, nose pointing out to sea.

TIDAL POOLS

1 PISCINAS NATURAIS, SÃO MIGUEL

These tidal pools are formed along the coast, just outside Calhetas, in the lava frozen mid-flow before the sea. The water is crystal clear as there is no sand. Step inside, between the waves, at low tide for a glorious swim.

→ In Calhetas follow signs to Piscinas Naturais and then signs to Zona Balnear.

10 mins, 37.8238, -25.6064

2 PISCINAS NATURAIS CANEIROS, SÃO MIGUEL

Tidal pools formed by the volcanic rock along the coast. Some of the pools get very deep, make sure you come at low tide when they are calm. Great for wild waves at high tide. Sunbathe on the warm rocks to dry off.

→ From Mosteiros walk 300m N along the coast.

3 mins, 37.8981, -25.8222

3 BISCOITOS, TERCEIRA

Volcanic rocks form wild sculptural forms and tidal pools on the N coast of Terceira.

→ From Biscoitos town take the road down towards the beach.

2 mins, 38.8027, -27.2571

4 POÇA DO SIMÃO DIAS, SÃO JORGE

The lava field of Fajã do Ouvidor along the N coast of São Jorge is slowly eroding. Many caves and grottoes have been formed as the sea encroaches on the rocks, as well as tidal pools, the largest of which is Poça de Simão Dias. The water is deep and crystal clear, perfect for a wild dive and snorkelling.

→ From the village of Norte Grande head W to the coast.

10 mins, 38.6786, -28.0552

5 SANTA CRUZ DA GRACIOSA

Several tidal pools in the volcanic rocks provide sheltered swims. Nearby is a small fishing harbour.

→ Take the N1-2 into Santa Cruz da Graciosa and turn towards the coast after Rent-a-Car-Graciosa.

1 min, 39.0872, -28.0073

6 CARAPACHO, GRACIOSA

A 19th century spa by the sea with warm, sulphurous water (between 36C and 40C) which has been used for rheumatism and skin diseases down the ages. There are also tidal pools, open to all, with crystal clear water.

→ Rua Doutor Manuel de Sousa Menezes,

Carapacho, 9880-152 Santa Cruz da Graciosa +351 295 730 505, Graciosahotel.com

2 mins, 39.0127, -27.9593

7 SANTA CRUZ DAS FLORES PISCINAS NATURAIS

Several tidal pools in black rocks provide safe oases for a swim. Views out across sea to the mysterious Corvo island.

→ Take the R1-2 into Santa Cruz and follow brown signs for the pools.

2 mins, 39.4593, -31.1265

HOT SPRINGS

8 PONTA DA FERRARIA, SÃO MIGUEL

Here the cliffs give way to a wide black belt of volcanic stone, a *fajã*, level with the sea. The rocks arch to form wild bridges where the waves crash under. But only 20m beneath this bedrock stirs molten lava and magma. At low tide, large rock pools fill with seawater warmed by bouts of heat issuing from these volcanic sea caves. Come at night, low tide, and take a dip under a canopy of stars. Feel the hot and cool waters mingle around you as you gaze up at the heavens and hold onto a tight rope as your body is gently pulled back and forth by the tide. There is an excellent

12

11

restaurant in the spa nearby with rich regional dishes and Açorean wines. Try the *alcatra*, Açorean pot roast, made with octopus, dark red meat or beans. A healing place.

→ Take the N9-1A N past Ginetes, turn L at signs for Ferraria. Park by the Termas and walk down the steps to the L of the swimming pool to the natural pools. Rua Ilha Sabrina, Ginetes, 9555-102 Ginetes +351 296 295 669, Termasferraria.com

2 mins 37.8603, -25.8538 🏖️🌊🍴📍

9 TERRA NOSTRA, SÃO MIGUEL

There has been a garden in the Furnas valley

for over 200 years but this valley is, in fact, a crater over 7km in diameter. Furnas became popular towards the end of the 18th century, due to the growing interest in the use of mineral water to treat health problems. It has hundreds of small springs and streams, all with different properties. The Terra Nostra garden is located in the midst of this crater's magnificent water system. Take a dip in their warm, muddy sulphuric swimming pool or explore the gardens and volcanic flora.

→ From Furnas follow signs for Terra Nostra. 15 mins, 37.7729, -25.3145 🏖️🍴🌊€

10 POÇA DA DONA BEIJA, SÃO MIGUEL

A network of five different hot springs of varying temperatures and health properties. The pools, streams and tumbling waters are outside, under willow trees. Plenty of places to rest and relax.

→ Take the N1-1A into Furnas. Lomba Das Barracas, 9675-044 Furnas +351 296 584 256, Pocadadonabeija.com 2 mins 37.7692, -25.3190 🌊€

SURF & COVES

11 PRAIA DA SANTA BÁRBARA, SÃO MIGUEL

Big waves at this surfers' beach and also

popular with bodyboarders. To the W of this beach, where the black rocks start, are hidden bunkers constructed under these rocks in 1942 to house artillery. You can explore a little of their remains, and look out to the bright beach from their dark casements. For surfing lessons/boards: Azores Surf Center +351 915 970 726, azoressurfcenter.com. Or skyxpedition@gmail.com for paragliding.

→ From Ribeira Grande follow signs. 2 mins, 37.8166, -25.5490 🍴🏖️

12 PRAIA DA VILA FRANCA DO CAMPO, SÃO MIGUEL

A black sand beach just up from the harbour. There are a couple of cafés and, although less wild, a safe stretch of sand with much smaller waves.

→ From Vila Franca do Campo follow signs to the harbour and walk E from here. 10 mins, 37.7168, -25.4276 🏖️🌊🍴

13 PRAIA DA RIBEIRA QUENTE, SÃO MIGUEL

A stretch of blackish-grey sandy beach under dramatic hills, where the Ribeira Quente meets the sea. It's known as the 'Hot River' as its waters are warmed by the volcanic springs at Furnas. A protected beach with a number of little cafés and big, rolling waves.

16

→ Take the N2-2A into Ribeira Quente and follow signs for Praia. Parking.
1 min, 37.7338, -25.3013 🍴✎

14 PRAIA DE AGUA D'ALTO, SÃO MIGUEL
A sandy cove with views of the steep wooded hills while you take a dip.
→ From Agua de Alto follow signs to 'Praia'.
2 mins, 37.7157, -25.4636 🅱✎⚓🍴

SECRET BEACHES

15 PRAIA DOS MOSTEIROS, SÃO MIGUEL
This is a black sand beach and, although fairly empty, is popular mostly with locals. There are views out to four mysterious rocks called Ilhéus dos Mosteiros, so called as they resemble traditional Celtic sea monasteries. The sun sets just behind them.
→ From Mosteiros follow the road to the shore.
4 mins, 37.8880, -25.8238 ✎⊞◻

16 RIBEIRA DAS TAINHAS, SÃO MIGUEL
A black sand beach in a tiny cove between cliffs. Within easy swimming distance is a black rocky island jutting up from the waves. Locals jump from its many ledges.
→ From Ribeira das Tainhas town follow signs

to Praia. Parking.
3 mins, 37.7165, -25.4102 ✎🍴◻🐚

17 PRAIA DA AMORA, SÃO MIGUEL
This is a wild, black sand beach beneath the cliffs and rock strata. A beautiful place to gather the *pau santo*, the sacred and deeply scented wood which falls from the trees. It has big, crashing waves and is a good place to collect a pumice stone.
→ Signed off the M527 from Ponta Garça. Park by the old fountain and walk down dirt track. After 300m turn R down steps.
10 mins, 37.7220, -25.3566 ✎✎⚠⊞◻

18 PRAIA DA AREIA, CORVO
This is the only sand beach on the island of Corvo. A sheltered little cove with sand grey from the volcanic ash and eroded basaltic rock.
→ From Vila do Corvo follow signs W towards Praia.
1 min, 39.6731, -31.1216 ✎✎

HIDDEN WATERFALLS

19 A BARQUINHA, SÃO MIGUEL
A rocky promontory formed by lava flow and accessed along a dramatic cliff-side path.

15

The Ribeira do Preto cascades alongside the path and reaches the sea, forming several small pools along its way. According to the chronicler Gaspar Frutuoso (1522-1591) it was once called the 'Black Cave' and a mysterious hermit lived here. Seagulls wheel overhead, heather and lichen cover the rocks and seaweed is caught in the clear waves. A perfect hermit's refuge.
→ From Lomba da Maia follow signs to Praia da Viola and park at (37.8396, -25.3591) when you reach the cliffs. Follow walking signs for Praia da Viola.
5 mins, 37.8401, -25.3618 👤🧍⚠✎◻

20 PARQUE NATURAL DA RIBEIRA DAS CALDEIRÕES, SÃO MIGUEL

Here you can find the Cascata da Achada waterfall, with its thundering freshness, but also several smaller waterfalls falling into natural pools. It has paths and a café, tended flora and an old watermill. There are private and secluded spaces for a dip and, although it is a tended park, its preservation of nature's wilder beauty is enchanting.

→ Follow signs towards Achada on the N1-1A; at Achada take the road inland and follow signs. Parking.

15 mins, 37.8421, -25.2672 ⚡🚻🚶🍴🚏

21 SALTO DO CABRITO, SÃO MIGUEL

Known as the 'Goat's Leap', this is a waterfall darting over 40m-high rocks like an arrow into the glassy, green pool below, bordered by ferns and slippery stones. Steep stairs follow the sheer rock up to a narrow bridge over the gorge. The stream sparkles through dense woodland.

→ From Ribeira Grande take the N5-2A towards Lagoa do Fogo; after 3km there is a sign to your L. Follow track until parking and walk upstream. The stairs lead from behind the hydropower plant.

2 mins, 37.7965, -25.4989 🚗🍴🚻🚶🏔🔽

22 RIBEIRA DO MALOÁS, SANTA MARIA

A strange geological formation which resulted from contact of the sea with a flow of lava. The rocks resemble a row of giant eels standing bolt upright. A waterfall plunges 20m over them and rushes down over its steps and ledges to the sea ahead.

→ From Malbusca take the coastal road S for 1km. Look out on R for short walking path.

10 mins, 36.9305, -25.0649 📱🔵🏖

23 CASCATA DO AVEIRO, SANTA MARIA

This waterfall streams over 100m of lichen and sheer rock into a deep pool. It flows on to fill several other tiers of bathing pools.

→ From Santo Espírito take the EN1-2A to the SE tip of the island, follow road L and N up the coast for 3km, park at end of road.

1 min, 36.9481, -25.0212 🏔🔽

24 FAJÃ DA CALDEIRA DE SANTO CRISTO, SÃO JORGE

This low, green belt of land, level with the sea is a special ecological area, and the only place in the archipelago where clams, a local delicacy, grow. There is a beautiful waterfall and pool along a signed walk from here. The blue lagoon and beach is also a sanctuary for

bodyboarding and surfing.

→ From Fajã da Caldeira follow signs to beach.
5 mins, 38.6269, -27.9281 🏊🅿⛰🏄

25 CASCATA DO POÇO DO BACALHAU, FLORES

A monumental waterfall slicing between craggy peaks and rushing into a myriad of cascades to fill a deep green bathing pool.

→ From Fajã Grande take the road N for 1km. The waterfall is on your R.
2 mins, 39.4586, -31.2561 🍴🏞🏊🔆🔅

SKINNY DIPS

26 CASCATA DA RIBEIRA DA SALGA, SÃO MIGUEL

A secret waterfall, little known, tumbling over thick rock strata to fill a bathing pool. Hidden by a deep grassy valley, it faces the sea. Follow the stream, jumping over rocks, until its journey ends at the beach 200m away.

→ From the coastal road from Salga to Lomba de Maia (37.8497, -25.3120) follow signs for Miradouro da Rocha. Park at the viewpoint and follow steep road downhill.
10 mins, 37.8573, -25.3073 🏊⛰🔆🍴🍷🅿🏖

27 LAGOA AZUL, SÃO MIGUEL

The blue lake, forming half of the Sete Cidades lagoon, where a wild peninsula reaches out into the water which fills the impressive volcanic crater and makes a perfect spot for a skinny dip. Deserted but for the birds; a path through woodland leads down to gently lapping water.

→ From N9-1 S, turn R before the bridge separating the two lakes and keep L. Park after 500m and walk down.
5 mins, 37.8602, -25.7841 🏞⛰🏊🏖

WILDLIFE WONDERS

28 SETE LAGOAS, FLORES

Within the wide and flowering volcanic cauldron of Flores, the *caldeira*, are seven lakes named for their features: Lagoas Funda, Branca, Seca, Comprida, Rasa, Lomba and Negra (Deep, White, Dry, Long, Shallow, Crest and Black Lakes, respectively). The last is 100m deep. There is a 7km linear walk passing some of these lakes and ends at beautiful Poço do Bacalhau in Fajã Grande.

→ The walk begins at the *miradouro* (viewpoint) between Caldeira Negra and Lagoa Comprida. Follow the path which skirts the lagoon.
3 hrs, 39.4397, -31.2239 🚶⛰🏊🏖

29 WHALES & DOLPHINS, SÃO MIGUEL

The Azores are currently one of the world's largest whale sanctuaries. Take a fishing boat out, along with a marine biologist, to see resident and migrant species, common and rare, that can be spotted around these islands. For those who want to plunge in, swimming with dolphins is also an option.

→ Contact Futurismo +351 296 628 522 Futurismo.pt or Picos de Aventura +351 912 525 356 Picosdeaventura.com. Both companies leave from the harbour of Ponta Delgada and must be pre-booked.
3 hrs, 37.7396, -25.6648 🚤

The green lake which forms half of the Sete Cidades lagoon, there's a picnic park and a fountain of fresh mountain water here. Take a dip in the cool, deep lake and look up at the wooded sides of the volcanic crater. A 17km circular walking trail around Sete Cidades passes along here.

→ From N9-1 S, head to Sete Cidades and turn L before the bridge over the lakes. Follow as far as picnic park.

1 min, 37.8446, -25.7846

32 LAGOA DO FOGO, SÃO MIGUEL

A blue lagoon reflecting the sky from the Água de Pau crater. Take a scrabbly track down through flowering bush and scrub to the still blue water. A perfect swim with long stretches of pebbly beaches and a dense overpowering silence.

→ From Ribeira Grande take the N5-2A to Lagoa do Fogo. Park at the signed viewpoint and walk down.

15 mins, 37.7626, -25.4925

33 ILHÉU DE VILA, SÃO MIGUEL

Bounce over the waves to Ilhéu de Vila, an island off an island, with wild fig trees and a turquoise lagoon. Its horseshoe-shaped volcanic crater is filled by seawater. Bring

30 WHALE & DOLPHIN WATCHING, FAIAL

Hortacetáceos is a local company based in Horta with a resident marine biologist who accompanies you on the small boat. The sea here is home to many different species, so keep a beady eye out for Risso's dolphins and pilot whales.

→ Cais de Sta. Cruz, Marina da Horta, 9900 Horta +351 292 391 942, Hortacetaceos.com

3 hrs, 38.5293, -28.6266

CRATER LAGOONS

31 LAGOA VERDE, SÃO MIGUEL

goggles, there are hundreds of colourful fish.

→ Boats leave every hour from the harbour at Vila Franca do Campo and cost about €5.

15 mins, 37.7057, -25.4445

PICNIC PARKS

34 PARQUE DE MERENDAS, O TÚNEL, SÃO MIGUEL

A picnic park by the banks of Lagoa Azul. From here the discharge tunnel, built in 1937 to maintain the water levels of Sete Cidades, leads off to Mosteiros on the coast. A peaceful place with a little cave hidden to one side.

→ From Sete Cidades village follow the road along the W edge of Lagoa Azul for 1km.

2 mins, 37.8753, -25.7901

35 PARQUE DAS FRECHAS, TERCEIRA

A little picnic park by the Ribeira da Agualva stream. There are several tumbling waterfalls and a shady lawn.

→ Facing the church in Agualva, turn L down Rua dos Moinhos and walk for 800m.

3 mins, 38.7687, -27.1819

36 MIRADOURO DA BALEIA, SÃO MIGUEL

Known as the 'Whale Lookout Point', from

34

this peak you can survey great swathes of deep sea and easily imagine the dip and flick of a whale's fins. Several BBQs, picnic tables and fountains for communal use.

→ Signed from Algarvia.
1 min, 37.8516, -25.2312 🎪🛥

37 LOMBA DO CAVALEIRO, SÃO MIGUEL

A dramatic spot for a picnic on green grass overlooking fields towards the Atlantic Ocean and the Povoação valley.

→ From Povoação take the coastal road W for 3km towards Ribeira Quente. On your L.
2 mins, 37.7491, -25.2691 🎪🏔

38 MIRADOURO DA MADRUGADA, SÃO MIGUEL

This beautifully kept picnic place overlooks the ocean to the east. Come for a spectacular dawn over a blushing sea. Fountains and stone tables are hidden beneath oak trees.

→ Take the N1-1A S from Nordeste for 8km. Signed, parking.
1 min, 37.7891, -25.1465 🎪🏔📷

39 MIRADOURO DA FONTE GRANDE, SÃO MIGUEL

A beautiful picnic park overlooking the

Capelas cliffs, perfect for a sunrise. There is also a spring with sweet, cool drinking water.

→ Signed off the N1-1A between Santo António and Santa Bárbara.
3 mins, 37.8701, -25.7080 🎪📷

40 RESERVA DAS FONTINHAS, SANTA MARIA

A cool and tranquil woodland reserve with many trails and secret picnic spots at Pico Alto, the island's highest point.

→ From Almagreira take the N1-2A for 4km and look for signs. Parking.
3 mins, 36.9618, -25.0754 🚶🎪🛥

CLIFFS & PEAKS

41 RIBEIRINHA, SÃO MIGUEL

Cliffs fall away into the crashing Atlantic and a silver stream gushes over the edge, droplets are wind-flung and dashed into a mist.

→ From Ribeira Grande take the coastal road up along the cliffs and over the small roundabout. Park and walk 500m.
5 mins, 37.8339, -25.5076 📷🏔🍴

42 MONTANHA DA PICO, PICO

The giant volcanic Mount Pico can be seen

41

from almost every corner of Pico and various points of neighbouring islands. A 2,351m high basaltic stratovolcano and the highest point in Portugal. In its main crater is the lava cone Piquinho with many permanent, smoking fumaroles. There is a 4km trail up to the top of Pico. It is a challenge to reach this magnificent peak but the feeling of having conquered Pico is worth the effort.

→ Begin the walk at Cabeço das Cabras, the 1,231m peak in São Caetano parish. From São Caetano town, take the road N and the walk is signed after 9 km.
5 hrs, 38.4706, -28.4265 🚶🏔➕🏕

(44)

(45)

43 TORRE DE VIGIA, SÃO MIGUEL

A beautiful lookout tower over the Capelas cliffs as far as Calhetas. Just downhill there is a wonderful, upcycled bathroom made from two upturned fishing boat prows.

→ Turn into Capelas centro, then follow brown signs for miradouro. Park at bottom of coastal hill and walk up 300m.

2 mins, 37.8408, -25.6836 ▣▲⊞

44 PONTA DO ESCALVADO, SÃO MIGUEL

Amazing place to watch the cliffs turn pink and the Ilhéu dos Mosteiros darken at sunset.

→ From Várzea take coastal road N for 800m.

1 min, 37.8714, -25.8415 ▣⊼

VOLCANIC CRATERS

45 CALDEIRA DO VULCÃO DAS FURNAS, SÃO MIGUEL

Several cavities in the earth, with bubbling fumaroles or steaming pot-holes, crown the top of Furnas' volcanic rocks. This is the closest you can get to what feels like a sleeping dragon. These sulphuric springs and steams have long been known to have medicinal properties: breathe in the healing steams as they blow your way. A number of hot springs and cool fountains mingle their waters in streams running nearby. Some springs are sparkling, some sulphuric and others a mix.

→ From Furnas follow signs to Caldeiras signed off N1-1A. Parking. Walk downhill for the springs and follow steam for the fumaroles.

10 mins, 37.7726, -25.3043 ⚶◉❙❙

46 LAGOA DAS FURNAS, SÃO MIGUEL

A quiet lake with unquiet fumaroles. Listen to the rumble, bubble and hiss of the volcanic heat released through the ground. This is nature's very own kitchen: here locals bury *cozido* stews in the fumaroles, to be slow-cooked over the course of six hours in sulphuric heat. You can bring your own stew to cook (€3) or visit a nearby restaurant which brings their *cozido* to cook here. There are long picnic tables in shady woodland nearby.

→ Take the road along the N side of the lake, park and walk down.

2 mins, 37.7675, -25.3319 ⊞€⊞

47 CALDEIRA DE PÊRO BOTELHO, SÃO MIGUEL

An ancient fumarole with many legends: one is that of Pêro Botelho, an evil man who many years ago fell into this muddy, slippery volcano vent. He never returned and his echoing cries led to it being known as 'Boca do Inferno', Hell's Mouth. If you stand close, and stay quiet, you can hear a distant thud, like Earth's heartbeat.

→ See Caldeira do Vulcão das Furnas (see 45) and walk down the steps below the park.

5 mins 37.7729, -25.3030 ⚶⊞

48 LAGOA DO CANÁRIO, SÃO MIGUEL

Wild steps through mossy woodland lead to this deserted lake in a volcanic crater in the Serra Devassa. Mild, opaque water surrounded by dense woodland. There is a signed 12km trail which starts here and leads to Sete Cidades taking in amazing views.

→ From Covoada take road N towards Sete Cidades. After 7km turn R at signs for Lagoa do Canário. Parking. Walk down steps to L.
2 mins, 37.8367, -25.7583 🏊🚶🏕⛰

49 FURNAS DO ENXOFRE, TERCEIRA
See the most visible remains of the latest volcanic eruption on Terceira, in the 18th century. Hot, sulphuric vapours billow out.
→ From Angra do Heroísmo take the N3-1A and turn R at signs to Furnas do Enxofre.
3 mins, 38.7286, -27.2310 🏕⛰

50 MIRADOURO DO CALDEIRÃO, CORVO
A 300m deep crater with a diameter of 2km. Some say that inside, between the lagoons and small mounds, you can see the outline of the nine islands of the Azores. A 5km circular trail which begins at this viewpoint.
→ Take the main road from Vila do Corvo and follow signs L for Caldeirão. Park and walk in.
5 mins, 39.7083, -31.0983 🚶⛰♿

CAVES & GROTTOES

51 GRUTA DO NATAL, TERCEIRA
A 697m-long lava tube with magnificent stalactites. Surrounded by the hills of the Santa Bárbara and Mistérios Negros Reserve and just next to the lake and picnic spot Lagoa do Negro. There is a 5km circular trail which begins here and winds its way through purple heather, passing the Lagoa do Negro, several small lakes and Pico Gaspar hill.
→ Path signed outside Gruta do Natal Interpretation Centre along the M502 after it crosses the N3-1A.
1 hr 38.7374, -27.2687 🅿🧺⛰💶📷

52 GRUTA DAS TORRES, PICO
Explore one of the longest lava caves in the world. It was formed by the flow and cooling of subterranean magma rivers about 1,500 years old and is 5,150m long. Certainly an eerie passage. In high season there are five group tours a day, booking recommended.
→ Criação Velha, Pico +351 924 403 921
1 hr, 38.4944, -28.5025 🅿♿🚶🧺💶

WILD WALKS

53 TRILHO DO SANGUINHO, SÃO MIGUEL
This 4.5km circular route begins and ends in Faial da Terra and leads you through chestnut, acacia and densely perfumed woodland, past endemic sanguinho trees, along streams and old mills up to a magical

waterfall, Salto do Prego. The way is signed from the old village Faial da Terra by the river.
→ Once in Faial da Terra continue up the river until you see yellow and red signs for the walking route. Park here and begin.
2 hrs, 37.7494, -25.2019 🚶🏊🍴🍷🧺🏕⛰

54 CHÁ GORREANA TEA TRAIL, SÃO MIGUEL
This 6km circular trail begins and ends near the Gorreana Tea Factory. The family-owned estate dates from 1883 and is the oldest surviving tea plantation in Europe. Walk through tea fields, past old farmhouses and mountain and sea views. Restore yourself

with a cup of *chá* on your return.

➜ Along N1-1A between São Bras and Maia. Carefully cross the regional highway towards the main gate at the entrance of tea plantation. Keep straight until you see a sign to turn to L.

2 hrs, 37.8176, -25.4025 🏃🚲⊞🅿

55 CAMINHO DAS LAGOAS, PICO

The Achada plateau, on the E side of Pico, has around 200 volcanic cones and several beautiful lagoons. This linear trail, 22km long, passes Lagoas dos Grotões, Caiado, Rosada, Paul, Landroal, Peixinho and Negra.

➜ Begins at the crossroads next to the Forest Refuge along the N2, 11km inland from S.Roque and ends at Ribeirinha.

1 day, 38.4707, -28.3018 🏃🚲🏔🏕🅿🍴🚻⊞

56 CALDEIRA WALKING TRAIL, FAIAL

Caldeira means cauldron and this gigantic volcanic crater could serve as a bubbling cauldron for a witch of astronomical dimensions. Its smooth grassy sides open up to the heavens. Explore along a 7km signed circular walk.

➜ Walk begins at the *Caldeira* viewing point, signed from the N2-2A 5.5km N of Flamengos.

2 hrs, 38.5803, -28.7064 🏃🏔🅿⊞🧭

CAFÉS & CAKES

57 CAFÉ GREENLOVE

Just outside Sete Cidades village centre is this wilder option for a snack or a drink, with views out across the Lagoa Azul. Take a dip in the water or lay out on the grassy banks. Good Açorean cheese here. Or try the grilled *morcela*, blood sausage, with pineapple.

➜ Rua Arruamento Margem da Lagoa das Sete Cidades +351 296 915 214

37.8636, -25.7925 🍴🚲🅿

58 QUEIJADAS DA VILA FRANCA DO CAMPO, SÃO MIGUEL

From the divinely guided hands of the 17th century nuns at Convento de Santo André come these *queijadas de vila*, dense little cakes made with lemons, egg yolks and sugar. The recipe was for many years a secret but eventually it leaked through the convent's heavy stone walls and reached the ears of Eduíno Morgado Medeiro. His family has kept the tradition alive since. Try them at their little bakery, Do Morgado.

➜ Rua do Penedo 20, 9680-146 Vila Franca do Campo +351 296 581 183

37.7160, -25.4301 🍴

59 RESTAURANTE MOAGEM, SÃO MIGUEL

Mountain and sea views, with little tables outside, this is a great place to stop for some shade, a slice of pizza (with Azorean pineapple) and a beer.

➜ On the coast road running N of Salga. Estrada Regional 1, 9630-270 Salga +351 296 462 192

37.8504, -25.3004 🍴🏔

60 TASCA DO TRAGUITA, SÃO MIGUEL

A friendly, locals' place for a beer – Especial – and a *tosta mista*. Hundreds of coloured hats line the walls and photos of the hair-raising Red Bull Cliff Diving from Ilhéu de Vila.

➜ Rua Simões de Almeida 4, Vila Franca do Campo

37.7157, -25.4327 🍴

SLOW FOOD

61 RESTAURANTE O CHICO, SÃO MIGUEL

A rustic, family-run restaurant with great fish dishes. A good place to try *lapas*, wild limpets, octopus or the fresh catch from the nearby fishing villages.

➜ Rua da Ponte 7, Mosteiros +351 296 915 500

37.8894, -25.8212 🍴❗

62 CERVEJARIA CASCATA, SÃO MIGUEL

A beer-house with local brew Especial on tap, but also hundreds of local snacks and seafood dishes. You can choose *lapas* (limpets), *salada de búzio* (conch or sea-snails), *cracas* (barnacles) from the counter, or there are fresh local fish dishes chalked up on the boards. Eat outside on tables in the cobbled square by the church.

➜ Largo Gaspar Frutuoso 7, 9600-513 Ribeira Grande +351 296 473 162
37.8231, -25.5197 🍴🚻

63 RESTAURANTE AGUAS QUENTES, SÃO MIGUEL

A good place to try the *cozido nas caldeiras*, stew slow-cooked in the Furnas fumaroles for six hours. Each mouthful is heaven, with a slightly sulphuric edge. A shrine with electric candles and saints sits at the back – it should be made to the *cozido* chef.

➜ Rua Água Quente 15, 9675-040 Furnas +351 296 584 482
37.7675, -25.3187 🍴🚻

64 QUINTA DOS SABORES, SÃO MIGUEL

A working arable farm between Lagoa and Rabo de Peixe, with plenty of fruit and veg on sale. There is a gorgeous restaurant open in the evenings and culinary workshops.

➜ Caminho da Selada 10, Alminhas de Rabo de Peixe +351 926 333 114, Quinta-sabores.blogspot.com
37.7916, -25.5830 🍴🚻🏕🏔

65 RESTAURANTE OS MOINHOS, TERCEIRA

This is a great place to try *alcatra*, the beef or fish stew cooked in an earthenware pot and served on chunks of *massa sovada* bread. Lots of dishes cooked Açoriana style and good wines. Log fires in winter.

➜ Rua do Arrabalde, São Sebastião, Angra do Heroísmo +351 295 904 508, Restauranteosmoinhos.pai.pt
38.6645, -27.0856 🍴🚻🏕

66 MUSEU DO VINHO, TERCEIRA

The landscape of Biscoitos is filled with vineyards. A specific type of wine is made from the Verdelho grape grown here. Try the wine and the Chico Maria liqueur also made here.

➜ Canada do Caldeiro, 9760-051 Biscoitos +351 965 667 324
38.7927, -27.2587 🚻

67 RESTAURANTE QUINTA DAS GROTAS, GRACIOSA

A rural Açorean house in an idyllic setting serving creative regional fish and meat dishes and good wines.

➜ Caminho das Grotas 28, 9880 Santa Cruz da Graciosa +351 295 712 334
39.0560, -28.0379 🍴🏕🚻

68 ADEGA A BURACA, PICO

A wine cellar in a basaltic cavern where you can try Verdelho wines, local Pico wines and see how 'Picarotos' would traditionally have lived. There is a cooper's shop and a blacksmith's tent; workshops are run in straw, wool and wicker, all activities related to the wine-making process. Lodging available.

➜ Estrada Regional 35, 9940-232 Santo António São Roque do Pico +351 292 642 119, Adegaaburaca.com
38.5349, -28.3416 🍴🛏🏕🚻

69 RESTAURANTE PÔR DO SOL, FLORES

A cosy restaurant above the cliffs with amazing sunset views. They serve regional dishes such as *linguiça, a morcela*, yams and sweet potatoes and *o bolo tijolo*, brick cake.

➜ 9960-110 Fajãzinha +351 292 552 075
39.4336, -31.2540 🏕🍴🚻📷

72

71

76

78

79

70 RESTAURANTE O TRAINEIRA, CORVO

A family-run restaurant is the place to try local fish and seafood: stewed octopus, limpets and crabs, among others. Enjoy local cheese and homemade puddings.

→ Rua da Matriz , Vila do Corvo, 9980-020 Corvo +351 912 632 127

39.6714, -31.1115

WILDER CAMPSITES

71 PARQUE DE CAMPISMO DA FEIRA, SÃO MIGUEL

A beautiful, wilder campsite by the River Guilherme. Walk a few metres down to old mill-houses and a secluded swim spot. A signed walking route passes through here.

→ Boca da Ribeira, 9630 Nordeste + 351 296 488 680

37.8400, -25.1522

72 QUINTA DAS LARANJEIRAS, SÃO MIGUEL

A great campsite, lovingly run by Renato, a true Açorean, and his dog Mordor. There is a communal kitchen with wood fire, a collection of walking maps and books on the island, chestnut trees, rainwater collection and several hidden camping areas and tipis. At the end of the garden you can survey the hills and coast from a lookout tower. Perfect for a sunset. Your country's flag will be hoisted upon arrival (his mother stitches every one).

→ Canada Roda do Pico 30, Areias, 9600-097 Rabo de Peixe +351 962 823 766, Azorescamp.com

37.7995, -25.5907

73 PARQUE DE CAMPISMO DOS BISCOITOS, TERCEIRA

A simple campsite by the sea and close to the tidal pools.

→ Caminho de Santo António, 9760-051 Biscoitos +351 965 235 417

38.7994, -27.2565

74 PARQUE DE CAMPISMO CALHETA, SÃO JORGE

A camping park in São Jorge just metres from the ocean with dazzling views across to Faial and Pico. There is also a natural swimming pool, ideal for a dive.

→ Rua Cabo Vicente Dias, Faja Grande, 9850-072 Calheta +351 295 417 366 camping.cht.sjz.2014@gmail.com

38.6073, -28.0333

HEALING RETREATS

75 TERRA NOSTRA GARDEN HOTEL, SÃO MIGUEL

Set within the Terra Nostra gardens of the Furnas crater are hot springs and healing sulphuric waters. Its botanical garden has a naturally heated geothermic pool which, if you visit in the evening once the day visitors have left, you can have all to yourselves.

→ Rua Padre José Jacinto Botelho 5, 9675-061 Furnas +351 296 549 090

37.7728, -25.3142

76 CASA DA LAGOA, SÃO JORGE

Situated between the steep green slope of the hills and the blue sea, this is the perfect couples' retreat. A typical Fajã house with a wood oven, sleeps two. Walking trail, surfers' beach and lagoon all nearby.

→ Fajã da Caldeira +351 919 828 685, Azorescasadalagoa.com

38.6247, -27.9289

HISTORIC HOUSES

77 HOTEL TALISMAN, SÃO MIGUEL

In the historical centre of Ponta Delgada, this 17th century building, made of traditional volcanic stone, has windows that open out to the sculptural trees and palms in the square.

→ Rua Marquês da Praia e Monforte 40, Ponta Delgada +351 296 308 500, Hoteltalisman.com

37.7389, -25.6719

78 CASA TI' JOSÉ BORGES, TERCEIRA

Stay in a 19th century farmhouse complete with a stone oven and a 'praying hands' chimney. A lovely retreat for a young family. Help on the farm, hand-milking the cows. Donkeys in nearby fields.

→ Rua Tio José Borges 10, 9760-279 Lajes, Praia da Vitória +351 295 517 367, Tijoseborges.com

38.7606, -27.0995

79 ALDEIA DA CUADA, FLORES

Flores is one of the wildest islands of the Açores. Escape to a small village with only the chirruping of birdsong to disturb your peace. Aldeia da Cuada was abandoned in the 1960s but Teotónia and Carlos Silva have rebuilt the village – there are now a number of little cottages for holiday rentals, and donkeys live in the nearby fields again.

→ 9960-070 Lajes das Flores +351 292 590 040, Aldeiadacuada.com

39.4404, -31.2557

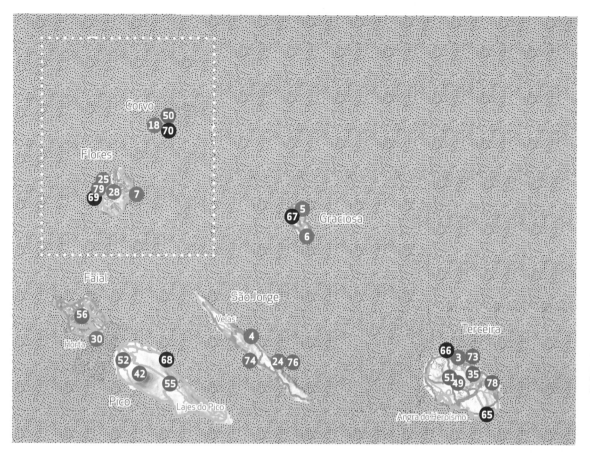

Corvo

18 50
70

Flores

25
79 28 7
69

5
67
Graciosa
6

Faial

56

Horta 30

São Jorge
Velas
4

Terceira
66
3 73
51 35
49 78

52 68
42
55
Pico
Lajes do Pico

74 24 76

Angra do Heroísmo 65

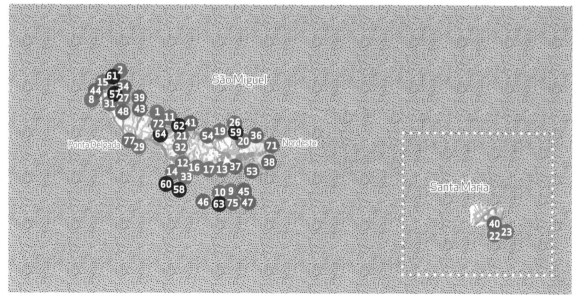

2
61
15 34
44 57
8 31 27 39
48 43
1 11
72 62 41
64 21
77 32
29

São Miguel

26
54 19 59
20 36
71 Nordeste
38
53

Ponta Delgada

12 16 17 13 37
14 33
60 58
10 9 45
46 63 75 47

Santa Maria

40
22 23

**Wild Guide
Portugal**

Words:
Edwina Pitcher

Photos:
Edwina Pitcher
and those credited

Editing:
Michael Waterton Lee

Proofreading:
Siobhan Kelly

Design:
Daniel Start
Tania Pascoe

Distribution:
Central Books Ltd
1 Heath Park Industrial
Estate, Freshwater Road,
Dagenham, RM8 1RX
Tel +44 (0)208 8525 8800
orders@centralbooks.com

Published by:
First edition published in
the United Kingdom 2017 by
Wild Things Publishing Ltd.
Freshford, Bath, Somerset
BA2 7WG, UK
ISBN 9781910636114

WILD guide

the award-winning, best-
selling adventure travel
series, also available as
iPhone and Android apps:

- South West England
- South East England
- Lakes and Dales
- Scotland
- Wales (2018)
- Scandinavia
- Portugal

hello@wildthingspublishing.com

Author acknowledgements:
I would like to thank Diana Matoso, who appears throughout this book and without whose knowledge of Portugal's wild places and inexhaustible spirit of adventure, this book would not have been possible.

For their generous support I would like to thank Carmel Fitzsimons, Richard & Elena Bridges, Tito & Cristina Manto, Lucinda & Patrick Horton, Michael & Solidade Harris, Pip & Harry Morton, Jenny & Lisa Wong, Hannah Fair, Helena Morrissey, Lindsay Nicholson, Gilli Fryzer, Ana Rita Sarzedas, Nikki Jones, Joe Duggan, Paul Nuki, Teresa Matoso, Kitty Walsh, Ginny Gascoigne, Nikolaj Munk Nielsen, Telma Pinto, Joe Fleming, Natasha Cossey, Charlotte Rixon, Carlos Leiria, Jota Susana da Costa Pinto and Chris Brennan.

I would also like to thank Instituto da Conservação da Natureza, Casas Brancas, Turismo dos Açores, Ecomuseu de Barroso, Alfredo Noronha Peres. For their guidance Tania, Daniel and Michael Lee. For countless rescues when I arrived half feral on doorsteps - Daniela Neta Fonseca and Maria Olivia Neta. For wild spirit, love and support Ellie Doney & Terri Merceica, Tiago Fonseca, George & Mobbs Pitcher, my brothers, my cousins.

Health, Safety and Responsibility:
Like any water-based activity, wild swimming has risks and can be dangerous. The locations featured in this book are prone to flood, drought and other changes. The locations may be on private land and permission may need to be sought. While the author and publisher have gone to great lengths to ensure the accuracy of the information herein they will not be held legally or financially responsible for any accident, injury, loss or inconvenience sustained as a result of the information or advice contained in this book. Swimming, jumping, diving or any other activities at any of these locations is entirely at your own risk.

Other books from Wild Things Publishing:

Bikepacking

France en Velo

Hidden Beaches

Lost Lanes Southern England

Lost Lanes Wales

Only Planet

Wild Garden Weekends

Scottish Bothy Bible

Wild Guide - Devon, Cornwall
   and South West

Wild Guide - Lakes and Dales

Wild Guide - Scotland

Wild Guide - Southern and
   Eastern England

Wild Guide - Portugal

Wild Guide - Scandinavia
   (Norway, Sweden, Iceland
   and Denmark)

Wild Ruins

Wild Running

Wild Swimming Britain

Wild Swimming France

Wild Swimming Italy

Wild Swimming Spain

Wild Swimming Sydney
   Australia

Wild Swimming Walks
   Around London

Wild Swimming Walks
   Dartmoor and South Devon